TENTH EDITION

CONNECTICUT

OFF THE BEATEN PATH®

DISCOVER YOUR FUN

CINDI D. PIETRZYK

Globe Pequot

Guilford, Connecticut

All the information in this guidebook is subject to change. We recommend you call ahead to obtain current information before traveling.

Globe Pequot

An imprint of The Rowman & Littlefield Publishing Group, Inc.
4501 Forbes Blvd., Ste. 200
Lanham, MD 20706
www.rowman.com

Distributed by NATIONAL BOOK NETWORK

Maps by Equator Graphics

British Library Cataloguing in Publication Information available

Library of Congress Cataloging-in-Publication Data available

ISBN 978-1-4930-3761-2 (paperback)
ISBN 978-1-4930-3762-9 (e-book)

∞™ The paper used in this publication meets the minimum requirements of American National Standard for Information Sciences—Permanence of Paper for Printed Library Materials, ANSI/NISO Z39.48-1992

Printed in the United States of America

To Charley, Samantha, and Kailey—my love for you is immeasurable, my faith in you boundless, my hope for you never-ending

To Steve—May we never run out of adventures

Contents

Acknowledgments

Authors often say a book can't be written without the help of many people, but I'm not sure readers always appreciate just how true that statement is. Trust me, it's true! When I agreed to write this edition, my first thought was, "How will I find places to include?" As I began my research, I thought, "How am I going to fit all of this into one book?!" Connecticut is one of those little spaces that packs a whole lot of punch. There are so many hidden gems that uncovering them all would be impossible for one person. In that vein, I'd like to thank all those people who gave me suggestions, sent me in the right directions, visited places for me, and answered my questions.

Specifically, I'd like to thank Stephen Wood of CTMuseumQuest.com for blazing a path through Connecticut. There weren't many places I discovered to which Steve hadn't already been. His write-ups were always helpful and entertaining. Check out Steve's blog and follow his ramblings around the state.

A huge thank you to all the grassroots community groups who have pulled together and saved so many historic sites. Without them, there just might not be a Connecticut off the beaten path.

Thanks to my first editor, Kevin Sirois, for having faith in me to do my first edition. To Sarah Parke and Alex Bordelon, for their patience and guidance with this edition. Thanks to everyone at GPP who do what they do so well!

And finally, I need to thank my husband, Steve, and my daughters for once again putting up with my hours away from them, the missed moments, and the frantic scramble to meet my deadline. Your love and support got me through the late nights and moments of thinking I'd never get it done. We got it done.

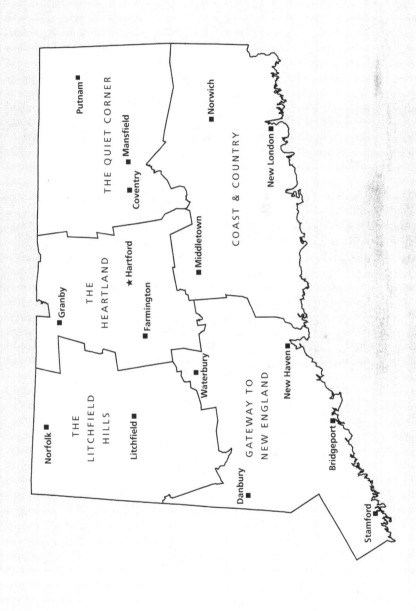

THE LITCHFIELD HILLS

Norfolk■

Litchfield■

THE HEARTLAND

Granby■

Farmington■

★Hartford

Danbury■

GATEWAY TO NEW ENGLAND

Waterbury■

Stamford■

Bridgeport■

New Haven■

Middletown■

THE QUIET CORNER

Putnam■

Coventry■ Mansfield■

COAST & COUNTRY

Norwich■

New London■

Introduction

Twenty years from now you will be more disappointed by the things
you didn't do than by the ones you did do. So throw off the bowlines,
sail away from the safe harbor. Catch the trade winds
in your sails. Explore. Dream. Discover.

—Mark Twain

Nestled between the much larger states of New York and Massachusetts, Connecticut is not to be overlooked. While our state occupies only a bit more than 5,000 square miles along the coast of Long Island Sound, it packs a punch. The third-smallest state in the Union, Connecticut has more to offer than you might think. Nowhere in America can the traveler find so representative a history, so rich a culture, and so great a physical diversity packed into so small an area.

Connecticut's history is rich and varied. The Native Americans who lived in the region for millennia before the arrival of the first Europeans called it Quinnehtukqut ("Beside the Long Tidal River" or "Long River"). About 20,000 Native Americans lived in the area when the Dutch discovered the Connecticut River in 1614. As settlers and natives clashed, many of the tribes were forced to work together, and tribal lines were blurred. Many Native peoples who live today have a mixed heritage from more than one of these tribes.

constitutionstate

Connecticut is called the "Constitution State" because the Fundamental Orders, a governing principle based on the will of the people, is considered one of the first written constitutions of a democratic government. You can see these orders at the Museum of Connecticut History in Hartford.

English Puritans from Massachusetts began to move into Connecticut in 1633, and in 1638–1639, the towns of Hartford, Windsor, and Wethersfield adopted the Fundamental Orders of Connecticut, setting up a government for the new Connecticut Colony. About the same time, the colony of New Haven was founded farther west along the coast of Long Island Sound. The two colonies were joined in 1662, and the state gained—roughly—its current outline.

Since then, the history of Connecticut has largely marched with that of America. The state has played a vital role in American experiences, such as the settlement of the frontier, the winning of the Revolutionary War, the adoption of the Constitution, the Union victory in the Civil War, and that vast upheaval known as the Industrial Revolution.

Connecticut's part in the American pageant has left a lasting mark on the state. Its towns have been ravaged by America's wars. Its language and culture

Connecticut River

The Connecticut River is one of fourteen waterways designated American Heritage Rivers by former vice president Al Gore.

The Connecticut River is 410 miles long—about 5,551 football fields.

Today's Connecticut River came into being between 10,000 and 13,000 years ago, after the Wisconsin Glacier receded from the New England area.

Connecticut developed about 220 million years ago in the late Triassic period.

have been molded by the nation's immigration patterns. Its geography has been altered by the spread of industrialization. Its economy has been shaped by the growth—and demise—of such industries as whaling, railroading, shipbuilding, and textile manufacturing. It has been, in many ways, a microcosm of America.

Sometimes known as the "Land of Steady Habits," Connecticut has taken as its official designation the title "Constitution State." George Washington called it the "Provision State" because it fed his army during the darkest days of the American Revolution.

It is also called the "Nutmeg State," a sobriquet just as common as the official designation and perhaps more representative of Connecticut's history and culture; the name "Nutmegger" was often applied by the residents of neighboring states to Connecticut peddlers, who were famous for selling bogus nutmegs carved from local wood in place of the imported (and more expensive) real thing.

Whatever you call it, Connecticut is a land of odd contrasts and strange delights that have accumulated over centuries. Modern Connecticut has something to excite the whim and tickle the fancy of almost every traveler. Its diverse geography runs the gamut from sandy beaches and teeming marshlands of its coastal plains and fertile meadows of its central lowlands to the forested hills of the eastern and western uplands and the craggy granite cliffs that characterize its northwestern reaches. The many eras of its history are enshrined not only in countless museums, galleries, and restorations but also in numerous historical structures that are still part of the everyday lives of its people; this is, in fact, one of the few places in America where you can find real Cape Cod saltboxes, Victorian Gothic mansions, and Art Deco roadside palaces of the early automotive era all happily residing cheek by jowl.

In fact, residents of Connecticut take their history seriously. Again and again strong Yankee ingenuity has been put into action, as dedicated Nutmeggers work to save historical property after historical property. Many times over, community action has resulted in the wonderful museums and galleries or historic neighborhoods you'll have the honor of exploring as you traverse this great state.

The densely populated cities along Connecticut's southwestern coast and the navigable portions of its major rivers are home to many of the state's inhabitants and give the state an urban flavor that stands in stark contrast to its rural uplands. This clustering of settlements along coasts and rivers explains why, even though Connecticut is the seventh-most densely populated state in the US (with an overall density of almost 740 persons per square mile), roughly sixty percent of the state is forest land. Most of the trees in these forests are northern hardwoods about 60–100 years old, and they are purely glorious in fall. In addition, approximately twelve percent of Connecticut is farmland.

In terms of amenities for the traveler, Connecticut has few equals. Though modern accommodations abound, this area, like most of New England, is famous for its quaint inns and bed-and-breakfasts (or B&Bs), many of which are housed in buildings that have been around longer than the state. The eclectic cuisine, both cosmopolitan and casual, reflects the cultural and gustatory gifts brought to the state by succeeding waves of immigrants. Its great wealth and emphasis on tourism make Connecticut a shopping paradise; establishments range from some of America's largest and most attractive malls, to mom-and-pop operations offering only-in-Connecticut crafts, to factory outlets that fairly shout "bargains."

For the traveler who likes to venture off the beaten path, Connecticut is an especially satisfying venue; one constantly discovers the odd, the interesting, and the truly unique tucked away in the most unexpected places. Whether it be a mere whimsy, such as a roadside rock painted to look like a startlingly realistic giant frog, a truly spine-chilling gothic mystery, such as Groton's Gungywamp, or something just plain honest and daring at East Haddam's Two Wrasslin' Cats Coffee House, you can never be entirely sure what you will find around the next bend.

We like to think of Connecticut as representing all the best of America in vest-pocket size: gilded beaches that would be the envy of California; rolling hills better than any in Virginia; pastoral farmland that makes you think you're in Indiana; downtown chic that rivals New York; and some of the friendliest people on Earth. A truly dedicated traveler could experience the full diversity of the state in one day. You could jump-start your day with an espresso in West Hartford, drive down to the shore for a few hours of sun and sand capped by a lunch of fried clams or lobster at the shore, and take an afternoon jaunt up into Litchfield County to browse the antiques shops before driving over to the

Quiet Corner for a hayride through its fields and glens. You'd be tired, but you could do it.

Geography isn't the only source of variety in Connecticut. Its northerly location and long coastline conspire to produce a multiplicity of seasonal variations in the weather. Each season brings its own wonders and offers its own characteristic activities. Winter means New England main streets dressed for the holidays, pure white candles glowing in many-paned windows. Spring is the season for strolling along one of eastern Connecticut's back roads, watching farmers plow rolling farmlands, listening to the first few notes of birdsong, and sniffing the green tang of growing things in the air. Summer is a time for the shore; for golden beaches, the hiss of the waves, the crunch of fried seafood, and the sugary-sweet smell of cotton candy. Fall means amber and cinnabar hills, quintessentially New England white clapboard churches poised against the fiery reds of nearby sugar maples, and the sweet taste of fresh-pressed cider and cider-glazed doughnuts.

Regardless of the season, traveling in Connecticut is easy, although traffic congestion has become an increasingly prevalent problem, especially during the summer, so you should build in extra time if you are planning to attend an event that has a specific starting time. Interstate highways crisscross the state, with I-95 (the Connecticut Turnpike) running the length of its shore, I-91 bisecting the state from north to south, I-395 winding along its eastern border, and I-84 running from Danbury through Waterbury to Hartford and then through the northeastern counties to the Massachusetts Turnpike. The interstate highway system is complemented by an excellent system of state highways. More often than not, this book takes you off the interstates and puts you on the smaller roads that evolved with our state's history from Indian trails to two-lane paved roads. Some of these back roads may seem isolated. But never fear; no matter how far into the outback it feels, you're never more than half an hour from a major highway that will quickly return you to more populated areas.

Clearly, no one book can do justice to Connecticut's 350 years of history or to the diverse delights packed into this one small state. As in most of life, some judicious editing is necessary. Thus, you won't find herein detailed descriptions of the well-known delights of Mystic or the popular casinos at Foxwoods or Mohegan Sun. Nor do we devote much space to the major attractions in the state's larger cities. These items are well documented online. We do not pretend to compete with the State of Connecticut in offering general travel information or describing nationally famous attractions. Instead, we offer a directory of out-of-the-way places you might not know to look for if you're not native to the area. We've done the research for you and pulled it all together in this one convenient place. What is that historic building you're passing? Where does that trail lead? Where should I eat? Is that antiques store really worth the stop? We may miss some of the major attractions, but if it's funky, funny, little known, or out of the way, you'll probably find it here.

For the purposes of this book, we've divided the state into five chapters, matching Connecticut's major geographic, historical, and cultural divisions. Within those chapters are smaller sections to help keep things organized. However, we have not laid things out, necessarily, in travel order. For example, it may make more sense for you to visit an attraction in western East Haddam and then move west to Haddam before visiting an attraction on the eastern side of East Haddam, but we have included all the East Haddam attractions in one section. Then we list the Haddam attractions, and so on. We suggest that when planning a trip, you pull out a Connecticut state map and look at all the surrounding towns. Decide where you'd like to go, then use a nifty route planner, in which you plug in street addresses (all of which we have provided for you), and have the computer map your route for you. You can see at a glance the best way to see everything on your list and how much time it will take.

In today's world, social media sites are invaluable for up-to-the-minute news on all your favorite places. We strongly suggest you "like," "follow," and "subscribe" to places you plan to visit. This way you'll know about special events, pricing, and closings ahead of time.

Fall Foliage

In most of Connecticut, fall foliage hits its peak around Columbus Day. Areas in the north, northwest, and northeast see peak color a little earlier. Starting in late September, you can get a daily fall foliage update by visiting ct.gov/deep/site/default.asp and clicking on the Fall Foliage link; you can even sign up for text and/or e-mail updates.

Food in Connecticut

Here in Connecticut, our cuisine is an amalgam of rugged colonial dishes leavened with ethnic foods, the heritage of the immigrants who helped transform our state. It all makes for a diverse and heady cuisine. Try to sample some of these emphatically Connecticut foods when you visit.

Chowder. The origins of its name, *chaudière* (large kettle), may be French, but this hearty soup is all New England. You won't find as many fish chowders in Connecticut as in other parts of New England, but we make stellar clam chowders.

- **New England clam chowder** is a milk- or cream-based soup full of potatoes, onions, whole clams, and salt pork and seasoned with thyme. It's probably the version you think of when someone mentions clam chowder.

- **Rhode Island clam chowder** is New England clam chowder lightened with just enough pureed tomatoes to turn the soup a rosy pink.

- **Southern New England clam chowder** is a bracing, briny broth loaded with clams, potatoes, and onions—no milk or cream.

- **Manhattan clam chowder** is a tomato-based veggie soup with a few clams.

Lobster roll. In some New England states, a lobster roll is lobster salad (cold lobster, mayonnaise, seasonings) served on a toasted hot dog bun. But in Connecticut, a lobster roll is a spiritual experience: fresh, hot lobster meat, dripping with melted butter, served on a sesame-seed hamburger bun or toasted hot dog bun. Be sure to try one, and don't forget the extra napkins for wiping butter-drenched chins and fingers.

Grape-Nuts pudding. Baked custard served in a sweet shell of Grape-Nuts cereal; one version features a swirl of Grape-Nuts throughout the pudding. Much better than it sounds. Check out Zip's Dining Car in Dayville for Zip's recipe for Grape-Nuts pudding.

Indian pudding. A robust dessert dating back to colonial times, it's a mix of cornmeal, molasses, and warm spices cooked for hours at a low temperature until thick and amber-colored. Some heretics add raisins or apples. Served with vanilla ice cream or a rivulet of heavy cream. The Griswold Inn in Essex usually has Indian pudding on its fall and winter dessert menu.

Pizza. New Haven is the pizza capital of Connecticut, maybe of the US. New Haven pizza has a thin and crunchy crust and doesn't wallow in toppings. Pepe's and Sally's are the traditional top choices among New Haven pizza palaces. In Hartford County, the pizza at Harry's in West Hartford Center is glorious.

State Symbols

- **Official designation:** Constitution State

- **Indian name:** Quinnehtukqut—"Beside the Long Tidal River"

- **State motto:** He who is transplanted still sustains

- **State flower:** mountain laurel

- **State bird:** American robin

- **State tree:** white oak

- **State animal:** sperm whale

- **State insect:** praying mantis

- **State mineral:** garnet

- **State song:** "Yankee Doodle"

- **State ship:** USS *Nautilus*

- **State shellfish:** eastern oyster

- **State composer:** Charles Edward Ives

- **State poet laureate:** Dick Allen

- **State fossil:** *Eubrontes giganteus,* an eighteen-foot-long carnivore

- **State hero:** Nathan Hale

- **State heroine:** Prudence Crandall

Places to Stay & Places to Eat Price Codes

At the end of each chapter are area accommodations and restaurants you'll want to check out.

The rating scale for accommodations is based on double occupancy and is as follows:

Inexpensive: Less than $100 per night

Moderate: $101 to $200 per night

Expensive: More than $200 per night

The rating scale for restaurants is based on the price of an entrée without beverages, desserts, tax, or tip, and is as follows:

Inexpensive: Less than $10

Moderate: $11 to $20

Expensive: More than $20

Please remember, these are rough guidelines and should not be considered actual rates. Always call ahead to confirm. For museums and places that charge admission, we indicated if an admission is charged but now how much, as those change often. We have also indicated if a museum is a member of the Blue Star Program, which gives active-duty military members and five members of their family free admission from Memorial Day through Labor Day.

The Heartland

The upper Connecticut River Valley is a broad, fertile meadow-land ideal for farming and grazing, and the state's Puritan settlers were naturally drawn to it. It was the first part of Connecticut to be colonized, and those original settlements thrived and expanded until they finally merged to form what is today Greater Hartford, a vibrant metropolitan area of just under 125,000 people.

Bounding Hartford County's urban and suburban core on the north and west are the rural Tobacco and Farmington Valleys. To the east is pastoral Tolland County, and to the south are New Haven County and Connecticut's Coast & Country areas. Within these rural boundaries is Connecticut's heartland, the seat of its government and one of its most important commercial centers. As you might suspect, the majority of the attractions in this area are historical and cultural; in addition, you can find the commercial activities and entertainments of a large metropolitan area.

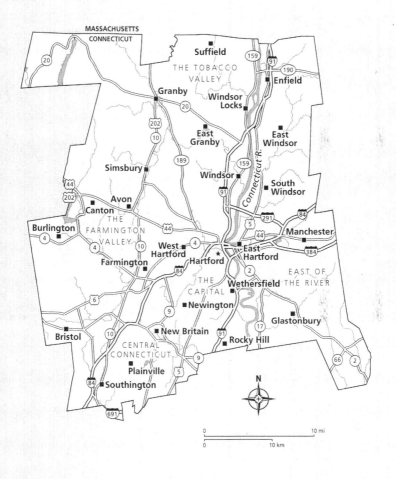

MASSACHUSETTS
CONNECTICUT

Suffield

THE TOBACCO
VALLEY

Granby

Windsor
Locks

Enfield

East
Granby

East
Windsor

Simsbury

Windsor

South
Windsor

Avon

Canton

THE
FARMINGTON
VALLEY

Manchester

Burlington

West
Hartford

East
Hartford

Farmington

Hartford

THE
CAPITAL

Wethersfield

EAST OF
THE RIVER

Newington

Glastonbury

Bristol

New Britain

Rocky Hill

CENTRAL
CONNECTICUT

Plainville

Southington

Connecticut R.

N

0   10 mi

0   10 km

The Capital

Hartford

Officially settled in 1635, **Hartford** was important in the nineteenth century as a center of the abolitionist movement and the tobacco industry. A hub of activity, Hartford played an integral part in shaping our nation's history. Merchants traded molasses, spices, coffee, and rum along with the tobacco from warehouses throughout the city. The Colt Firearms Factory, maker of the Colt Revolver, "the gun that won the West," called Hartford home.

That history can be explored at the ***Museum of Connecticut History*** (231 Capitol Ave.; 860-757-6534; museumofcthistory.org), which has a great collection of items from our state's past, including an exhibit on the role Connecticut and its residents played in World War I; so many guns from so many years of Colt Manufacturing's history; Memorial Hall, where the portraits of the state's past and present governors hang; and the Mitchelson Coin Collection, reportedly one of the best in the world.

You can truly spend hours here trying to absorb it all. The best part? Admission is free. Open Mon through Fri, 9 a.m. to 4 p.m.; Sat, 9 a.m. to 2 p.m. Closed on state holidays and on Saturday when a holiday observance falls on a Friday or Monday. Call ahead to be sure. There are metal detectors as you enter the building, which you will have to pass through. When you do enter, the Connecticut Supreme Court is on your right, the Connecticut State Library is on your left. Straight ahead you will see a double staircase that leads off in both directions and will likely be roped off. The museum is located directly through the center of these staircases.

One of our favorite exhibits here was the ***Connecticut Freedom Trail Quilt Project***. Connecticut residents fought for freedom on more than one front throughout the state's history. While some went to battlegrounds throughout the region and fought on the front lines, many stayed home and fought for freedom on a different level—a secret, underground level. As a tribute to these early freedom fighters, a member of the Freedom Trail Planning Committee suggested the quilt project. People from across the state created squares for the final product, each piece representing one of the sites along the trail. Quilting is a long-standing tradition, in fact, quilts were often hung outside safe houses to alert those in need that help was available within.

If this period in our history interests you, head to cultureandtourism.org and click on the link for the Connecticut Freedom Trail Brochure to download information on the places around the state that played an important part in the antislavery movement. Be aware, though, that many of these places are now privately owned, restricting you to a simple drive-by in appreciation.

When you are done exploring the museum, head across the street to the State Capitol building. With its eight-sided gilded cupola gleaming in sunlight, **Connecticut's State Capitol** (210 Capitol Ave; 860-240-0222; cga.ct.gov) greets your eyes when you come into Hartford by way of I-84. Designed by Richard M. Upjohn, primarily a cathedral architect, this High Victorian Gothic–style colossus—completed on its hilltop site in 1878—is a marble-and-granite riot of pinnacles, turrets, columns, bas reliefs, statues, heraldic emblems, arches, and porticoes. In addition to state executive offices and legislative chambers, the capitol building offers a variety of historic exhibits, including the figure-head from the USS *Connecticut*, which sailed around the world on a good-will mission ordered by President Theodore Roosevelt in 1907. The ship was destroyed in 1923, but the figurehead was spared and presented to Connecticut to be displayed. Also on display is a brownstone statue of a Union soldier acquired in 1895 by two Connecticut residents after it was rejected for higher purposes because of incorrect foot positioning. You'll find a model of the *Hartford*, built by a US Navy veteran with one arm! It took him two and a half years of patience and determination to complete. History buffs may know it was from the *Hartford* that Admiral David Farragut commanded the famous words, "Damn the torpedoes, full speed ahead!" in 1864. (Someone may want to tell the powers that be in Hartford that they misspelled "torpedoes" on their plaque.)

Visitors can take a hour-long guided tour of the premises between 9:15 a.m. and 1:15 p.m. on weekdays year-round (to 2:15 p.m. in July and Aug). Tours are funded by the League of Women Voters of Connecticut Education Fund. Visitors can also do a self-guided tour Mon through Fri, 8 a.m. to 5 p.m. Tour information can be found in the Capitol outside room 101 and also on the first floor of the Legislative Office Building, near the west entrance. The Capitol and Legislative Office Building are closed on weekends and major holidays.

If you haven't had your fill of history yet, we highly recommend you take the time to stop by **Connecticut's Old State House** (800 Main St.; 860-522-6766; ctoldstatehouse.org), especially if you have little ones in your group who need to expend some energy. The hands-on children's exhibits in the Emily Seymour Goodwin Holcombe Center on the bottom level of this historic building will surely do the trick. Emily Holcombe was a dedicated activist and preservationist who organized many campaigns to save Connecticut landmarks and preserve our history, including working diligently to save the Old State House when it was marked for demolition. The education center here is a fitting memorial to her. Here at this center, antsy little ones can build their own capitol on the Lego table; explore a farm yard with interactive, child-size farm animal statues, and more! There are lots of bells and whistles to grab their attention and exercise their minds for a bit before you take them upstairs to the more historical exhibits. You can always entice them with a promise to see the two-headed calf at the ***Museum of Curiosities***, where you will also find African tribal masks, sharks' jaws, a stuffed cobra, giant tortoise shells, artfully impaled tropical insects, a wing-spread bat under glass, a crocodile's head, drawers full of birds' eggs and wide-ranging diverse exhibits that were part of the former collection of local painter Joseph Seward. But first, take the time to explore the original state House of Representatives on one side of the upper level and the chamber of the state Senate on the other. There's an inspiring speech from P.T. Barnum that you can read aloud and feel as if you're speaking to a group of aspiring lawmakers and making a difference, but mostly it's just cool to stand where our forefathers stood hundreds of years ago as our state was taking shape. On the lower level you'll also find an informative exhibit on the *Amistad* and the trial that ensued. It all adds up to great fun in the least stuffy historical site/museum you're likely to come across.

The building itself has a long and interesting history. Construction began in 1792 but was not completed until 1796 due to various financial obstacles. It has faced the wrecking ball many times, but each time Nutmeggers rallied and saved this important part of their history. In 1961, the Old State House was named a National Historic Landmark. In the late 1970s, the Old State House Association set forth to turn the building into the museum you see today. You can take a guided tour, or opt for a tour on your own, which is pretty easy with the set up they have. You'll start with a video, if you wish, that offers a brief overview of the history of the area. You are then on your own to explore and appreciate.

Hartford is often referred to as the "Insurance City," a reputation that dates back to the city's thriving merchant district, from which many ships set sail to England and other far-off ports. As business grew, so did the need for protection from pirates, storms, and accidents. In 1810, the Hartford Fire Insurance Group was created, and it still operates today. Other insurance entrepreneurs followed suit. In 1846, the Connecticut Mutual Life Insurance Co. of Hartford was formed even as local clergy declared the practice of insuring lives immoral. They came around, however, when in 1851 religious leaders joined business and civic leaders in founding the American Temperance Life Insurance Company, now The Phoenix Companies, Inc. The Hartford Steam Boiler Inspection and Insurance Company came along in 1864, and by 1898, the first automobile insurance policy, at a staggering cost of two cents, had been issued by Travelers Insurance Company. Hartford's insurance companies continued to prosper and build their reputations by paying in full and on time when claims arose. Recent history has seen some challenges to the city's

never know this. The inside is still beautiful, though, and creative. Although the house was scoffed at by those who misunderstood it, we think it's pretty cool.

Austin died in 1957 at the age of fifty-six from lung cancer. His wife, Helen Goodwin Austin, remained in the house. In 1985, she and her two children donated the house to the Atheneum.

Tours of the house can be arranged through the Atheneum and are conducted on the second and fourth Thursday and third Saturday of each month at 3 p.m. Admission.

If you are in the downtown area of Hartford, be sure to check out Connecticut's own Alexander Calder's *Stegosaurus*. You really can't miss this huge, red steel construction that towers over the Alfred E. Burr Memorial Mall, a pocket park between the Wadsworth Atheneum and Hartford City Hall. This fifty-foot-tall treasure was built in Waterbury and installed in Hartford in 1973 as a memorial to Alfred E. Burr, founder of the *Hartford Times*. In 2016, the structure received a facelift overseen by artist Abigail Mack in collaboration with the owners of the artwork, the Ella Burr McManus Trust (Alfred was Ella's father). Workers carefully removed decades of paint right down to the steel. A zinc-based primer was then applied and new coats of red paint, carefully matched to Calder's original color, were added. The pedestrian areas around the sculpture were cleaned and *Stegosaurus* once again stands proud.

As you continue north, turn left onto Gold Street and watch for this unexpected and ingenious work of art. Carl Andre's **Stone Field** sculpture has always been a subject of conversation in Hartford. It consists of thirty-six large rocks arranged in rows on a slope of lawn. Some critics consider it a statement of minimalist art; some witty citizens call it Hartford's Meadow Muffins. When Andre conceptualized the sculpture, he claimed he wanted to offer city residents a refuge from the noises of the city, a place in which to contemplate and relax. George Athanso, the city's mayor at the time, didn't buy the idea and thought the sculpture would cause the city to be a laughing stock. Of course, it didn't help matters that after using a scant $13,000 to quarry and transport the boulders from a Bristol quarry, Andre pocketed the remaining $87,000 of the $100,000 commission he was paid to create the work of art. See, as we said, ingenious.

After you contemplate a while in *Stone Field,* walk over to the four-acre **Ancient Burying Ground** (60 Gold St.; 860-337-1640; theancientburyingground. org). This cemetery was created in 1640 and holds the bones of some of Hartford's most prominent citizens, including Thomas Hooker. It's also the site of the **African-American Memorial** that honors the unmarked graves of more than 300 African Americans, including five governors, who are buried here. If you're a fan of early American art, the tombstones are a treasure trove of colonial death imagery and epitaphs. The cemetery is open Apr 1 through Nov 30, Mon

Freedom Fighters and Groundbreakers

Old North Cemetery (N. Main St. at Mather St.) contains the graves of numerous African-American Civil War soldiers. Some served in the state's all-black 29th Regiment, some were from the 31st Regiment US Colored Troops, and some came from other units. Many of the headstones have since gone missing, but at one time there were almost 30 military-issued headstones here. Take notice of headstones that are generally made of marble (or granite) and have a rounded top; these are usually military issue. The soldier's name typically will appear at the top with his company, regiment, date of death, and age.

Also located in Old North Cemetery is the grave of *Mary Townsend Seymour*, a civil activist and leader in Hartford. She is credited with cofounding the city's chapter of the National Association for the Advancement of Colored People (NAACP), fighting for women's rights, and being active in local and state politics. In fact, she was the first black woman to run for a state office. Seymour fought tirelessly throughout her life and in 2006 was inducted into the Connecticut Women's Hall of Fame. You'll find her family plot on the left side of the drive if you enter the cemetery from Main Street and walk toward the back gate.

Since you're in the area and cemeteries are your thing (as they are mine, welcome to the club), be sure to stop and explore *Spring Grove Cemetery* (2035 Main St.). Here you'll find the final resting place of *William Henry Jacklyn*, Hartford's first African-American firefighter, along with that of *Laurent Clerc*, founder of the American School for the Deaf. Both cemeteries are open from dawn to dusk.

through Fri, 8:30 a.m. to 4:30 p.m.; Sat, 9 a.m. to 5 p.m. Walking tour brochures can be found on the website.

Next to the State Capitol building on Jewell Street is *Bushnell Park* (166 Capitol Ave.; bushnellpark.org), the oldest publicly funded park in the country, and one of the first plots of land in America acquired through eminent domain for use as a park. The vision of *Rev. Horace Bushnell*, the park was first known as City Park and was designed not by Fredrick Olmstead as many think, but by *Jacob Weidenmann*, a Swiss-born architect. Olmstead was busy on New York's Central Park when Reverend Bushnell asked him to work on the project, and he recommended Weidenmann instead. Now, more than a hundred years later, the renamed Bushnell Park continues to be "a place of life and motion," as its creators intended. Fun activities are always taking place somewhere in the park, but there are also plenty of places to sit quietly and enjoy the beauty. Whatever your plans, definitely take the time to explore this park's treasures, including the 1914 *Bushnell Carousel* (1 Jewell St.; 860-585-5411; thecarouselmuseum.org), whose forty-eight antique Stein and Goldstein horses revolve beneath 800 twinkling lights. The band organ is a refurbished 1925 Wurlitzer, and yes, you really can try to catch a brass ring. While the park is open year-round, the carousel closes from Jan through Mar. It is run by the **New England Carousel Museum**. The carousel is usually open Sat and Sun, 11 a.m. to 5 p.m., but hours can be erratic, so it's best to check ahead. There's a small charge to ride, but it's well worth it.

The Historic *Hartford Courant*

Founded in 1764 by **Thomas Green**, the **Hartford Courant** (once the Connecticut Courant) is America's oldest continuously published newspaper. It is, in fact, older than our nation. It has been around long enough to report the Boston Tea Party as breaking news, and was a pro-patriot publication. This is an important distinction considering Boston newspapers were shut down by the Crown and much of what was coming out of New York was pro-British.

Green was a printer and worked diligently to keep the fledgling paper afloat. He owned a storefront out of which he sold dry goods and clothing and ran the news-paper out of an office in back. He had an assistant, Ebenezer Watson, who even-tually purchased the business from Green. Watson ran the paper until 1777, when he died of small pox. His wife, Hannah Bunce Watson, then stepped in to keep the paper going. This was no small feat considering Hannah had five young children to care for and the Loyalists were chomping at her heels; they burned down the paper mill she used and would not allow the *Courant* to be exported to the colonies. Hannah fought the good fight for two years before getting help from her new hus-band, Barzillai Hudson, in 1779.

Hannah Bunce Watson died in 1807 at the age of 57. She is buried in the Old South Burying Ground (Maple Ave at Benton St.) in Hartford next to Barzillai Hudson. The name on her gravestone is Hannah Hudson.

The paper continued to play an important part in the country's news-making machine and the history recorded therein is priceless. In 1783, Connecticut resident Noah Webster published his Blue-Backed Speller in the *Courant*. In 1796, a Virginia farmer named George Washington advertised in its real estate section to lease part of his land at Mount Vernon. The paper was embroiled in the messy and confusing case of libel brought about by Thomas Jefferson's administration (no charges were filed). In the mid-nineteenth century, the paper enthusiastically supported Abraham Lincoln and proclaimed his victory in 1860. At the turn of the twentieth century, the paper presented its Sunday edition, something that would become a household tradition across the area and continues today with a circulation in excess of 180,000. In 1954, it ran a doomsday scenario that proclaimed "Hartford Destroyed," with smaller print explaining that it hadn't actually happened. In 2013, the *Courant* won a Pulitzer Prize for its coverage of the shootings at Newtown, Connecticut.

Today, the *Hartford Courant* continues to be a leading newspaper in the area with a daily circulation of more than 120,000. Its offices can still be found in Hartford at 285 Broad Street.

hartford trivia

While the carousel is a well-publicized park attraction, there are also some hidden jewels in the park that are often overlooked (or just under appreciated). Take the trees, for example. In his original design for the park, Weidenmann included a whopping 157 varieties of trees and shrubs, spanning more than 1,000 specimens from across the world. Over the years, that number sadly shrunk to less than 340 due to disease, neglect, and damage. Thanks to the efforts of the **Bushnell Park Foundation**, the number of specimens has risen to 750 in recent years. So, as you're strolling through the park, see how many of the more unusual specimens you can find, like the largest turkey oak (*Quercus cerris*) in New England, a 500-year-old Chinese Toon (*Cedrela sinensis*), or the first-generation offspring of the state's original Charter Oak. Readers are welcome to attempt this search on their own by picking up a free tour brochure at the Capitol Building, but for those wanting a little help, check out the half-hour guided "Tree Tours of Bushnell Park," which runs seasonally. For more information, visit bushnellpark.org.

Visitors will also want to stop and appreciate the history behind the monuments within Bushnell Park. Various volunteer-led tours are available throughout the year. Check the website for the latest availability. If you decide to go it alone, here's a touch of what you'll find.

From May until the end of October, you can not only walk beneath the 1886 **Soldiers & Sailors Memorial Arch**, but if you happen to be in the park between noon and 1:30 on a Thursday, you can take a tour of the monument and learn little-known facts such as that the ashes of arch creator George Keller and his wife are buried in the east tower. Also be sure to check out the eight-foot-tall statues set into the arch. These represent residents who walked away from their lives to fight in the Civil War. You'll find a student, a farmer, a freed slave, a stone mason, a carpenter, and a blacksmith.

In the eastern portion of the park, near the pond, is an 1874 statue of **Horace Wells**, a Connecticut dentist who is my hero for pioneering the use of nitrous oxide anesthesia in 1846. Wells went on to have a few difficulties, including experiencing a bad episode after an overuse of chloroform. He unfortunately committed suicide in 1848, but was posthumously recognized for his achievements in 1870. He continues to be celebrated seasonally at the **Hartford Stage** in a play title *Ether Dome*, all about his life and tragic death.

The 1899 ***Corning Fountain*** was a gift from John Corning (of Corning Glass Works of New York). He commissioned this beautiful thirty-foot-tall fountain as a way to honor his father who operated a grist mill in Hartford.

Keep exploring to find the 1874 bronze monument to ***Israel Putnam***, the Connecticut resident who is credited with the famous line, "Don't fire until you see the whites of their eyes," on Bunker Hill in 1775. He also has some other history with the state, but we will revisit that in another section.

When you come across a statue of a torch-holding angel, check out the size of her feet! This is the **Spirit of Victory**, a ***Spanish American War Memorial*** that pays tribute to the soldiers who fought in the Spanish American War from 1898 to 1899. The feet needed to be made so large to keep the statue standing upright.

If you're done exploring Bushnell Park and want to get out of the elements for a bit, head south to Summit Street and the campus of ***Trinity College***. One don't-miss here is the college's chapel. Completed in 1932, the ***Trinity College Chapel*** boasts stained-glass windows, a cloister, arches, and carved pews in keeping with the best medieval tradition. The chapel's most interesting elements are seventy-eight ***hand-carved oak pews*** that face each other across the nave. It took more than thirty years to complete all the carvings, most of which were the work of ***J. Gregory Wiggins***, originally of Pomfret. Wiggins was a self-taught wood carver who began his trade as a young boy when he and his brother used to whittle wooden soldiers to play with. While it wasn't his full-time job—he also taught at St. Paul's in Concord, New Hampshire—Wiggins's carving gained great acclaim and can be found in many New England churches and even some private homes. He always put great thought into what he was creating, which is why his carvings are so unique. Wiggins was also a friend of Trinity President Remsen Brinckerhoff Ogilby, who held the position from 1920 to 1943. It was through this friendship that Wiggins was able to explore and expand his talent into the pews you see today. He once told Ogilby that he wanted to create humorous pieces for the church since "the act of smiling in church should not be considered a crime." Take the time to appreciate his carvings even as you take in the beauty of the chapel. The Charter Oak Pew shows Captain Joseph Wadsworth hiding the Connecticut Colony's royal charter in an ancient oak tree to prevent its recall by Royal Governor Edmund Andros (not a beloved figure in Connecticut history). There are carvings of animals, ships, soldiers, and warriors, as well as scenes from history. Wiggins continued to create works for Trinity until his death in 1956. He is buried at the Christ Episcopal Church Cemetery in Pomfret.

If your stomach is rumbling and you're in the mood for some hearty food, head to the **Polish National Home of Hartford** (PNH) (60 Charter Oak Ave.; 860-247-1784; polishhomect.org). This place offers some of the best Polish (and American) food in the area. It is often referred to as "Hartford's worst-kept secret," because it's not, in fact, a secret at all. Built in 1930 and designed by Hartford architect **Henry F. Ludorf**, the brick building in which the restaurant is located was meant to be a social center for the city's large Polish American community. Located next to the Capewell Horse Nail Company, which had been making horseshoe nails in the city since 1881 and employed a large number of Poles, the club enjoyed a robust business. As times changed and the demand for horseshoe nails dwindled, Capewell expanded into other areas and was acquired by the Hartford/Standard Machine Screw Company in 1970. Eventually, the horseshoe nail division was sold in 1985 and the plant closed altogether in the late 1980s. This brought on difficult times for the PNH as people began to branch out of the city and into the suburbs, leaving the once-thriving social club with a bit of an identity crisis. It held on through the years, though, and the current board of directors, some who have fond memories of many an afternoon spent with family at the club, are making strides to meet the needs of new generations. The club has opened its membership up to those of any ethnicity and now offers beer and wine tastings, business meeting space, and some, not all, lighter fare on its menus. The 1903 Romanesque Revival-style Capewell building has been renovated into luxury apartments that come with a complimentary one-year membership to the club. They have made updates to the aging Art Deco building, which is now a National Historic Landmark.

While you will find a few American dishes on the menu, the not-so-food-adventurous (such as yours truly) will want to bring along someone (such as a Polish husband or brother-in-law) who will appreciate the rest of the menu, which features true treasures from the homeland. The *Polski Talerz Luksusowy* (Polish Plate Deluxe) is a popular choice and includes fresh Polksa kielbasa, *bigos* (aka Hunter's Stew, which is sauerkraut and shredded cabbage simmered in a meat-based broth, usually pork but not always, and, I'm told, delicious), two pierogis (cheese and potato), *golabki* (stuffed cabbage), and delicious dill potatoes. It's a lot of food, but it's a nice sampling of what the PNH has to offer. The food is authentic, heavy, and delicious, and the owners do not apologize, as a sign behind the bar states, "Thousands in Poland are over 100 years old. It ain't the yogurt." You can check out their full menu online. Any choice you make pairs well with the local craft or imported beers available from the bar. Open 11:30 a.m. to 3 p.m. Tues through Wed, 11:30 a.m. to 11 p.m. (kitchen closes at 9 p.m.) Thurs through Sat, and 11 a.m. to 6 p.m. (kitchen closes at 5 p.m.) on Sun.

Elizabeth Park (1561 Asylum Ave., West Hartford; 860-231-9443, ext. 104; elizabethparkct.org), which first opened in 1904, is home to the first municipally-owned rose garden in America. The park itself, however, has been around since 1897 and was made possible when Charles Murray Pond donated his country estate to the city of Hartford. The park is named in honor of his wife, Elizabeth Aldrich Pond. Mr. Pond also left funds to design and maintain the park and to purchase additional property if desired. The city hired Theodore Wirth to design the park. Wirth consulted with the firm of Frederick Law Olmsted, and his influences can be seen throughout the property along with Wirth's. Today the property consists of 101 acres (90 of those were Pond's) and is lovingly cared for and maintained by the **Elizabeth Park Conservancy**, which was formed in 1977 and brought the park back from serious disrepair. They continue to work as a nonprofit and raise funds to keep the park not only beautiful but also thriving. Due much to their efforts, the park is now listed on the National Register of Historic Places and is visited by thousands annually.

The park offers something special during every season, but the approximately 15,000 rose bushes are at their peak between late June and early July. In those few brief weeks, Elizabeth Park is an experience that overwhelms the senses. The many varieties of roses come in all sizes and hues, and the mingled scents, from the sweetly-scented traditional American hybrids to the elegantly fragrant damask roses, are indescribable.

The park features amazing gardens with flowers of all varieties, including a perennial garden, a tulip and annual garden, a shade garden, and a horticulture garden. Fans of history and architecture should make time to explore the ground's historical buildings, many original to the Pond farm. Even the restrooms are architecturally interesting, built and designed in 1935 by Hartford architects Smith & Bassett. There is a gazebo that dates back more than a hundred years and feels like a gateway into another world. The maintenance buildings were WPA or possibly CCC projects. There are also greenhouses, ponds, and bridges to explore. And don't be so blinded by the flowers that you forget to check out the trees, too. Walking trails meander throughout the property. There are also six tennis courts, lawn bowling, basketball courts, playgrounds, and ball fields.

Elizabeth Park is open daily, year-round, dawn to dusk. Admission is free, but the conservancy always appreciates donations. Check their website for more information on the myriad special events and fundraisers happening throughout the year.

Back in 1874, the great American humorist and novelist **Mark Twain** (aka Samuel Langhorne Clemens) began summering in Hartford in a rambling, three-story, nineteen-room Victorian mansion that he had built to his eccentric specifications. In 1881, he had the place redecorated in an even more eccentric style by Louis Comfort Tiffany. For the next quarter century, this was the Twain family summer home, which Twain himself often described as "part house, part steamboat." It was the place where the author wrote some of his best works, including *The Adventures of Tom Sawyer*, *The Adventures of Huckleberry Finn*, *The Prince and the Pauper*, and *A Connecticut Yankee in King Arthur's Court*.

The restored **Mark Twain House and Museum** (351 Farmington Ave.; 860-247-0998; marktwainhouse.org) is now a museum and storehouse of Twain memorabilia. The unmistakable redbrick building, with its startling three-color slate roof, many gables, monumental chimneys (it has eighteen fireplaces), and flamboyant exterior walls painted in red and black Chinese stripes and trimmed in dark red, looms over the Farmington Avenue commuter traffic, almost like a lingering sardonic comment from the famous humorist. Inside, the unique rooms have been restored as close to their 1881 condition as possible. About half of the original furnishings remain or have been acquired, including Twain's Venetian bed, whose ornate headboard so intrigued the author that he slept with his head at the foot of the bed so he could see the intricate carvings.

While the Twain family spent many happy years at this house in Hartford, Twain himself experienced much heartache. He and his wife lost their first son, Langdon, to diphtheria at the tender age of two in 1871, the same year they moved to Hartford. They had a daughter that same year (Susy) and two more daughters (Clara in 1874 and Jean in 1880) and spent the next seventeen years at this home. In 1891, the Twains moved their family to Europe while keeping ownership of the Hartford house. In 1896, on a trip back home to Farmington Ave, Susy contracted meningitis and died at the age of twenty-four. The family never moved back to the house, unable to be where they had lost their beloved daughter and son. In 1904, Olivia passed away from an illness. In 1909, Jean died from complications due to epilepsy. Twain was left with only Clara until he died a year later in 1910 at the age of seventy-four. It seems he never really found happiness again after the loss of his children. This unrest is evidenced in the harshness that his writing took on in the later years, and it seems to permeate the house, even among the beauty.

This Blue Star Museum features a welcome center, exhibition galleries, a theater, and classrooms. While the welcome center and exhibits are self-guided, admission to the Twain family home is by guided tour only. There are a variety of tours to choose from, including holiday tours (highly recommended), Graveyard Shift Ghost Tours (learn what *Ghost Hunters* investigators discovered . . . if you dare), Get a CLUE tours, and the Living History House tours. Visit the website for more details. Open daily, 9:30 a.m. to 5:30 p.m. (last tour at 4:30 p.m.). Closed Tues, Jan through Feb. Also closed on major holidays. Gift shop. Admission.

Across the lawn from the Mark Twain House is the home where Twain's friend and famous author Harriet Beecher Stowe once lived. Today, the ***Harriet Beecher Stowe Center*** (77 Forest St.; 860-522-9258; harrietbeecherstowe.org) has a visitor center in an 1873 carriage house, The Stowe House, a museum shop, beautiful historic gardens, a research library, and the Katherine Seymour Day House. Day was Stowe's grandniece and she was responsible for the creation of the Harriet Beecher Stowe Center in 1941. Purchasing and moving into Stowe's house in 1927 (it had passed out of the family upon Stowe's death in 1896), Day lived there until her death in 1964, collecting all things related to her aunt and creating much of the collection you see today.

marktwaintrivia

Twain was fascinated by technology and incorporated many of the day's latest inventions in his home, including central heating and gas lighting fixtures. So it is fitting that the new museum center at the Mark Twain House was the first Leadership in Energy and Environmental Design (LEED)–certified museum in the country and the first LEED building in Connecticut. Among the many cutting-edge environmental features are the geothermal walls as the predominant cooling source.

Twain's ill-advised investment in a typesetting machine called the Paige Compositor resulted in such a devastating financial loss that he was forced to leave his Farmington Avenue home and move his family to Europe.

The Adventures of Tom Sawyer was the first novel in America to be written on a typewriter.

This collection of artifacts and buildings offers a vivid glimpse into Stowe's life, the life of the woman who helped galvanize the abolitionist cause with her novel *Uncle Tom's Cabin.*

In 1941, Day also purchased the 1884 mansion that sat next door to the Stowe House in order to save it from demolition. Today, known as the Katharine Seymour Day House in her honor, it holds the center's research library and administrative offices.

There are specialty tours and events throughout the year at the center, including Spirits at Stowe: An Otherwordly Tour (Oct) and The Preservation Tour, which focuses on the Victorian finishes in the house. The grounds of the Stowe Center are open year-round, dawn to dusk. The Stowe House is open year-round, Mon though Sat, 9:30 a.m. to 5 p.m.; Sun, noon to 5 p.m. Tours begin at 10 a.m., noon on Sunday. Admission. Free for active military during the summer. Not every building on site is handicapped accessible.

Connecticut Historical Society Museum and Library (1 Elizabeth St.; 850-236-5621; chs.org) was founded in 1825 and is one of the oldest historical societies in the country. Designated a Blue Star Museum, they offer exhibits that help visitors learn about history and understand today through interpretation of the past. They have rotating exhibits, including one on how our state fared and changed through World War I, one on signs for inns and taverns of the state, and more. Open Tues through Thurs, noon to 5 p.m.; Fri and Sat, 9 a.m. to 5 p.m. Admission.

The craft beer scene has taken Connecticut by storm, with new breweries popping up all the time. ***City Steam Brewery Cafe*** (942 Main St.; 860-525-1600; citysteam.biz) is located in the 1877 Cheney building designed by H.H. Richardson. This former home of the Brown Thomson and Company department store is loaded with character and City Steam has capitalized on that by creating a unique dining and brewing experience. With nine levels of space, they offer an outdoor beer garden, a pool and game room, private dining rooms, and, of course, a bar. They keep more than a dozen hand-crafted beers on tap at any given time. You might find their Naughty Nurse, Hoppy Harrington, Colt 45, and White Wedding if you're lucky. They also serve food and have gluten-free offerings, Sunday brunch, as well as typical bar fare. Open Mon through Thurs, 11:30 a.m. to 12 a.m.; Fri and Sat, 11:30 a.m. to 1 a.m.; Sun, 11 a.m. to 10 p.m.

Hog River Brewing (1429 Park St; 860-206-2119; hogriverbrewing.com) is a love story about Ben and Joy Braddock and their dream of owning a brewery. And it looks like they're doing it right, on all accounts. The beers are poured "direct from tank to your pint," and include such creations as a German wheat Summer Dusk Hefeweizen, Saison de Hartford (brewed in collaboration with Hanging Hills), and a Pixie Dust IPA that features citrus and passionfruit flavors. Hog River offers live music every Thurs, 7 to 9 p.m., no cover (they call them "Twang Thursdays"). They also invite food trucks on a regular schedule and hold special events throughout the year. Open Wed, 3 to 8 p.m.; Thurs and Fri, 3 to 10 p.m.; Sat, noon to 10 p.m.; Sun, 2 to 7 p.m. They suggest using 30 Bartholomew Ave. as your destination address for more accurate directions from your GPS. The entrance to the taproom is on Bartholomew, in the five-story white building on the corner of Park. Parking is available in the lot across the street.

Hanging Hills Brewing Company (150 Ledyard St.; 860-263-7033; hanginghillsbrewery.com) evokes an old legend about the black dog of Hanging Hills in Meriden. The story goes that a black ghost dog haunts the woods of Hanging Hills. Should you encounter him once, you will have a good day and good fortune. Should you meet him a second time, well, your day will not be so good. Should you encounter him a third time, your time on Earth comes to an end. But the folks at Hanging Hills were inspired by the adventure of this tale rather than the impending doom. Life is made up of chances and mystery and they embrace that.

They run a rotating tap list and offer pints, growlers, and cans of beer in their tasting room, as well as a calendar of special events best checked out on their Facebook page. Their beers include such deliciousness as B-Side IPA, Constructive Summer, June Bug Saison, Lulu L'Orange Sour Ale, Metacomet IPA (a nod to the hiking trail that runs through the Hanging Hills), Mail Truck, New England Sea Hag IPA, Saison de Hartford (in collaboration with Hog River) and so much more. Open Thurs, 5 to 8 p.m.; Fri, 4 to 10 p.m.; Sat, noon to 10 p.m.; Sun, 2 to 8 p.m. May your day be bright and your sightings of the ghost dog be rare. Drink on.

West Hartford

Granby has ponies, East Granby has turkeys, **West Hartford** has the cows, which makes sense considering this is where CowParade Holdings Corporation is located. There were actually two cow parades in town, one in 2003 and one in 2007, and money raised benefitted numerous charities. You can see some of the herd still in town.

But, of course, cows are not all that this swanky town has to offer. First settled in 1679, West Hartford stands in the shadow of Hartford but has a personality of its own. From the upscale Blue Back Square, where one can spend hours strolling the sidewalks and exploring the myriad shops and eateries to the down-home **Westmoor Park**.

Proud of its history, town officials installed a sign on **Goodman Green** (Farmington Ave and South Main St.) that lists thirty-nine historic West Hartford sites with a short history and a map location for all. The green itself is a historic site, too. Donated to the West Hartford Parish of the Congregational Church by Timothy Goodman in 1747, this parcel of land has long been the center of activity for this community. Now maintained by the town (but still owned by the parish), Goodman Green is host to special town events and ceremonies. While traffic can be busy on both Farmington Ave and South Main St., the green is worth the visit. For a preview of the list, visit westhartfordct.gov.

Across Farmington Ave from Goodman Green in Veterans Park, you will find **Connecticut Veteran's Memorial**, a memorial to all members of the US armed forces from King Philip's War to the present. This circular memorial of black granite is titled "The Wall of Peace," and symbolizes the passage of time. Each conflict involving the US is reflected with a breaking of the wall. The names of West Hartford residents who were killed are etched in the stone. There is also a Walk of Remembrance that leads to an inner area of reflection.

A short trip up Farmington Avenue and down Trout Brook Drive brings you to **The Children's Museum** (950 Trout Brook Dr.; 860-231-2824; thechildrensmuseumct.org), a great hands-on place to visit with the kids. They claim it's "where science and nature are fun," and they're right! Most kids we know like the giant walk-in kaleidoscope, but just as many love Conny the Whale, the giant, walk-in sperm whale (which is, of course, Connecticut's state animal). Voted *Hartford Magazine*'s "Best Kid's Attraction," the center offers the NASA-funded Blue Planet Red Planet exhibit, a planetarium (separate admission required), a wildlife sanctuary (very cool with lots of neat animals to see), an indoor forest that changes with the seasons, Turtle Town and Lizard Lair where critters can be seen and studied, and so much more. There are hands-on rooms, too, for those little ones with the wiggles. And don't forget the cool gift shop. Open Mon through Sat, 9 a.m. to 4 p.m.; Sun, 11 a.m. to 4 p.m. Closed major holidays. Admission for adults and children age 2 and older.

If you head south from the museum or Goodman Green, you can head to the **Vintage Hi-Fi Museum** (485 New Park Ave.; 203-877-2409; vintagehifimuseum.blogspot.com), where "everything vintage is new again." The folks here want to share their knowledge of high-fidelity music, vinyl records, and analog audio systems with American-made parts with those who are interested. Their focus is from the 1950s through the 1970s. Only open Wed, 11 a.m. to 2 p.m.; Sat, 9 a.m. to 3 p.m. Blue Star Museum.

And, since you're there, you should go next door to **New Park Brewing** (485 New Park Ave.; 860-232-2033; newparkbrewing.com), whose creations include Foliation, a pale ale brewed with flaked wheat and pilsner malt, and Expression Ten, with flavors of fresh pine needles, orange peel, and grapefruit. They have regular can releases, as well as food truck visits that are listed on their website. Monthly events include a Soul Brunch, which offers an array of soul, jazz, and R&B music, and includes a food truck and coffee roasters to complement the beer offerings. There's also a Funk Night that showcases special musical guests. Both events are free. The brewery is open Thurs, 5 to 9 p.m.; Fri, 4 to 10 p.m.; Sat, noon to 10 p.m.; Sun, noon to 5 p.m.

If you head north from the museum or Goodman Green, you can visit 162 acres of natural diversity at **Westmoor Park** (119 Flagg Rd.; 860-561-8260; westmoorpark.com). It's a great place to take the kids or the nature lover in your family. You will find a demonstration farm complete with farm animals; seasonal flower, herb, and vegetable gardens; a wildflower meadow; two ponds; an indoor discovery room with a parrot, geckos, turtles, and lizards; and three miles of nature trails all tended to by knowledgeable and talented staff. The park was made possible by the generous gift of Charles and Leila Hunter, who bequeathed the property to the town. The farm is open daily 9 a.m. to 4 p.m. year-round. The trails open at 7 a.m. and close at dusk. Fishing, picnicking, and dogs are not permitted in the park.

Newington

The town of Newington got its start as an industrial enclave of Wethersfield. The source of the town's first industry is portrayed on its town seal. Go ahead, go take a look. We'll wait.

Yep, you saw that right. It's a waterfall. A really, really small waterfall, about fifteen feet actually. But **Mill Pond Falls** (123 Garfield St.) is where everything started for the fledgling settlement. In 1677, before Newington was Newington, four men secured the right to build a saw mill on Mill Pond so they could make barrel staves (the beveled sides of the barrel). They must have been onto something; the business lasted for a century before the wood supply dwindled and the business diminished. Today, the falls are surrounded by Mill Pond Park, a gathering place for many in town with a playground, sports fields, and walking trails.

The Newington Historical Society (860-666-7118) manages two historic houses at 679 Williard Ave. The first one, **Kellogg-Eddy House & Museum**, is where the society is headquartered. It was built in 1808 by Captain Martin Kellog for his son and daughter-in-law, Martin and Mary Kellog. While Captain Kellogg died in 1753, his descendants lived in the house until 1913, and even then it was sold to a distant relative, E. Welles Eddy. In 1975, the town acquired the house from Eddy's widow and today it is listed on the National Register of Historic Places. Only open the first Sun of each month, 1 to 3 p.m., or by appointment.

The second historic home is the 1799 **Enoch Kelsey House**, which features hand-painted wall designs (like wallpaper, but real painting). It was also hiding a secret. Four *trompe l'oeil* paintings were discovered and society members knew immediately they had to save this house, which was slated for demolition. In 1979, they

newington trivia

Newington means "new town in the meadow," and residents adopted it as they made their departure from Wethersfield.

succeeded, and the house was moved from its original location to its Williard Avenue home. The paintings were cared for and preserved, and the house was lovingly restored as a unique example of this early-American art form. Tours are available by appointment and the house is sometimes open during public events.

If you have a ham-radio fan in your life, you'll want to visit the headquarters for the ***American Radio Relay League*** (225 Main St.; 860-594-0200; arrl.org). Founded in 1914, the ARRL is the national association for amateur radio, with more than 170,000 members. It is not only a mecca for ham-radio operators but also the official voice of amateur radio. In these days of lightning-quick communication, you may think of ham radio as merely an interesting hobby, but during natural disasters, ham radios provide vital information while our cell towers may be inoperable. Beside the administrative offices of the ARRL, you'll find ***W1AW***, the league's amateur-radio station. Ham operators come from all over the world to operate from W1AW (you need to have your license with you if you do). Tours are available Mon through Fri, 9 a.m. to noon and 1 to 4 p.m. By the way, there's no one story as to why operators are called hams. Some people say it's because the radio gives operators a chance to "ham it up"; others say it comes from the ham-fisted way early operators pounded their code keys. The most likely story is that "ham" is derived from "am," an abbreviation for "amateur."

Wethersfield

East of Newington is Wethersfield, once known as "Oniontown" because the crop, especially the red onion, grew so well within its confines and its scent permeated everything. In fact, the red onion still has a strong presence here. And, while Wethersfield boasts the motto of "ye most auncient towne in Connecticut," it is actually one of three towns settled in 1635, the first year of our colony. Wethersfield shares the distinction with Windsor and Hartford, each represented by a grapevine displayed on Connecticut's flag.

There is a friendly rivalry between the residents of these towns as to who was first; but no matter if it was first or not, Wethersfield was an important port on the Connecticut River as the town grew. Then, in 1692, a flood changed the course of the river forever and destroyed all but one warehouse in the prosperous river town. Adjustments needed to be made, the former shipping port was now a cove and the river was deep enough to allow ships to bypass Wethersfield and sail right into Hartford. Industrious residents shifted their port from the newly formed cove out to the new river side (the area that is now Rocky Hill), allowing them to remain active in the shipping industry into the nineteenth century.

Today, Old Wethersfield, the remnants of the original town, has more than 300 historic homes, many bearing the names of early sea captains and some dating back to before the Revolution. With so much history in one place, it's difficult to decide where to begin. The ***Wethersfield Historical Society*** (150 Main St.; 860-529-7656; wethersfieldhistory.org) offers some good advice on interesting narrated tours and exhibits to whet your appetite.

You can also choose to explore the **Wethersfield Heritage Walk**, a three-mile, self-guided tour of many of the historic sites. There are interpretive plaques along the walk that provide more information as well. To find an online map of the heritage trail, head to the town website (wethersfieldct.gov). You can park for free at the **Keeney Memorial Cultural Center** (200 Main St.; 860-529-7656; wethersfieldct.gov), where you will find more maps, public bathrooms, drinking fountains, historic exhibits, and a museum shop.

wethersfieldtrivia

Old Wethersfield was the setting for two amusing novels of gothic horror—*The Other* and *Harvest Home*—written by Wethersfield native Thomas Tryon.

Also on Main Street you'll find the **Old Wethersfield Country Store** (221 Main St., 860-436-3782; owcsct.com), named "Best General Store in New England" by *Yankee Magazine* in 2017, for good reason. Inside, you'll find a delightful menagerie of local food and products; 300 kinds of candies and chocolates (yep, 300); more than seventy different types of cheese; a nice selection of non-GMO, vegan, gluten-free, and organic foods; toys, gifts, and gift baskets for every occasion; and oh so much more, including ice cream. Owners Megan and John Jakubowski, who opened the store in 2014, are always looking for suggestions from their customers of what they'd like to see in the store. As the *New England Traveler* says, this store "takes the hit-and-miss out of finding locally made goodies and gifts." Open Tues through Fri, 10 a.m. to 7 p.m.; Sat 10 a.m. to 6 p.m.; Sun, 10 a.m. to 5 p.m.

If you have a seafood lover among you, you need to stop at **City Fish Market** (884 Silas Deane Hwy.; 860-522-3129; cfishct.com). Part fish market, part seafood restaurant, City Fish has been a fixture on the Silas Deane Highway since 1967. Owner John Anagnos is the third generation of the Anagnos family to operate the market; his four children who work alongside him are the fourth. It's family tradition for children to start working at the market at an early age to learn the ropes from the bottom up, and John started when he was nine.

When John's grandfather Genos came to America from Greece, he opened his fish market in Hartford. That was in 1930. In the 1940s, when war caused meat rationing, the seafood industry was not affected, allowing business to do well. As landscapes and populations changed, it was necessary for the family to think about relocating, and they picked Wethersfield. They purchased the building at their current address and retrofitted it to suit their needs.

Fresh seafood is available daily in their market, having been trucked in from Massachusetts seaports. If you don't see what you're looking for in their vast freezer cases, just ask; chances are they might have it in the back. If you'd rather have the cooking done for you, have a seat in the restaurant and enjoy the huge portions and friendly service. The market is open Mon through Fri, 7 a.m. to 6 p.m.; Sat, 7 a.m. to 5 p.m. The restaurant is open Mon through Fri, 9 a.m. to 6 p.m.; Sun, 9 a.m. to 5 p.m. City Fish also supplies many area restaurants with fresh seafood, so don't be surprised when you see their orange/yellow trucks on the highway going to and fro.

Independent bookstores are havens in our busy world. Of course you can always order from online, but there's nothing quite like that new book smell as you peruse the shelves for your next purchase, or that personal greeting as you enter the store. ***That Book Store*** (446 Silas Deane Hwy.; 860-529-5500; thatbookstore.com) was recently opened by mother-and-daughter-team Karen and Isabelle Opper. This new-to-the scene store is operating on a love of books and personal attention to its customers. They carry the bestsellers as well as books by local authors that you might not find at the larger stores. Open Mon through Sat, 10 a.m. to 7 p.m.; Sun, 10 a.m. to 5 p.m. Check their website for special events and book club information.

Rocky Hill

Leaving the nineteenth century behind, we travel to nearby ***Rocky Hill,*** and to another time in our history.

In 1966, while clearing ground for the construction of a new state building in Rocky Hill, bulldozer operator Ed McCarthy uncovered some unusual rocks. They had strange markings and scorings on them. It turned out that these were the tracks of dinosaurs that prowled the area 185 million years ago. In those days, this part of Connecticut was a mud flat on the shore of a huge lake, rich in fish and small crocodilians—good eating for a growing dinosaur.

After covering the initial excavation to preserve 1,500 tracks, the state excavated an additional 500 tracks, enclosed them in a geodesic dome, added an audiovisual facility that offers a neat presentation, and called the result ***Dinosaur State Park*** (400 West St.; 860-529-8423; dinosaurstatepark.org). Inside the dome, you'll be greeted by a full-size reconstruction of a carnivorous dinosaur called *Dilophosaurus,* but the big attraction is the amazing collection of tracks. Most of the impressions are three-toed, and they run up to sixteen inches long. There's also a hands-on Discovery Room with many things to explore.

The eighty-acre park also has two miles of nature trails and picnic tables, and a place where you can make your own dinosaur casts out of plaster (check the website; you'll need to bring your

connecticuttrivia

Purchase a Heritage Pass at Dinosaur State Park, Fort Trumbull (in New London), or Gillette Castle (in East Haddam) and receive unlimited admission into all three parks during the entire calendar year for two adults and four children.

own supplies). The Exhibit Center is open Tues through Sun, 9 a.m. to 4:30 p.m. The grounds close at 4 p.m. Admission.

The **Rocky Hill Historical Society** (785 Old Main St.; 860-563-6704; rhhistory.org) is located in the 1803 **Academy Hall**, the former school designed and built by architect Abraham Jaggers to teach sailors the art of navigation. The society has a few interesting exhibits showcasing artifacts from Rocky Hill's history, including a Danforth Pewter collection. Open Tues, 10 a.m. to noon; Sat, 12:30 to 3 p.m., or by appointment. There is no charge to visit.

The Rocky Hill–Glastonbury Ferry (293 Meadow Rd.; 860-625-8473), spanning the Connecticut River and linking one part of Route 160 (Ferry Lane) to the other, has been in operation since 1655. That makes it the oldest continuously operating ferry in America. It's also a good place to cross the river if you want to avoid the usually heavy traffic around Hartford's bridges. Service is provided by a tug called the *Cumberland*, which tows a barge called the *Hollister III*.

In 2011, this ferry, along with the Hadlyme–Chester Ferry, was almost shut down by the state in an effort to reduce the ever-present deficit. Nutmeggers again rallied—politicians were motivated, grassroots groups sprung up, voices were heard, and the decision was reversed. The Rocky Hill–Glastonbury ferry operates Tues through Fri (weather permitting), 7 a.m. to 6:45 p.m.; Sat and Sun, 10:30 a.m. to 5 p.m., Apr 1 through Nov 30. Cost is $5 per vehicle on weekdays and $6 on weekends, and $2 for pedestrians and bikers; special commuter rates are available.

And, since you'll be taking the ferry, why not stop at **Still Hill Brewery and Tap Room** (1275 Cromwell Ave., Building C; 860-436-6368; stillhillbrewery.com) and taste the creations of Scott Barbanel before leaving town. While relatively new to the professional brewing scene, Barbanel is no stranger to making home brews. He began experimenting at his family home on Still Hill in Glastonbury, carrying on the tradition that gave the hill its name back in the day when one of Glastonbury's founding fathers operated a still there. Although Scott was not brewing moonshine, his beers consistently drew compliments from his family and friends and they encouraged him to make the leap into professional brewing. He did. He opened the brewery and tap room early in 2016 and says it's his job to "craft high-quality kick-ass beers," and that it's our job to enjoy them. Well, okay, if we have to. Still Hill is open Thurs and Fri, 4 to 8 p.m.; Sat and Sun, noon to 6 p.m. Time to go to work.

The Collins family of **Fair Weather Acres** (1146 Cromwell Ave.; 860-529-6755; fairweatheracres.com) has farmed the Connecticut River Valley for more than a century. The present generation, Chris and Mary Collins and their son Billy, started Fair Weather Acres in 1988 and went on to become the largest green bean grower in New England. In 1997, Fair Weather Acres relocated to the site of the original Collins Farm and business boomed until superstorm Irene hit the state in 2011. True to their roots, the Collinses recovered from the damage, diversified their business, and today they thrive once more. Their farm produces more than 200 varieties of fruit, vegetables, and herbs. They have a farm market, offer a CSA program, and host a large annual festival in the fall. The farm has seasonal hours as follows: Apr and May, Sun, 9 a.m. to 5 p.m.; Mon through Sat, 9 a.m. to 6 p.m.; June through Aug, Sun, 9 a.m. to 5 p.m.; Mon through Fri, 8 a.m. to 7 p.m.; Sat, 8 a.m. to 6 p.m.; Sept and Oct, Sun, 9 a.m. to 5 p.m.; Mon through Sat, 9 a.m. to 6 p.m.; Nov and Dec, Sun through Fri, 9 a.m. to 5 p.m.; Sat, 9 a.m. to 6 p.m.

You simply cannot leave Rocky Hill without stopping at **Scoops & Sprinkles** (2229 Silas Deane Hwy.; 860-436-3031; scoopsandsprinklesct.com). The Rocky Hill Chamber of Commerce voted them Best of 2018 in customer service and we couldn't agree more. This family-owned and -operated ice cream shop features more than forty-five flavors of premium ice cream, sherbet, and sorbet. Oh, did we mention they have a variety of gluten-free, nut-free, and dairy-free options as well? But what makes them stand out from the others is their commitment to their community. Owner Shane Aforismo and his staff go above and beyond in supporting local causes, boosting fellow businesses, holding fundraisers, doing whatever they can to lend a hand. You'll often see them and their Scoops & Sprinkles Ice Cream Cart at farmers markets and outside other's businesses in an effort to draw customers in. Open daily, year-round. Summer hours are Mon through Sat, 11 a.m. to 10 p.m.; Sun, noon to 10 p.m. In the spring they are open Sun through Wed, noon to 9 p.m.; Thurs and Fri, noon to 9:30 p.m.; Sat, 11 a.m. to 9:30 p.m.

East of the River

Glastonbury

When Senator John Quincy Adams received a petition signed by forty women in **Glastonbury**, he probably had no idea what he was dealing with. The petition was circulated by sisters Julia and Abby Smith and their mother, Hannah, to protest slavery. But the women didn't stop there. They, along with the other members of the Smith family, used their home, known as **Kimberly Mansion** (1625 Main St.), as a base of operations for their work for freedom, including hosting antislavery lectures and abolitionist meetings, and distributing literature throughout the area. In 1994, the Glastonbury family was inducted into the Connecticut Women's Hall of Fame to honor their tireless work. Kimberly Mansion is now a National Historic Landmark. You can drive by the home, but please respect the present owners' privacy, as the home is privately held and not open to the public.

Today, Glastonbury is home to many farms and orchards. A complete list with addresses and crops they offer, as well as a crop calendar can be found on the Glastonbury town website (Glastonbury-ct.gov). Many of these farms have pick-your-own options or roadside stands. It's always a good idea to have cash with you in small bills, as sometimes the farm stands are on the honor system and no one is there to give you change.

If you're lucky enough, you'll choose to visit one of the two farms whose crops also include grapes. For example, the ***Joseph Preli Farm & Vineyard*** (235 Hopewell Rd.; 860-633-7333; josephprelifarm.com) has a farm stand *and* a winery. Head to the farm stand to pick up some fresh garlic, fresh-cut flowers, radishes, plums, or yellow squash. Or maybe you want to pick your own blueberries or blackberries. Then you can head to the vineyard and find the outdoor tasting area. Sounds good, right? The winery is open Fri, Sat, and Sun, noon to 6:30 p.m.; the farm stand is open Fri, Sat, and Sun, 8 a.m. to 6:30 p.m.

Crystal Ridge Winery (257 Belltown Rd.; 860-657-1004; crystaldridgewinery. com) is another fine wine choice. This vineyard was established in 2004 on a two-hundred-acre estate in South Glastonbury. In 2018, Crystal Ridge added a tasting room where you can do a tasting of five wines (Estate Tasting) or four (Reserve Tasting) of their red, white, and rose wines, made right on the premises. The winery is truly a family venture with everyone lending a hand to make things run smoothly. Matriarch MaryAnn James passed away in 2016 after a battle with cancer, and the family continues in her honor.

Open Thurs and Fri, 4:30 to 8 p.m.; Sat, noon to 8 p.m.; Sun, noon to 6 p.m. Hours may change with the seasons, so be sure to check their website or Facebook page to be sure. They also hold special events and have a calendar on their website.

East Hartford

Any Connecticut guidebook will tell you that the ***Makens Bemont House*** (307 Burnside Ave.; 860-568-5188) in ***East Hartford***'s Martin Park is an excellent example of a restored colonial house. They'll talk about the gambrel roof and the vaulted dormer windows. What they won't tell you is that the house has ghosts, albeit friendly ones. When the house was moved in 1971 from its original location on Tolland Street to the park, workers started reporting seeing the ghost of a lady in a blue dress. Then, as construction to restore and anchor the house to its new site began, work was frequently disrupted by the loud sounds of crashing, knocking, and hammering, even when the house was empty.

The occurrences became so regular, workers dubbed the haunt "Benny," and the foreman made out a daily work list for the ghost. Some believe the ghost or ghosts are the original residents of the house, Edmund and Abigail Bemont. Edmund built the house for his wife and son, Makens, in 1761. Descendants lived there into the nineteenth century, so who knows who haunts the residence now. The house was donated to the **Historical Society of East Hartford** in the late 1960s. The all-volunteer society offer limited tours, so it's best to call ahead. Maybe you'll get lucky and have the chance to meet the spirits who roam the rooms and go bump in the night.

East Hartford is also home to the ***Hockanum River Linear Park Trail*** (hockanumriverwa.org), a four-and-a-half-mile trail that runs from Hillside Street to the Meadow Hill Station on Pitkin Street. Parking is available at designated spots along the trail and on the website the trail is mapped, broken into sections according to these parking places.

One of the parking places is a destination in itself. ***Great River Park*** (301 East River Dr.; riverfront.org/parks/great-river-park) is part of the movement to recapture the riverfront, and it's lovely. It features an amphitheater in which many special events and concerts take place, sculptures, nearly two miles of walking trails that are paved and lighted, a boat launch, and access to fishing in the river. And, if you choose, you can walk across the ***Founders Bridge Promenade*** into Hartford from the park. Parking is free and off street, but may be limited during special events. The park is open year-round.

Family is always welcome at the table, but food needs to earn its place. That's the motto at ***Granny's Pie Factory*** (103 School St.; 860-291-1164; grannyspiefactory.com), owned and operated by Joan and Anton Harovas along with their son, Niko. They make pie—and only pie—and they do it right. Believing that traditions are made around the family table, they want to make it a little easier for people by giving them a delicious reason to gather around that table. Any one of their pies will bring family members out of the woodwork and off their electronics. Give them a try and reconnect with your loved ones.

Manchester

Manchester is the fifteenth most populated town in Connecticut, and the eighty-fifth largest, so that tells you a little something about this interesting community. Originally home to the Podunk Indians, this area didn't see English settlers until 1673. The area then proceeded to go through an identity crisis as it grew and more people arrived in the area. It was part of Hartford for a while, known as the Five Mile Tract; then it became Orford Parish and was part of East Hartford. This was about a decade before the turn of the eighteenth century, and there were about 1,000 residents in the area, including ***Captain Richard***

Pitkin who, along with his sons, had supplied gun powder to the Continental army. As a thank you to the Pitkin family for their service, the newly minted State of Connecticut awarded the family a twenty-five-year monopoly on the manufacturing of glass. The *Pitkin Glass Works* was formed in 1783 and dominated the glass trade in the area until about 1830, mainly manufacturing bottles, flasks, and inkwells. The remains of the glass works building can still be seen on the corner of Putnam and Parker Streets.

While you're there at the corner of Putnam and Parker, turn west toward the traffic island. There, hidden within a stand of arborvitaes is a sign that designates this as the site of the 1775 *Pitkin Tavern*. It was here, the sign says, that Richard Pitkin and his wife Dorothy fed twenty-six Manchester volunteers who "answered the Lexington Alarm." Mrs. Pitkin is also credited with feeding General Rochambeau's army in 1761 as they headed to Yorktown. So not only did the Pitkins supply gun powder to the troops, they kept them fueled with food as well!

The Pitkin family was joined by other families who made their living in the area. According to the **Manchester Historical Society**, the town had two churches (Congregational and Methodist), five schools, four taverns, five saw and grist mills, one unsuccessful copper mine, three paper mills, and several woolen and cotton factories throughout the years. The town applied for incorporation in 1812, but was not successful until 1823, when Orford Parish officially became the town of Manchester.

One of the more successful manufacturing endeavors in Manchester belonged to a gentleman by the name of *Richard N. Mather*, who owned and operated Mather Electric. Originally in Hartford, Mather moved his business to Manchester when he built an impressive new mill on Hilliard Street, close to the New England Railroad that ran through the area, in the summer of 1887. At that time, generators and light bulbs were the backbone of Mather Electric. Mather was known in the industry as an "electrical genius," securing more than twenty patents in his life, including one in 1883 for the first generator. His light bulbs, known then as "lamps," graced the Chicago Opera House in 1885 when they made the switch from gaslights. Mather continued to enjoy success for the next ten years before trouble struck. In 1893, a company by the name of General Electric accused Mather of infringing on Thomas Edison's patent for the light bulb. Mather struck back, saying the GE wanted a monopoly on the industry and was trying to put him out of business.

The battle raged in the courts for close to a year before Mather had to stop making his light bulbs. At one point, even the street lights in the north end of the city went dark. Mather Electric revamped and reorganized and continued making machinery for a time in their fancy building on Hilliard Street, but the company and the man were never the same.

As a way to make ends meet, the company leased some of its building space to other manufacturers, including the Norton Electrical Instrument Company, which saw success during the war years as it made anti-mine apparatus among other things; there was a company in the building in 1896 that built "horseless carriages," a typesetting equipment manufacturer named Unitype that moved to the building for the tax benefits offered by the town to lure them here. The **Orford Soap Company** rented space on Hilliard Street after their Oakland Street building was destroyed by a fire in 1899. They liked it so much that they ultimately purchased the entire plant from Mather in 1903.

After the soap company ceased operations at Hilliard Street, other businesses moved in and out of the building over the years with ownership changing periodically but the buildings remaining more or less intact. In 1980, the Train Exchange and Miniature Corner operated here, featuring a miniature railroad room on the second floor. Today, **Time Machine Hobby** (71 Hilliard St., 860-646-0610; timemachinehobby.com) occupies the building and continues the tradition of the upstairs train room, with the **Silk City Model Railroad Club** coming in every first and third Sunday of the month from 1 to 4 p.m. to build, add on to, and operate the huge layout, which is now the largest in New England.

Downstairs on the first floor you will find so many toys and hobbies from today and yesteryear. From model cars to spud guns, from therapy putty to stuffed animals, from board games to card tricks, there's something for everyone. The prices are competitive and the staff knowledgeable and eager to help. Stop in and enjoy the toys and trains, but also take a moment to appreciate the building and the history it has witnessed. They are open year-round Mon through Wed, 10 a.m. to 6 p.m.; Thurs, 10 a.m. to 8 p.m., Fri through Sun, 10 a.m. to 6 p.m.

Manchester's **Fire Museum** (230 Pine St.; 860-649-9436; thefiremuseum. org) is home to the **Connecticut Firemen's Historical Society**. The museum was born out of a concern that our state was losing its firefighting history to other outside collectors. On March 20, 1970, a group of concerned firemen met to discuss forming a watchdog group with the intent of collecting and preserving artifacts of the fireman's life. The society held its first official meeting early in 1971. There were representatives from each county in the state and their first order of business was to find a home. While the search was on, artifacts and treasures were already being secured with a special attention to a man named **Clarence Baldwin** who already had an impressive collection of fire and police memorabilia. When asked, he agreed to leave his entire collection to the society.

Manchester's town manager, Bob Weiss, alerted the society members that the old fire station in his town was slated to be demolished unless a suitable use for it could be found. The members jumped at the chance and in the spring of 1979 the society signed a 100-year lease for the property, which was in desperate need of some love. It took four years, a state grant, hundreds of hours of work from volunteers, and a little help from the US Navy Sea Bees for the museum to finally open. The dedication took place on October 29, 1983, thirteen years after the idea was first conceived.

Built in 1901 and located at the corner of Pine Street and Hartford Road, the building served as a fire station until the mid-1960s, using only horse-drawn equipment until 1910. In 1921, an Ahrens Fox pumper was installed and is still working and on display at the museum, along with a 1912 Seagrave Chemical engine that was also operated at this fire station. You'll also find old leather fire buckets, ornate marching hats, wooden water mains and a rare eighteenth-century fire warden's staff among other artifacts on the museum's three floors. There's even a collection of old prints and lithographs of fires, from the pre-photographic era when the artist and lithographer were as important as the reporter to the process of communicating the news. The museum is open from the second Sat in Apr through the second Sat in Nov, noon to 4 p.m. Fri and Sat. Other dates and times may be available by appointment. Suggested donation of $5 for adults; children under 12 are admitted free.

If you have time to drive around Manchester, take note of these two houses should you pass by them (both are now private properties, so you must admire them from the street). The first is the ***Walter Bunce House*** (34 Bidwell St.), which was built by ***Alpheus Quicy***, an African-American stonemason, and is the only such building of his that still stands today. Quicy, his father, and his brother are credited with building important fieldstone homes and several dams in the Manchester area.

The second home of note is the ***Hart Porter House and Its Outbuilding*** (465 Porter St.), built sometime between 1840 and 1845 and believed to be a stop on the Underground Railroad due to a full basement in the outbuilding that is accessible only through a trapdoor. This leads us to the question, who was Hart Porter? We know he was born in 1812 and died on October 4, 1891. He worked as a farmer and married Martha Miner on January 12, 1837, in the in the same Manchester Methodist Church where Frederick Douglass spoke in 1843. Does this tie him to the abolitionist movement? The church's pastor, Reverend V.R. Osborn, often preached the importance of the abolitionist movement, but were Porter and his family in the audience? Besides the clues left behind in the house he built on the street named for him, it appears that Hart Porter was an inconspicuous man who went to remarkable lengths, at great risk to himself, to help others find freedom.

If you are in the area and have the kids with you, why not let them burn off some energy with a visit to the *Lutz Children's Museum* (247 S. Main St.; 860-643-0949; lutzmuseum.org). Founded by a former art teacher and located in a former school building, this place is designed for children. The emphasis here is on "please touch" science and natural history exhibits including live animals rescued by the museum. If the animals can be rehabbed, they are cared for and released back to the wild. If their injuries are such that they would not be able to care for themselves, they become residents of the museum. There is also an art exhibit here with rotating collections. Owing much to the museum's founder's belief that we need to encourage our children to display their creations, the museum has a partnership with area teachers who show their students' artwork here. The museum also sponsors several excellent programs throughout the year including classes, trips, outreach programs, and summer camp. Open year-round, Tues through Fri, 9 a.m. to 5 p.m.; Sat and Sun, noon to 5 p.m. Closed Mon. Admission except for those younger than one.

The Tobacco Valley

South Windsor

Jem's Gardens (1062 Pleasant Valley Rd.; 860-550-4652) is a roadside food stand run by mom-and-daughter team Ellen and Jordan Marouski, offering delicious homemade sandwiches made right there at the snack shop. Choose from the J.P. Melt (turkey, spinach, tomato, caramelized onions, peppers, and melted American cheese); a wrap with seasonal veggies and hummus; a panini with caramelized onions, red pepper hummus, Swiss cheese, tomato, and spinach; and more! If you're in a hurry, you can call ahead and they'll have your order ready when you arrive. Be sure to save room for ice cream, which they serve here as well. They will also do customized dessert trays with advance order and holiday pies. Open Mon through Sat, 11 a.m. to 9:30 p.m.; Sun, 2 to 9 p.m. Sandwiches are served until 6 p.m. (no sandwiches on Sun).

South Windsor is also home to *Carla's Pasta* (50 Talbot Ln; 860-436-4042; carlaspasta.com), a company started in 1978 by Carla Squatrito and now run with the help of her two sons, Sandro and Sergio. Carla knows what she's doing in business as well as in the kitchen—the National Women Business Owners Corporation has recognized her as Outstanding CEO every year since 2010. Housed in a 100,000-square-foot manufacturing facility, the company pumps out pounds of award-winning pasta daily, which you can find in many of the grocery stores across the county as well as from their food truck as it makes the rounds (follow them on Facebook to see their schedule). They provide recipes for many of their pastas on their website.

East Windsor

The **Connecticut Trolley Museum**, **Connecticut Fire Museum**, and **Connecticut Motor Coach Museum** (58 North Rd.; 860-627-6540 for Trolley Museum or 860-623-4732 for Fire and Motor Coach Museum) in East Windsor offer you the opportunity to visit three great museums for one price in one location. How can you beat that?

The Trolley Museum is run by the nonprofit **Connecticut Electric Railway Association** and has a collection of more than seventy pieces of rail equipment, some dating back to 1869. The collection includes freight and passenger cars, interurban cars, elevated railway cars, locomotives, and more. While most of the trolleys are from New England and Canada, there are some from as far away as Illinois and Ohio and one from Rio de Janeiro. The museum offers a car-barn tour and a three-mile trolley ride. Special events are held throughout the year including Storytime Mondays and Lego building contests. There are also special holiday rides, including Winterfest in December, which features leisurely rides along a one-and-a-half-mile route decorated with twinkling colored lights. Santa has also been known to make an appearance.

The Connecticut Fire Museum is operated by the **Connecticut Antique Fire Apparatus Association** and has a collection of about twenty fire trucks built between the early and late twentieth century. The adjacent Motor Coach Museum, also run by the Connecticut Antique Fire Apparatus Association has a variety of transit busses on display.

The museums are open sporadically depending on the season, but weekends are your best bet. Check their website ct-trolley.org for the latest. Admission.

Halloween Spooktacular

Maybe it's the scudding clouds posed against a full harvest moon. Maybe it's the whirling wisps of ground fog whipped along by a shuddering wind. Maybe it's the weight of all those years of history. We're not sure what it is, but in New England we enjoy Halloween a lot.

The Connecticut Trolley Museum in East Windsor offers "Rails to the Darkside" Fri and Sat at 7 p.m. The rides take you out on the rails when few dare to join you. According to trolley records, a cemetery was relocated due to the construction of the Hartford & Springfield line to Rockville. Perhaps some of the spirits are not so happy in their new homes. Will they choose to let you know about it? Visit ct-trolley.org/events/darkside.php for more details . . . if you dare.

Windsor

Once upon a time, every town had a *Bart's Drive-In* (55 Palisado Ave.; 860-688-9035; bartsdrivein.com). Today they are scarce, but you'll find one in *Windsor*. Once you find a place like Bart's, you become a customer for life. Bart's started as a hot dog stand, eventually expanded to include an indoor dining area, and has now expanded even further to include the Beanery Bistro right next door. Whether you're craving a chili dog, fresh fish, an ice cream cone, or maybe a gourmet coffee and a muffin, you'll find it here. Watch for Seafood Sunday, when all seafood is delivered and prepared fresh daily. There are picnic tables that overlook the river, and you can usually spot anglers fishing from the shore or in boats, so after a meal it's fun to sit awhile and watch or stroll down the sidewalk that runs along the river. Open Mon through Fri, 7 a.m. to 8 p.m.; Sat, 8 a.m. to 4 p.m.; Sun, 11 a.m. to 4 p.m.

The *Windsor Historical Society* (96 Palisado Ave.; 860-688-3813; windsorhistoricalsociety.org) was founded in 1921 and continues to preserve the town's history and share it with all those who visit. The society operates a museum and library where you can explore and discover myriad permanent and changing exhibits, including old journals and maps, an 1800 highway survey, and an original payroll list of the Windsor residents who answered the rebel alarm in Boston in spring 1775. The museum also contains a variety of Native American relics and a display of Americana. Open Wed through Sat, 11 a.m. to 4 p.m. Admission.

The society cares for two historic houses in Windsor. The first, the *Dr. Hezekiah Chaffee House* (108 Palisado Ave.), was built around 1767 and was home to the doctor and his family. It is said that John Adams had dinner here in 1774. The house now belongs to the town of Windsor, and the society began leasing it in 1992. They opened the first floor to the public in 1993 as a museum with period furnishings and household items. Visitors can also learn about the lives of slaves owned by the Chaffee, including Elizabeth Stevenson, who was emancipated, and Nancy Toney, who was the last surviving slave in the state when she passed away in 1857.

Dr. Chaffee's offices were attached to the family's home and are available for viewing today. Visitors can view medical instruments and learn about medicinal practices during that time. Chaffee's daughter, Abigail, was married to Colonel James Loomis. Their son, James Chaffee Loomis, went on to become a senator and founded the **Loomis Institute** along with his siblings. Back then the institute separated boys and girls, and The Chaffee House housed the girls' division, which went on to become the Chaffee School. The two branches reunited in 1970 to form the **Loomis-Chaffee School**.

The historical society also manages *The Strong-Howard House* (96 Palisado Ave.). This historic home (formerly the Fyler House) experienced a bit of an identity crisis when it was renamed in 1999. The house was scheduled to be demolished in 1925, but was saved thanks to the efforts of the historical society which raised $750,000 for restorations. In their research to do just that, the society discovered that while the home sat on land belonging to Lieutenant Walter Fyler, the current structure was actually built by the Strong family 118 years after the Fylers were in residence and later substantially updated by Captain Nathanial Howard. Hence, the new name.

The house now reflects the way of life at the beginning of the nineteenth century, but you don't have to be careful of fragile artifacts in this museum. In fact, touching and exploring is encouraged! That's because the furniture and household objects are actually accurate reproductions. Each item was carefully researched and created to reflect the time period. So go ahead and sit on that bed! Guided tours of both homes are available Mon through Wed, at 11 a.m. and 1 p.m.

Windsor Locks

For anyone interested in the history of aviation, the *New England Air Museum* (36 Perimeter Rd.; 860-623-3305; neam.org) in nearby *Windsor Locks* is a must. The museum features an extensive collection of aircraft, memorabilia, and exhibits housed in three large heated or cooled (depending on the need) hangars. Some of the larger aircraft are kept outdoors. One of the oldest aircrafts is a beautiful wood-and-canvas Bleriot XI monoplane, dating from 1911. There is also an extensive collection of World War II fighters and bombers, and even supersonic jets. The museum also features smaller items of interest, including a variety of engines, cockpit simulators, and a collection of flight memorabilia. Many of these items, acquired from area aerospace companies, can't be seen anywhere else. Open daily 10 a.m. to 5 p.m., closed on Mon after Labor Day. Don't miss their Open Cockpit and Veterans Day programs; they are a family favorite. Gift shop. Admission. Museum passes cannot be used on special event days.

westsuffieldtrivia

West Suffield is the site of the first cigar factory in the country. Built in 1810, the site of the factory is now marked by a mere gravestone-like monument on the front lawn of a residence on Ratley Road, just south of Spruce Street in West Suffield.

Suffield

A few miles up Route 75 from the New England Air Museum is another museum commemorating quite a different era. The restored 1764 home on *Suffield's* beautiful Main Street (Route 75) is the *King House Museum* (232 S. Main St.; 860-668-5256). The building is filled with period furnishings, including a four-poster bed that formerly graced the Jonathan Trumbull house in Lebanon, and features six original fireplaces. Displays include an assortment of Bennington pottery, a tinware collection, and, appropriately enough for the Tobacco Valley, a collection of cigar and tobacco memorabilia. The King House Museum is open Wed and Sat, May through Sept, from 1 to 4 p.m. Admission is free, but donations are welcome.

Enfield

About twenty minutes east of Suffield is the town of *Enfield* and the site of Connecticut's only community of Shakers. This community thrived in Enfield from 1792 to 1917. Based on the premise of direct communication between man and God, Shakers did not believe in praying through a church, priests, or other men of cloth, but members would sit and meditate until they received a sign from God personally. At this point, they would begin to tremble or shake, hence the name "Shaking Quakers," which was eventually shortened to Shakers and adopted by the group. While it may have started off as a derogatory term, it came to symbolize quality and integrity.

Facing serious opposition in England, Shaker leader Ann Lee set sail for America with some of her supporters in 1774 and began spreading word of their religion on the shores of America. First visiting Enfield in 1781, Mother Ann, as she was known, was met with opposition and barely escaped being tarred and feathered. She risked a second visit the following year and again met with opposition that broke out in serious riots. Not to be deterred, however, Ann returned to Enfield in 1783. While this visit was much more peaceful than the previous two, Mother Ann would not live long enough to enjoy it. She died the following September at the age of 48. She had laid the seeds in this community, however, and in 1792, the first Shaker community was established in Enfield.

Throughout the years, the Enfield community grew to include five families who lived on nearly 3,000 acres in town. The group held true to its beliefs in feminism, pacifism, and freedom. It became an important stop for fugitive slaves in their quest for justice, as evidenced by a diary of a member that chronicles the visit of one Sojourner Truth. The community thrived through the first half of the 1800s, but then things started to decline. The stringent demands of the religion began to take their toll, and one by one the families disbanded or merged until only eight members were left. When they could no longer survive on their own, they moved to other established Shaker communities.

Today, only a few buildings built and owned by this Shaker community remain. Some are privately owned, and the rest, unfortunately, are not open to public access, as they are on the grounds of the state Department of Corrections facilities on Shaker Road in Enfield. Visitors can, however, learn more at Enfield Historical Society's **Old Town Hall Museum** (1294 Enfield St.; 860-745-1729) and the **Martha A. Parsons House Museum** (1387 Enfield St.; 860-745-6064) or by visiting enfieldhistoricalsociety.org.

Like every other successful business, Powder Hill Farm in Enfield was feeling the need to diversify to survive. For this working dairy farm, the 1990s brought falling milk prices and struggling times. Owners Jack and Mavis Collins decided to open **The Collins Creamery** (9 Powder Hill Rd.; 860-749-8663; thecollinscreamery.com) in 1997. The business took off and today is managed by Jack and Mavis's daughter and son-in-law, Tony and Michele Bellafronte, which is funny because Tony doesn't eat ice cream. They do just fine, however, by offering more than 20 flavors of the richest, creamiest ice cream we have ever tasted. For those of you who can't handle the high-test stuff, there is also frozen yogurt, fat- and sugar-free, and soft serve. While there is no indoor seating, you are welcome to stay and enjoy your frozen treat at the picnic tables among the beautiful farmland. Open daily, noon to 10 p.m. Remember to bring cash; they don't do plastic here.

East Granby

When **East Granby** was first settled in 1664 it was known as the Turkey Hills Ecclesiastical Society, and the town really embraces this history. The turkey is on the town seal, there's a Turkey Hills Road that runs through town, and in 2008 when the town was celebrating its 150th birthday, they took a page from Granby's campaign of the painted ponies called "Giddy Up to Granby," but they put their own spin on it. They trotted out the turkeys. Fiberglass turkeys, that is. Sponsors were able to decorate their turkeys to their liking and these Toms started popping up all over town. There are about forty in total and they stand about five feet tall; you will see them outside of businesses and on private lawns. See how many you can find!

One place you won't find a turkey is the **Old New-Gate Prison &
Copper Mine** (115 Newgate Rd.; 860-653-3563). "Copper mine" and "prison"
are not usually two things linked together, but such is the case here. Originally
chartered as the first copper mine in America in the early 1700s, the town's
mine didn't produce the results necessary to make it profitable, although not
for lack of trying—fifty years of trying, in fact! Work was finally abandoned in
1750. The mine, with all its holes and tunnels, sat empty for over twenty years
until 1773, when it was decided by the General Assembly that the dark, dank
environment might be just the place to deposit criminals. On December 22,
1773, New-Gate Prison (its notorious namesake being in London) welcomed
its first prisoner—John Hinson. (He escaped eighteen days later, but he was
still the first!) The prison operated as our nation's first state prison until 1827
and during that time proved to be a nasty, cruel, and horrible place, gaining a
reputation as "the worst hell-hole in North America." The site is now a National
Historic Landmark and a State Archaeological Preserve. It was reopened to the
public in July 2018 after an eight-year restoration. The preserve includes forty-
five acres of land on which stand the one-acre prison yard surrounded by a
twelve-foot-tall stone wall. Inside the wall you'll find the entrance to the underground copper mine, a guardhouse, the ruins of a chapel, two workshops,
and a cell block. While the prison had a substantial complex of aboveground
buildings, the prisoners were confined fifty feet belowground in the dank
passageways of the old mine. Disease claimed many. Others committed suicide
or went insane. In fact, some people say that spirits of the men and women
who met their demises here still haunt the tunnels to this day. Visit if you dare!
Open July through Oct, Fri, 1 to 5 p.m.; Sat and Sun, 10 to 5 p.m.; Mon, 10 a.m.
to 1 p.m. Admission for those older than 12; Blue Star Museum.

Across the street from the prison stands the **Viets' Tavern**, an eighteenth-
century house that was home to Captain John Viets, first warden of the prison,
and his wife, Louis Phelps, who prepared food for the prisoners at one time.
Captain Viets died in 1777 of small pox at the age of sixty-five. He and his wife
are both buried near the tavern and their tombstones can be seen there. Tours
of the unrestored tavern are offered the last Sunday of each month.

You'll spot the "Viets" name elsewhere in town. Take a ride to **East
Granby Farms Recreation Area** (79 North Main St. [Route 187]) and head
to the entrance where you can't miss the bright blue silo with the words "L.
H. Viets & Sons Cattle & Horses" painted on it. The L.H. is Leon Hastings, the
son of Anna and Charles Viets, who owned the 500-acre farm that is now the
recreation area. Leon worked alongside his father, even after he married his
wife Grace and had three children of his own. When the farm ceased operating,
the town acquired the land and turned it into a recreation center and park. As

a nod to its former use and owners, they decided to leave the silo and adorn it with a mural of the farm. It is a striking sight.

The bungalow style house located at the entrance to the park once belonged to Leon's parents. It was a **Gordon Van Tine mail-order house** that the Viets ordered late in 1920. Gordon Van Tine houses, manufactured home kits that needed to be assembled (like IKEA furniture), rivaled Sears in the mail-order home business. Charles presented Anna with the deed on Christmas morning as a gift to her. They lived in the smaller house on the farm while one of their sons and his family lived in the main farmhouse.

If you need a glass of spirits to calm your nerves after visiting with spirits at the prison (see what we did there?), then **Brignole Vineyards** (103 Hartford Ave., 860-653-9463; brignolevineyards.com) can help you out. This fifteen-acre, family-owned vineyard boasts a beautiful new winery. They offer different events throughout the year, so be sure to check their Facebook page and website for the latest. Even if you choose to simply enjoy your wine on their beautiful deck, you really can't go wrong! Open Wed through Fri, 1 to 7 p.m.; Sat, noon to 7 p.m.; Sun, noon to 5 p.m.

Granby

You will see many places in **Granby** that reference Salmon Brook, which is a village in Granby named for the original British settlement in the area. There is also a Salmon Brook that runs to the east and south of the village. Whether the stream was named for the settlement or vice versa, we're not sure. But the area is still rich in history. A stop at the **Salmon Brook Historical Society** (208 Salmon Brook Street; 860-653-9713; salmonbrookhistoricalsociety.com) allows you to literally walk through that history. You can start at the 1732 **Abijah Rowe House**, donated to the historical society in 1966 by Colton sisters Mildred and Carolyn, whose father had purchased the house in 1903. The house has been restored to what it would have looked like in the early nineteenth century. Period furniture from the area was donated and added to original features of the house, including a corner cupboard in the parlor and the front door. Upstairs there is a collection of Victorian artifacts, such as antique dolls. The Rowe House is believed to be the oldest structure left from the original British settlement. Also onsite is the 1790 **Weed-Enders House**, home to the society's office and museum store. This primitive saltbox house was moved from its original location in Enders State Forest to the society's property in 1974. Once there, it was restored to its original condition as a farmhouse with a Victorian parlor containing a stereopticon and an Edison Phonograph.

Your next stop at the museum can be the 1870 **Cooley School House**, the only remaining one-room schoolhouse in town (at least the last one that hasn't been renovated into a private residence or store). This building was moved to its current location in 1980 after being donated to the society by Merrill Clark, whose mother was a teacher at the school. It now gives visitors a good idea of what a nineteenth-century schoolroom would have looked like.

The last building on our tour is the newest, the 1914 ***Colten-Hayes Barn***. Built by tobacco farmer Fred M. Colten, the barn holds a lot of history, including antique tools, Native American artifacts, a replicated village store, exhibits on the history of voting in town and the town churches, and so much more. Like we said, you can literally walk through history.

A trip to Granby is not complete without a visit to the 300-year-old ***Dewey-Granby Oak*** on Day Street, off Route 20. This tree, while not the biggest or even the oldest tree in the state, is definitely the coolest. It's prominently displayed on Granby's town seal, which appears on everything from official stationery to town vehicles. It even has its own website (salmonbrookhistorical. org/granby.htm), which tells you all about this beautiful tree that has seen so much. In fall, the oak is especially attractive and worthy of a photograph, as numerous artists and photographers can attest.

Once you've had your fill of the Dewey-Granby Oak, perhaps a stop at ***Grassroots Ice Cream*** (4 Park Pl.; 860-653-6303; grassrootsicecream.com) is in order. This artisan ice cream shop, as they like to call themselves, is located in the old Avery's General Store and is family-owned and -operated by Lee and Eliza Florian and their children.

The business name has special meaning to the Florians. They tragically lost their two-year-old son to a disease called adrenoleukodystrophy, a disease that could have been treated had their newborn been screened. Determined to spare other families the pain they were going through, the Florians formed a grassroots campaign to have a bill passed in Connecticut requiring the screening. Needing a distraction from her grief, Eliza jumped at the chance to start a new project when she noticed a for rent sign in the old Avery's General Store building. They began renovations and put their plan for an ice cream shop into motion.

Due largely to their efforts, the bill requiring newborn screening for adrenoleukodystrophy passed in the Connecticut Legislature on July 3, 2013. Grassroots Ice Cream opened the next day. No one taught the Florians how to make ice cream, and they didn't really have any experience in running a business. By all accounts, they should have failed. But they did quite the opposite. By experimenting and coming up with their own unique flavors, they have amassed an almost cult-like following. You never know what flavors you're going to find when you walk in the door at Grassroots. From Pear Lavender sorbet to Banana Caramel Cup to Boysenberry Jasmine. And flavors don't always stay around for long. When one runs out, they just replace it with a different one. They can scoop up to thirty-six flavors a day, but they have so many that they are listed alphabetically on their website. As one article on the ice cream shop warned, if you have trouble making a decision, you may want to prepare before heading into Grassroots. Open through the summer, Mon through Thurs, 11 a.m. to 10 p.m.; Fri and Sat, 11 a.m. to 10 p.m.; closed on Sun. Winter hours depend on the weather, so be sure to check their website or Facebook pages before traveling.

As you drive around town, watch for the smattering of life-size painted ponies. These were part of the 2006 fundraiser called "Giddy Up Granby" hosted by the **Granby Artists Association** (granbyartists.org) Each horse (and there are more than forty) has a name and a theme. A drive along Salmon Brook Street will bring you past "State Line Colt" by Sally Melrose at State Line Propane (500 Salmon Brook St.), "Stargazer," by David Guarco and Julie Wilson Foster at State Line Oil (514 Salmon Brook St.), and "Meadow Mare" by Diane Bannon standing not in a meadow at all, but under the porch for the residents at MeadowBrook of Granby (350 Salmon Brook St.). "Sparky & Friends," painted by Rosemarie Mendes, can be found outside the Salmon Brook Veterinary Hospital (136 Salmon Brook St.) if you are heading back that way. Some folks make a day of finding as many horses as they can. We've given you a start. Good luck!

When you've just about had your fill of painted ponies, find your last one of the day outside **Cambridge House Brew Pub** (357 Salmon Brook St.; 860-653-2739; cbh.beer). This horse, aptly named "IPA," was purchased through the donations of Cambridge's patrons and he stands guard at this pretty laid-back brew pub that has been creating delicious concoctions since 2005. As an example of just how laid back they are, they have a job opportunity on their website called "I'll do anything" for those who know they want to work in a brew pub, but aren't exactly sure what they want to do.

Their beers are crafted onsite and change often, so you never know what will be available, but you know it'll be good. Food portions are generous and delicious and the atmosphere is relaxed and family-friendly. Open Tues and Wed, 11:30 a.m. to midnight, with the kitchen closing at 9 p.m.; Thurs and Fri, 11:30 a.m. to 1 a.m., with the kitchen closing at 10 p.m.; Sun, 11:30 a.m. to 11 p.m., with the kitchen closing at 9 p.m. Closed on Mon. Live music is offered most weekends.

If you're in a shopping frame of mind, you'll find your fill at **Old Mill Pond Village** (383 Salmon Brook St., 860-653-3433; oldmillpondvillage.com). This cool conglomeration of shops is fun to explore. There's the **Big Red Gift Barn** that is jam packed with everything you'd expect to find in a New England gift shop—clothes, jewelry, home decor, jams, jellies, and kitchen items. Then there's *The Christmas Shop* that will transport you to December the minute you walk in the door, even if it's a 100°F August day outside. This shop also carries enough Halloween decorations to satisfy any fan, a selection of outdoor decorations from garden flags to porch benches, and a nice assortment of indoors furniture, too! Even if you don't purchase anything, you can walk off some of that Cambridge Brew. Open Tues through Sat, 9:30 a.m. to 5:30 p.m.; Sun, noon to 5 p.m. Closed Mon. Check the website for vacation closings before traveling.

If you like to stroll through rooms full of items from years gone by, don't drive by *Salmon Brook Shops* (563 Salmon Brook St.; 860-653-6587) without stopping. While it admittedly doesn't look like much from the outside, the inside is packed with stuff. You can browse through old records, estate jewelry, furniture, postcards, books, linens, dishes, movie posters, advertising art, and more. Former First Lady Laura Bush stopped by here a few years back on her way to a speaking engagement. The staff said she was polite and personable as she perused the store with her security detail in tow. So, if Mrs. Bush deemed this store worthy of a stop, then we concur! Open daily, 10 a.m. to 5 p.m.

Another great place to stop at in the area is *Sweet Pea Cheese* (151 East St.; 860-653-4157) in North Granby. Located on the Hayes family farm known as the *House of Hayes*, this operation churns out cheese and other products made from their own goats and cows. They regularly supply local restaurants and can be found at many farmers' markets throughout the state. After eight generations of family farming, we're pretty sure they know what they're doing! Open daily, 8 a.m. to 6 p.m.

If you're ready for an amazing farm-to-table experience, visit *Lost Acres Orchards* (130 Lost Acres Road; 860-653-6600; lostacres.com). Purchased in 1975 by Ginny and Tom Wutka, these lands have been producing fruit since 1812! The Wutkas have expanded the orchards and found new ways to share them with visitors. The family operates their Farm Kitchen, which offers fresh soups, hot and cold sandwiches, salads, and even pizza, all made with the freshest ingredients (some, when possible, just minutes off the vine!). There's even a kid's menu! And you can enjoy it all on their huge wrap-around porch while overlooking the beautiful grounds. If you love what you had for lunch, there are plenty of pastries in their bakery for you to take home and enjoy later.

Don't be fooled by the relaxed atmosphere, though. Running an orchard is a busy, year-round endeavor. Rhubarb is harvested in May; June brings the berries (strawberries, blueberries, and raspberries); in July there's basil, parsley, and early vegetables; August is peach season; and September through October brings apples, pumpkins, squash, and mums! September also brings the beginning of cider time and the pressing continues until the apples run out, which is typically right around the holidays. Then it's time for baking pies and cookies. The winter months find the Wutkas making apple butter and other jams and jellies, as well as hot soup for the restaurant. When it starts to warm enough, they start the vegetable seedlings in the greenhouse and the cycle starts all over again. Phew.

As if that wasn't enough, Ginny also offers "Quilt Happenings" three times a year, an opportunity to listen to and talk with master quilters and purchase quilts, both finished and unfinished, as well as quilted pillows, fabrics, and other handmade items. Check the website for dates.

The bakery is open year-round, Tues through Sun, 9 a.m. to 5 p.m.; the deck is open, weather permitting, May through Oct. Please note that while the Wutkas grow many crops, the apples are the only ones that are pick-your-own.

If you're in the area on a weekend evening, continue down the road to **Lost Acres Vineyard** (80 Lost Acres Rd., 860-324-9481; lostacresvineyard. com), a completely separate business with no relation to the orchards and completely worth a stop. Husband and wife team Kevin and Michelle Riggott purchased the land in 2008 with plans for a vineyard. Two years later, they opened the tasting room. Today, Kevin continues to make all the wines on the premises using mostly their own grapes. Red grapes don't fare too well with New England's climate, so those are imported from California and the wine is made here.

Tastings of the white, red, rose, and apple wines are available and include five choices and a complimentary glass to take home. Once you choose your favorite, you can move to the deck overlooking the vineyards to enjoy it al fresco or sit fireside and listen to the live music that's offered some nights. Guests can bring in their own food or purchase a cheese plate or antipasto right there at the vineyard.

The Riggotts are big supporters of the arts and they choose artists each year and feature their art in the vineyard's tasting room as well as hosting the Granby Land Trust's annual Juried Art Show. They also hold special events throughout the year, so be sure to check the website often to see what's coming up next! Open Apr through Dec, Fri and Sat, noon to 6 p.m., and Sun, noon to 5 p.m.

If you opted to head west from the Salmon Brook Historical Society on Route 20 (Simsbury Road) instead of north, you have other options. If you have the kids with you and they need to burn off some energy, head to **Holcombe Farm** (111 and 113 Simsbury Rd.; 860-653-5554; holcombfarm.org) where you will find 312 acres that are home to a working (and historic) farm, recreation areas, and miles of trails on which to explore and enjoy nature. According to the website, you should head east for easier walks through fields and forest and head west for more challenging hikes up ridges and along the brook. Whichever you choose, birdwatchers in your group will be thrilled with the more than sixty species of birds that live at the farm, and if you're lucky, you'll see other wildlife too, including deer, turtles, and more. If **geocaching** is your thing, you'll find several caches at the farm as well. You can download a map from the website to take with you. The trails are open year-round from dawn until dusk.

If you have a cooking aficionado in your family, a stop at *The Garlic Farm* (76 Simsbury Rd.; 860-264-5644; garlicfarmct.com) may be in order, although this farm is so much more than garlic. Farmer and owner Gary Cirullo started the farm in 1996 and is committed to "raising high-quality vegetables, herbs, and flowers according to sound and sustainable farming practices." And that's what he does. They sell almost everything they grow from their farm stand on the premises, including tomatoes, peppers (sweet and hot), eggplant, carrots, beets, squash (zucchini, yellow, and winter), German White garlic, onions, shallots, pumpkins, herbs, and flowers. They also offer a CSA. If you've always wanted to go organic and aren't entirely sure where to start, Gary has myriad recipes on his website to help you out. Gary also supplies local restaurants with his farm-fresh produce, so you can always have someone else do the cooking or you. Either way, it's a win.

The farm stand opens for the season the Sat after the Fourth of July and stays open through Oct, as long as the weather cooperates, from 10 a.m. to 6 p.m. daily. Gary doesn't accept plastic, so you'll need to bring cash or a check with you.

To the west of The Garlic Farm along Route 219 (Barkhamsted Road) you will find *Enders State Forest* (Route 219; 860-379-2469; ct.gov/deep), Connecticut's twenty-ninth state forest and home to the beautiful *Enders Falls*. The original 1,500-acre property was a gift from the Enders family in memory of their parents, John and Harriet Enders. Today the park contains more than 2,000 acres (thanks to land acquisitions by the state) and is enjoyed by thousands of visitors.

While the forest neighbors *McLean Game Refuge*, hunting is allowed only in certain areas of the park per the original deed from the Enders family. It is important, though, for you to be aware of hunting season and who else might be out there with you. Connecticut DEEP's website (ct.gov/deep) provides information on when and where hunting is allowed.

As you enjoy this beautiful state forest, please heed the warnings posted at the beginning of the trails. The purple-blazed trail takes hikers to the waterfalls, and we urge those headed that way to do so with caution. Enjoy the waterfalls, but please do it from a distance. The rocks above and around the falls are wet and slippery and can be dangerous. Stay on the trail and keep an eye on all those in your party, especially the young ones who may scamper off for a closer look at the beautiful falls that cascade over jumbles of rocks and form pools upon pools. It's not unusual in the warm weather to see adventure seekers sliding down the rocks and plunging into the refreshing pools below, but this is something that really shouldn't be attempted without proper equipment and training. The nearby Lost Acres Fire Department even does special training exercises in the area so they can be prepared for the numerous rescue operations they are called out to annually. Nature deserves to be respected in all its beauty and danger.

The park is open from 8 a.m. to sunset year-round. There is no fee and there are no facilities at this state park.

The Farmington Valley

Simsbury

Simsbury was settled in 1648 by a group of Windsor families who acquired the land from the Massacoe Indians. They called their new settlement Massacoh Plantation, a name that was eventually changed to Simsbury when the town was incorporated by the Connecticut General Court in 1670. In March 1676, when King Philip's War began to heat up, the entire village of about 40 dwellings was destroyed by Wampanoag Indians. The Wampanoag uprising was over by August, but it took two years for reconstruction to begin. Once it did, Simsbury quickly became an important factor in Connecticut's economy and politics. The first copper coins in America were struck here in 1737, and the first steel mill in America was built here in 1744. Hundreds of residents fought in the American Revolution, including Major General Noah Phelps, who, as America's first spy (he was just a captain then), entered Fort Ticonderoga in disguise to gather information for Ethan Allen; Allen then proceeded to capture the fort. By the 1820s, the town was a major stop on the Farmington Canal, which ran along the route of today's Hopmeadow Street (Route 10).

simsbury trivia

Simsbury's main avenue, Hopmeadow Street, gets its name from the fields of hops that once grew where the street runs today.

In 1737, Simsbury's Samuel Higley developed the first copper coinage in America. The Higley copper was worth two and sixpence (42 cents) in paper currency. The coin's motto was "I am good copper."

The first safety fuse, used for mining and exploration, in America was made in Simsbury in 1836 by Richard Bacon. Bacon, who ran the mine at Newgate, entered into a partnership with the English firm of Bickford, Smith & Davey.

Pettibone's Tavern has been a fixture in Simsbury since 1780, when it was built for Captain Jonathon Pettibone Jr. Situated conveniently along the major travel path from Boston to New York, the tavern saw its fair share of travelers, including George Washington, John Adams, Harriet Beecher Stowe, and Ethan Allen.

The house, however, was not the happy family home one would think. You see, Captain Pettibone was a whaling captain, which necessitated him being out at sea for long stretches of time. This left his wife, Abigail, home alone in the big house. As the story goes, Abigail took up with another man, and one evening the captain returned home early and found his wife with her lover. He allegedly killed both of them on the spot with an axe. Despite the fact that historical records don't really bear this story out, it is fun to speculate, and people do.

Throughout its long history, the building has switched between being a tavern and a private residence. A tunnel—now bricked over—from its basement to the basement of an old red colonial home across the street suggests it may have been a stop on the Underground Railroad at one time. Today, the tavern has been transformed into ***Abigail's Grille & Wine Bar*** (4 Hartford Rd.; 860-264-1580; abigailsgrill.com), an upscale and trendy gathering place for good food and good wine. There's also the restaurant's resident ghost, who has been known to give diners a friendly pat or poke now and again. There's a lot of speculation as to who the ghost might be. Is it Abigail Pettibone? Or perhaps someone who lost his life in pursuit of freedom in that tunnel? Whoever the ghost is, it appears to be friendly and has become a Farmington Valley tradition, with radio disk jockeys often spending All Hallows' Eve at the restaurant reporting on ghostly doings.

Open for lunch Mon through Sat, 11:30 a.m. to 4 p.m.; for dinner Mon through Thurs, 4:30 to 9:30 p.m.; Fri and Sat, 4 to 10 p.m.; Sun, 3 to 8 p.m. The tavern is open Mon through Thurs, 4 to 10 p.m.; Fri and Sat, 4 to 11 p.m.; and Sun, 4 to 9 p.m.

The ***Simsbury Historical Society*** (800 Hopmeadow St.; 860-658-2500; simsburyhistory.org) owns nine buildings on a two-acre complex in historic Simsbury, including **Phelps Tavern**, **Phelps Barn**, **Hendrick Cottage**, and a one-room schoolhouse. Explore these period buildings and enjoy interactive exhibition galleries, showing visitors what it was like to be a guest at the Captain Elisha Phelps House when it was an inn between 1786 and 1849. Three successive generations of Phelps tavern keepers are chronicled, along with the social history of New England taverns. Back then, Connecticut towns were required by law to have at least one tavern to accommodate travelers, who arrived by horse, stagecoach, and canal boat. Museum hours are limited and tours are only offered on Sat or by appointment. The grounds and gardens are open year-round during daylight hours. Admission. Blue Star Museum.

For much of Simsbury's early history, **Talcott Mountain** cut the region off from the meadowlands of the Connecticut River Valley to the east. This isolation ended when the Albany Turnpike was hacked across the mountain, but the state of mind engendered by that knife-edge of rock looming dramatically over the landscape remains. Though separated by only a mile, Simsbury, Avon, and even Farmington to the south, have far more in common with the small towns to their west than with the suburbs east of the mountain.

There has been a tower atop Talcott Mountain for most of the past 200 years. The first was built in 1810 but was destroyed in a windstorm in 1840. It was the inspiration for John Greenleaf Whittier's poem "Monte Video." Other structures followed until finally, in 1914, businessman Gilbert Heublein built a fourth tower atop the mountain, a grand white 165-foot-high edifice of steel and concrete anchored in the rock. For twenty years this so-called **Heublein Tower** was a summer home for the Heublein family. Today, the mountain and its tower are all part of **Talcott Mountain State Park** (Route 185; 860-242-1158). Four states are visible from the top of the tower on a clear day, but first you have to get there. The main public access route is off Route 185. A road leads partway up the mountain to a parking area, from which you can hike the 1.25-mile trail to the top. The early part of the climb is fairly steep, but there are benches for resting. Once you reach the tower, you'll have to make another climb up the stairs to the top; there are no elevators. There have been an increasing number of bear sightings in Connecticut as of late. The DEEP recommends, if you see a bear, to keep your distance, make your presence known by shouting and waving your arms and/or walk slowly away. Never feed the bears or any wildlife for that matter.

The park is open year-round from 8 a.m. to sunset. Heublein Tower is open 10 a.m. to 5 p.m., Thurs through Mon, Nov through Sept. For the month of Oct, they extend their hours from Wed through Mon, 10 a.m. to 5 p.m.

When leaving Talcott Mountain, turn left on Route 185 and drive west toward Route 10. A mile or so west of the access road, you'll come to an old iron bridge. On your right is a huge, witchy-looking tree whose branches loom over the road like some spectral presence. This is the **Pinchot Sycamore**, reputedly the oldest tree in Connecticut. Right before the bridge is the entrance to a small park where the tree resides. Take the turn slowly, as it's a bit steep as you enter the park. The tree is named for conservationist Gifford Pinchot and was dedicated to him in 1965. You'll be in awe as you stand under the tree that sports a twenty-three-foot-diameter trunk. You have to stop and wonder about all this beautiful sycamore has seen in its history.

Canton

Canton, like so many Connecticut towns, has a ghost. This one is supposedly in the shape of a Revolutionary War messenger who disappeared in the vicinity while conveying a payroll from Hartford patriots to French officers aiding the Americans. After a bleached skeleton was found under the Canton Tavern, where the man was last seen alive, stories began circulating that the innkeeper had murdered the hapless messenger and stolen the money. Shortly thereafter, people started seeing a headless horseman, presumed to be the ghost of the paymaster, riding west along the Albany Turnpike (US 44) toward Saratoga. They still do. So if you're down by the Canton Golf Course some dark and foggy night, and you notice that your headlights are shining through a ghostly horseman and his steed to illuminate the road beyond, don't pay it any mind. It's just the *Headless Horseman of Canton* on his perpetual journey.

If you have teens, or you consider yourself young at heart, you may want to consider a stop at the *Trading Post* (233 Albany Tpke.; 860-693-4679; tradingpostct.com) in Canton. Offering an eclectic collection of all things rock and roll, Trading Post is open Mon through Sat, 10 a.m. to 8 p.m., and Sun, 11 a.m. to 7 p.m. Inside you will find a huge selection of band T-shirts, CDs, DVDs, jewelry, women's clothing and accessories, posters, the requisite lava lamps, and so much more.

In the southern part of Canton on Route 179 is the village of *Collinsville*, home to *Antiques on the Farmington* (10 Depot St.; 860-693-0615; antiquesonfarmington.com), a multi-dealer shop with furniture and accessories displayed in room settings so you really feel as if you've walked back in time. Browse slowly and you may just find a bargain. Open daily, 10 a.m. to 5 p.m.

Collinsville received its name from the **Collins Company**, an eighteenth- and nineteenth-century manufacturer of axes and machetes that were sold around the world. The story of the Collins Company is recounted in a series of exhibits in the *Canton Historical Museum* (11 Front St.; 860-693-2793; cantonmuseum.org). This small museum houses a re-creation nineteenth-century general store, post office, barber, and blacksmith shop. There are collections of period clothing, furniture, household items, even a Civil War casket. There is also a striking 2,000-square-foot railway diorama accurately showing Collinsville and Canton as they appeared circa 1900. It is managed by the *Farmington Valley Railroad Society*. Open June through Nov, Fri, Sat, and Sun, 1 to 4 p.m.; Dec through May, Sat and Sun, 1 to 4 p.m. Admission.

Roaring Brook Nature Center (70 Gracey Rd.; 860-693-0263; roaringbrook.org) is affiliated with the Children's Museum in West Harford and aims to foster the relationship between humans and nature. They offer guided nature walks, hikes on snowshoes, maple-sugaring demonstrations, bird walks, and summer nocturnal walks on five miles of trails. If you want to go it alone, you can, as there are trail maps available in the Nature Center Store and on their website. They hold special events, too, throughout the year, including concerts and a Halloween children's fair. Open Sept to June, Tues through Sat, 10 a.m. to 5 p.m.; Sun, 1 to 5 p.m.; July and August, daily, 10 a.m. to 5 p.m.

Avon

Crossing into **Avon**, follow Town Farm Road to its end. If you turn right, you will quickly happened upon **Fisher Meadows** (800 Old Farms Rd.), a 205-acre natural area for hiking and walking, biking, fishing, canoeing, and picnicking. There are also recreational ball fields here. You have your choice of trails and you can download a map at Avon's town website (avonct.gov). The trail around Spring Lake is a good, flat walk. For a more strenuous hike, take the trail along the Farmington River, which offers lots of up-and-down walking, so it's not a good walk for small kids or tots in strollers. In the spring and summer, both trails offer great opportunities to spot wildflowers, such as the Virginia water-leaf, a declining species that is protected in Connecticut. Feel free to bring Fido, but please be sure he stays on his leash; it's the rule.

If you left onto Town Farm Road, you travel the narrow, winding roads past **Avon Old Farms School**. This private school for boys was designed by Theodate Pope Riddle of Hill-Stead Museum fame. The buildings are modeled after cottages in Great Britain's Cotswolds. There are no tours of the campus for the public, but you can drive through the campus to look at the buildings.

Heading north past Avon Old Farms along Nod Road, you'll eventually come to the **Pickin' Patch** (276 Nod Rd.; 860-677-9552; thepickinpatch.com). The land here has been farmed since 1666 and operates as a family-friendly farm stand and pick-your-own place. In 2012, when the Avon Cider Mill went out of business, the Pickin' Patch acquired their name, equipment, and product lines, adding cider donuts, jams, jellies, and more to their repertoire of items available.

The farm stand opens when the pansies start to bloom and stays open until Christmas Eve; open 9 a.m. to 6 p.m. daily. There is a crop calendar on their website, so you can check and see what's in season when. On October weekends, you can take a free hayride to the pumpkin patch or book a group hayride during the week for a small price and receive a sugar pumpkin, cider and doughnut holes, and a souvenir cider sipper. Perfect for those gorgeous New England fall days.

If you continue west on US 44, you'll pass **Old Avon Village** (1–45 E. Main Street; 860-680-5298; avonvillagemarketplace.com), where you'll see a huge Hitchcock-style rocking chair that is something of a local landmark. People give directions based on proximity to the rocker, and rival high school students often "chair-nap" it to celebrate a football victory.

Old Avon Village boasts a pretty neat history of revitalization that started in the early 1960s when old houses were converted into retail shops. The craze caught on, and over the next quarter century, more homes, barns, and other buildings were converted until there was the thriving retail and commercial district you see today with forty businesses throughout eighteen buildings.

This area of our state saw its first Congregational church organized in 1652. The **West Avon Congregational Church** (280 Country Club Rd.; 860-673-3996; westavonchurch.org), built in 1751, is the descendant of this congregation. But as more settlers arrived and the population grew, the community began to spread out. Residents found the trip along the Farmington River from their homes to the village of Farmington too arduous and dangerous in the winter months. They requested and were allowed to build their own church, known as the "Lord's Barn." Unfortunately, the structure burned down in 1817, and today, only a marker remains to mark the location on a knoll near the end of Reverknolls Road, about one mile north of the Cider Brook Cemetery.

By that time, however, plans for a new meetinghouse to serve the growing community were already under way—if only residents could agree on a location. Unable to come to a decision, the two groups began to diverge. Changes occurred within the General Assembly that allowed additional congregations to form. The society on the east side of the river assumed the title of Third Church in Farmington and their church was built, with the help of none other than David Hoadley, the future builder of many New England churches at the intersection of what are now Routes 44 and 10. You can read more of the fascinating history on their website.

Just west of the junction of Routes 44 and 10 North is Avon Park North, where you'll find the **Farmington Valley Arts Center** (25 Arts Center Ln.; 860-678-1867; artsfvac.org). Home to the **Fisher Gallery and Shop** and about twenty artists' studios, this arts center showcases pottery, basket weaving, printing, painting, leatherworking, and silversmithing. The center believes in promoting the arts and giving visitors the chance to experience the creative process from start to finish. What a wonderful way to inspire your inner artist! Studios are open the first Sat of every month from noon to 4 p.m., and at the discretion of the individual artists. The shop and gallery are open Mon, 10 a.m. to 2 p.m.; Tues through Fri, 10 a.m. to 4 p.m.; Sat, noon to 4 p.m.; they are closed for major holidays.

The **First Company of the Governor's Horse Guards** (280 Arch Rd.; 860-673-3525; ctfirsthorseguard.org) is the oldest cavalry unit in continuous service in the US, tracing its lineage back to 1658, when the Connecticut Colony founded a troop of mounted guards. In 1788, the Horse Guards were reformed as a company of Light Dragoons, modeled on the Royal Regiment of Horse Guards in England. When Connecticut joined the Revolution against the British Crown, the new state took over the Horse Guards. In those days, the unit's main function was to escort and protect visiting dignitaries, and it acted as an honor guard to President George Washington when he visited Wethersfield in 1789.

The unit saw somewhat more dangerous service as a mounted unit in the War of 1812 and the Spanish–American War. In 1916, it patrolled the Mexican border during operations against Pancho Villa. Dismounted and reorganized as a machine-gun battalion, it served in seven major engagements in France during World War I. At the end of the war, the Horse Guards were remounted as the 122nd Cavalry Squadron of the Connecticut National Guard; four days after Pearl Harbor, they became the 208th Coast Artillery and served as an anti-aircraft unit in the South Pacific.

Today, the Horse Guards' duties are once again mainly ceremonial. The company makes appearances at presidential and gubernatorial inaugurations. All horses are donated, and they include just about every breed except Clydesdales. On Thursday from 7:30 to 10 p.m., the public is invited to watch the unit practice its drills. These consist of intricate, beautifully choreographed precision maneuvers, often accompanied by music. The Horse Guards hosts an annual Open Horse Show in June as well as various community programs. The Second Company of the Governor's Horse Guards holds its summer practices in Newtown; see the Danbury entry in "Gateway to New England" for details.

Around the corner on Route 167, you can see the **Old Horse Guard Barn**, which dates back to 1880 and is currently being leased from the state by the Avon Historical Society. The society recently put a new roof on the building, which was used to house the Guard's horses from 1954 to 2002. They hope to use the barn to house exhibits in the future. You can't miss it, it's right on the road.

Miller Foods Market (308 Arch Rd.; 860-673-3250; millerfoodsonline .com), next to the Horse Guards headquarters, is a fourth-generation operation that produces some of the best turkeys in the region, but fresh birds are available only during the fall and winter holidays. At Thanksgiving, Miller's pitches its "turkey tent," an outdoor bazaar full of special goodies for your holiday table, including their "Turkease," a semi-boneless turkey that cooks three times faster than a whole turkey and "slices like a dream," according to Miller's. The turkeys sell like hotcakes, so call ahead to order. Outside the holiday season, Miller Foods sells other meats such as hams and smoked turkeys plus natural pet food in their market. Open Mon through Fri, 9 a.m. to 5 p.m.; Sat, 9 a.m. to 3 p.m.; Sun, 9 a.m. to 1 p.m.

Once a large dairy farm, **Riverdale Farms Shopping** (124 Simsbury Rd.; 860-677-6437; riverdalefarmsshopping.com) in Avon is now the site of one of the more interesting shopping centers in the area. This complex occupies several low hills under the eye of the Heublein Tower, atop Talcott Mountain to the north and east. Nineteen barn-like buildings, some original and renovated, some new, now house offices, stores, restaurants, and boutiques—and new ones are opening all the time. Most of the stores are crafts, gift, or fashion stores, but you'll also find a yoga studio, pet groomers and pet supply stores, dance studios, and so much more. Check out their website for a detailed list and a more in-depth history of this former farm.

Burlington

Burlington is home to the beautiful 1,148-acre **Nassahegon State Forest**, established in 1926 as watershed protection for the **Burlington Fish Hatchery** (34 Belden Rd.; 860-673-2340), which is still in operation today as the oldest fish hatchery in the state. They stock our waterways with brook, brown, and rainbow trout, as well as being the only producer of kokanee salmon fry.

Kokanee are a breed of the larger, Pacific Ocean sockeye salmon. Every fall, adult kokanee are transported from East Twin Lake and Lake Wononskopomuc in Salisbury to the hatchery for spawning. The eggs are incubated and the fry are cared for until late May when they are brought back to East Twin Lake, Lake Wononskopomuc, and added to West Hill Pond. It takes three years for the fish to mature into adults, which can be between twelve and sixteen inches long. The hatchery estimates that their kokanee salmon program results in 20,000 to 30,000 hours of recreational fishing annually. The hatchery is open year-round, 8 a.m. to 3 p.m. daily. Tours can be arranged by appointment or you can simply stop in and check it out for yourself.

Known simply as the Burlington Block of the Nepaug Forest until 1942 when it was officially renamed the **Nassahegon State Forest**, this area offers great hiking, including a portion of the Connecticut Forest and Park Association's **Tunxis Trail**, which travels a total length of seventy-nine miles from Southington to the Massachusetts border, but you can do a small portion of it through the forest. Make it a two-mile out and back, or, if you have the option, leave a car on each end and cut the hike in half.

Before you head to your parked car (or get ready to retrace your steps to Punch Brook Road), turn right on Stone Road and walk about 140 feet. On your right, you will come to an **old stone jailhouse**. This is a remnant of a camp built in these woods in 1934 for men who traveled from town to town looking for work during that difficult economic time. This camp could accommodate up to 250 men, who were required to put in at least twenty-four hours of work a week in exchange for board and a weekly paycheck of 90 cents. Residents of Burlington, who are old enough to remember, say that sometimes these men came into town and caused quite a ruckus. This is most likely where this "jail" came into play; it was basically a holding cell for those who might have had too much to drink or were not following the rules. They hung out here until they were under control again. In 1936, the Works Progress Administration (WPA) took over the camp and men lived and worked there until about 1938 when the National Youth Administration took over. Other agencies used the camp from time to time until 1944, when it was put to use as a forest headquarters until 1971, when DEEP was formed. Today, nothing more than foundations and a chimney exist along with the jail, oddly still intact, right off of Stone Road.

The **Taine Mountain Preserve** (burlingtonlandtrust.org) is another great hike, and further proof of how instrumental land trusts are in saving the open spaces in our state. In 2015, the **Burlington Land Trust** collaborated with the town and **Trust for Public Land** to purchase 150 acres that were adjacent to the 150 acres already in the preserve. A developer had also been interested in purchasing the land, which could have meant thirty-five to forty houses being built there. Today, the 300 acres are managed by the land trust and are open for us to enjoy and appreciate. There are two hikes available, the almost-two-mile Perry's Lookout Loop and the almost-three-mile Taine Mountain Double Loop. The terrain can be rocky (and wet during a thaw or rain) and some parts are steep, but it's generally not too bad if you take your time and wear the right shoes. There are some incredible views to be had at the summit as well. Please be bear aware and follow Leave No Trace practices. Parking is available along Venture's Way and Ryan's Way, directions are available on the website.

If ghost hunting is more your thing, then Burlington is your place. The first stop on our Burlington ghost tour is the **Seventh Day Baptist Cemetery** (Upson Road), but if you want to do more than drive by, you'll need to gain approval from the Burlington Police Department. A ghostly tale of a female apparition appearing and disappearing with a green mist at this cemetery has been told for years. There was speculation that the "Green Lady," as she is called, was Elizabeth Palmiter who walked this green earth in the nineteenth century. One stormy night, when Mr. Palmiter didn't arrive home in a timely manner from a trip into town, Elizabeth supposedly went out to look for him. She didn't get far before drowning in a swamp. It is said that now Elizabeth roams the cemetery presenting herself to unsuspecting (or suspecting) visitors. There have also been stories of Mr. Palmiter roaming the graveyard with a lantern looking for his beloved. Alas, these are just stories. Camp stories specifically. The reality of the situation is that the story of the Green Lady originated with a local camp leader who made up and told his campers the story all in good fun. But that doesn't mean there aren't other lonely spirits roaming the Seventh Day Baptist Cemetery.

The second stop on our ghost tour is the **Lamson Corner Cemetery** (Milford Street [Route 69]), where, the story goes, a hiker in the area noticed a young man standing at the top the hill of the cemetery and, thinking he was visiting a grave, called out to him to ask what time it was. He received no answer, and, in fact, the man turned and walked away. When the hiker, a bit perturbed, followed the man to get his answer, the man simply disappeared and where he stood was the grave of a World War II soldier. Numerous paranormal groups have visited the cemetery getting a variety of results, all up to interpretation. So if you're driving by and want to get out and take a stroll through the cemetery to pay your respects, just keep an open mind. Many of the gravestones are those of young children, possibly due to the small pox epidemic. Perhaps this explains the sadness that seems to thicken the air.

On a brighter note, let's make our way to **LaMothe's Sugar House** (89 Stone Rd.; 860-675-5043; lamothesugarhouse.com), one of just a handful of real old-fashioned sugar houses left in Connecticut. Here, during February and March, visitors can tour a working house and see the whole process of "sugaring off." There's a big old sap boiler that cooks maple sap into syrup, which you can then see blended with cream and butter and poured into molds to make creamy shaped candies (like Santas or maple leaves), or mixed with other ingredients to make maple taffy. The sugar house sells syrup, maple candy, and maple fudge. Visitors always get a sample of some type of maple sweet. In Connecticut, the peak season for sugaring off is late Feb or early Mar, but LaMothe's is open year-round, 10 a.m. to 6 p.m., Mon through Thurs; 10 a.m. to 5 p.m., Fri and Sat; noon to 5 p.m., Sun.

Farmington

We've found some unusual places in Connecticut, we've even encountered some spooky places, but **Shade Swamp Sanctuary** (Scott Swamp Rd.) in **Farmington** takes the cake as unusual and spooky. Located right off busy Route 6 in Farmington, this old abandoned zoo seems overhung with a prevailing sadness. It actually sits on an eight-hundred-acre preserve that is owned by the state but maintained by the Farmington Garden Club. You can park next to the Shade Swamp Shelter that is visible from Route 6 and you'll see a sign for the Blue Trail and then blazes on the trail. All this is pretty normal until you enter the woods and start to see the cages. Some are simply metal that is now bent with age and others are sort of dens that nature has begun to reclaim.

The state of Connecticut acquired 140 acres in 1926 as a donation from a Walter W. Holmes. In 1934, the Connecticut Department of Fish and Game opened the Shade Swamp Sanctuary as a place for endangered or injured native birds and animals. There were possibly some nefarious experiments going on during this time, but that only lasted for about four years. Structures, cages, and dens for the sanctuary were built by the Civilian Conservation Corps (CCC) as was the Shade Swamp Shelter, which is now listed on the National Register of Historic Places. As word got out about what the state was doing, people started bring nonnative species to the sanctuary in hopes of finding them a home. Alligators, monkeys, parrots, bears, and more were brought here, but, of course, it was impossible to house them in this environment. Mystery and speculation surround the sanctuary, but it is believed that facility was shut down in the early 1960s because of suspected "illicit activity."

If you'd like to explore the area, you have two choices of trails. One is the blue trail, which begins at the shelter off Route 6 and brings you through the abandoned zoo and over a footbridge. You'll pass by a kame terrace, a geological formation that resembles a hill with a flat top. It's made of sand and/or gravel left by a glacier, and if you had stood there thousands of years ago, you'd be looking at a large lake instead of the deposits it left there. The blue blazes then take you back to the start of the trail—just under a mile and a half in all.

The longer white trail is located on the west side of New Britain Avenue, with parking at near the gated entrance to the former DEEP site on the north side of Route 6 just west of New Britain Avenue. For your GPS, the address is approximately 198 Scott Swamp Rd. This DEEP headquarters is now decommissioned and you'll see the buildings as you hike by.

For maps and more information on these trails, visit Farmington's website (farmington-ct.org).

In the midst of 278-acre **_Farmington Memorial Town Forest_** there is a **memorial to US Army pilot 2nd Lt. Vincent H. Core**. In the spring of 1945, Lt. Core was on a training mission when he began to have trouble with his P47 Thunderbolt. Knowing he would have to make an emergency landing, the level-headed airman directed his plane toward the town forest in order to avoid the more populated areas below. Unfortunately, Core was unable to regain control over his aircraft and he hurtled through the trees, perishing in the crash. A Boy Scout troop from Bristol erected the memorial in the 1970s as thanks to Airman Core and his level-headed decision that saved countless lives on the ground. In 2014, Boy Scout William S. Sanford chose to blaze a trail with orange markers to the memorial so people could find it easily and pay homage to Core. The main access to the memorial is from Red Oak Hill Road (107 Red Oak Hill Rd., opposite 120 Red Oak Hill Rd.). If you were not able to secure parking on Red Oak Hill Road, your other option is to park on the cul-de-sac of Reservation Road.

Hill-Stead Museum (35 Mountain Rd.; 860-677-4787; hillstead.org) is so Farmington that it is almost impossible to imagine it existing anywhere else. Housed in a white clapboard 1901 replica of a neocolonial house built in an eighteenth-century English farm style is an amazing collection of French impressionist paintings, prints, antique furniture, porcelain, textiles, and clocks.

Hill-Stead was originally home to Cleveland iron mogul Alfred Atmore Pope. In keeping with his wealth and pretensions, Pope made sure that when it was time for daughter Theodate to go away to school, his child was entrusted to a proper eastern institution: *Miss Porter's School* in Farmington. Upon graduation, Theodate persuaded her father to forsake the Buckeye State and move east to the Nutmeg State. She also talked him into springing for a new house designed by the then-trendy architect **Stanford White**, with a sunken garden designed by landscape architect **Beatrix Farrand**. And since Theodate had an abiding interest in architecture, she assisted White in designing the new family manse. White was either a good businessman or he was truly impressed with Theodate's work, because he cut his fee by $25,000 in appreciation of her help. Miss Pope went on to become the first woman licensed to practice architecture in the US.

Like so many American captains of industry, Alfred Pope was a collector. This was an age in which America's newly rich raided the homes and galleries of Europe for furnishings, often buying art and antiques in wholesale lots. The Popes were fairly typical in this regard, and their tastes were certainly eclectic. Chippendale furniture, fine porcelain, contemporary bronzes, and pre-Columbian statuary all jostled for space in the Pope home. On the walls hung a Degas, a Manet, a Cassatt, and no fewer than three Monets. The piano was a custom-designed Steinway.

It was all gloriously excessive. And it is all still there, just as it was when Theodate died, leaving behind fifty pages of instructions for the house to be turned into a museum and maintained just as she left it. Hill-Stead Museum is open Tues through Sun, 10 a.m. to 4 p.m., with the last tour leaving at 3 p.m. each day. The grounds are open 7:30 a.m. to 5:30 p.m. Hill-Stead has a wonderful gift shop with prints of works exclusive to it, such as Monet's *Haystacks* and Degas's *Dancers in Pink*. Admission. Blue Star Museum.

Just around the corner from the Hill-Stead Museum is the **Stanley-Whitman House** (37 High St.; 860-677-9222; stanleywhitman.org), a beautifully restored 1720 colonial homestead. The original house, built to a typical early eighteenth-century standard, has a central chimney flanked by two chambers

on each floor; it was later expanded by the addition of a lean-to that gives it a saltbox shape. The wood-sided exterior was originally painted with a mixture of ox blood and buttermilk; the restoration has not gone to quite that extreme, but otherwise it seems authentic. Hinged access panels inside the house let you see details of the original construction and restoration. The house is filled with period furnishings and is surrounded by herb and flower gardens. The gift shop sells items of local historical interest. Tours are offered Wed through Sun, noon to 4 p.m., with the last one leaving at 3:15 p.m. If there are five or more in your party, the museum asks you call ahead to book a tour. The museum is open Wed through Fri, 9 a.m. to 4 p.m.; Sat and Sun, noon to 4 p.m. Admission. Blue Star Museum.

Farmington played an important role in the antislavery movement. Many abolitionists called the area home and offered their houses as stops on the Underground Railroad. In fact, Farmington gained the moniker "Grand Central Station" of the railroad. In 1841, the town hosted the slaves who fought for their freedom aboard *The Amistad* when they gained their freedom thanks to John Quincy Adams. Farmington abolitionists provided housing and education as well as raising money to get them back home. The **Farmington Historical Society** (138 Main St.; 860-678-1645; fhs-ct.org) offers monthly tours from May through Sept of places that played a part in helping the African Mendis and other slaves find freedom. There is a charge, details are on the website.

If you're in the Farmington area on a Wednesday, Saturday, or Sunday afternoon, don't miss a visit to the **Unionville Museum** (15 School St.; 860-673-2231; unionvillemuseum.org). The **Unionville** section of Farmington, located about five miles east of the center of town along Route 4 was an industrial center during the late eighteenth and early nineteenth centuries. Flints for Washington's army and guns for the War of 1812 were made here, as well as the pikes that Torrington native John Brown took with him to Harpers Ferry (he intended to use them to arm the Southern slaves he convinced to revolt). The museum has preserved some of this history and is continuously acquiring more. A recent acquisition includes advertising from a no-longer-existing Unionville movie house. **The Luxor** was located on Water Street and was quite the treat for residents, although not as flashy as theaters in larger cities. This movie schedule alerts patrons that *High Sierra* (with Humphrey Bogart and Ida Lupino), *Victor* (with Frederic March and Bettie Field), and *Andy Hardy's Private Secretary* (with Mickey Rooney, Lewis Stone, and Ian Hunter), among others would be playing. It also shows the movie house's phone number as 288-3. Ahh, such was the life in 1941. The museum has displayed chairs from the former theater. Open 2 to 4 p.m. Wed, Sat, and Sun.

Central Connecticut

New Britain

New Britain got its manufacturing start making sleigh bells. From these modest beginnings the city gradually branched out in the early 1800s and into the manufacture of other hardware products, until it eventually came to be known as the "Hardware City." With the industrial age came waves of new immigrants seeking jobs in the tool works. The Irish came first, then the Germans and Swedes, then the Italians. The biggest waves, though, consisted of Eastern Europeans, including Lithuanians, Ukrainians, and Armenians. Probably the largest group in this wave was the Poles. Even after the hardware industry moved abroad, Polish immigrants continued to arrive in New Britain. Today, the city's population of first- and second-generation Poles is greater than that of many cities in Poland. They have contributed their music, their language, and their food to the city.

In some places in New Britain, Polish is spoken almost as freely as English. And while you'll love the authentic Polish food at the Polish National Home in Hartford, there's something to be said for purchasing it in the midst of this cultural community. The perfect place to do that is *Podlasie* (188 High St.; 860-224-8467). It's like visiting a marketplace in Eastern Europe. You'll find Polish mineral water; dark, dense bread; newspapers; ingredients for Polish cooking; and some intriguing Polish chocolates on the shelves. The back of the store is given over to a dairy case (great country butter), a pastry case full of elegant-looking tortes and cakes, and a case for cheeses, herring, fresh meats, and cold cuts, many made in the store. Most of the shoppers are Polish, so you'll hear mostly Polish being spoken. There's usually at least one English speaker in the store who is happy to help you translate. Open daily 8 a.m. to 6 p.m. (There is another Podlasie in Bridgeport at 2286 E. Main St.; 203-335-0321.)

The Hardware City is not all about industry. There is also a true appreciation of the arts, evidenced by the *New Britain Museum of American Art* (56 Lexington St.; 860-229-0257; nbmaa.org). Established in 1903, this museum is the oldest in the US devoted solely to American art. Its more than 8,000 holdings include portraits by Cassatt, Stuart, Copley, and Sargent and the western bronzes of Solon Borglum, as well as works by the likes of O'Keeffe, Noguchi, Benton, and Wyeth. Its collection of American impressionists is second to none.

There are landscapes by Hassam, Inness, Bierstadt, Church, and Cole (including *The Clove*, with its mysterious disappearing figures), among others. Graydon Parrish's *The Cycle of Terror and Tragedy: September 11, 2001* is a truly moving experience. The 77-inch-by-120-inch painting covers most of the length of one wall of the building, making it life-like in size. The museum provides benches in front of the painting for visitors to sit and reflect. The feeling in the room as people pay their respects is almost tangible. The experience may be too intense for younger patrons, so please use discretion if you have children with you.

The museum also sponsors temporary exhibits throughout the year. One such exhibit, Lisa Hoke's *The Gravity of Color*, was an amazing kaleidoscope of color made almost entirely of plastic and paper cups. The two-story design graced the LeWitt Staircase beginning in 2008, and was even featured on the cover of *Art New England*. They have a pretty cool gift shop as well.

The museum is open Mon, Tues, Weds, Fri, and Sun, 11 a.m. to 5 p.m.; Thurs, 11 a.m. to 8 p.m.; and Sat, 10 a.m. to 5 p.m. Admission is charged except Sat from 10 a.m. to noon. This free window is a great time to introduce the kids to the art of this wonderful place without breaking the bank. Blue Star Museum.

New Britain's **Central Connecticut State University** is home to the small **Copernican Observatory and Planetarium** (1615 Stanley St.; 860-832-3399; ccsu.edu/astronomy), which offers free programs on a first-come-first-serve basis, on the first and third Saturdays of each month at 8 p.m. There is an obvious love of the subject matter by the presenters. It's a great way to gain an intro into all things astronomical. Did we mention it's free?

New Britain's moniker as the Hardware City is commemorated in the **New Britain Industrial Museum** (59 W. Main St.; 860-832-8654; nbim.org). It's a small but choice museum, put together by people who genuinely love New Britain and its industrial past. You can trace New Britain's past and see its future as you view the history of the companies that put New Britain on the map: Stanley Works, Fafnir Bearing, Landers, North & Judd, and American Hardware. Open Wed, noon to 4 p.m.; Thurs and Fri, 2 to 4 p.m.; Sat, 10 a.m. to 4 p.m. Admission (except for children 12 and younger) on Sat 10 to noon.

newbritaintrivia

The Copernican Observatory and Planetarium at Central Connecticut State University in New Britain houses one of the largest publicly available telescopes in the US.

ANNUAL EVENTS IN THE HEARTLAND

FEBRUARY

Connecticut Flower & Garden Show
Connecticut Convention Center, Hartford
(860) 240-6000
ctflowershow.com

MARCH

Connecticut Spring Antiques Show
Hartford State Armory
360 Broad St., Hartford
(860) 345-2400
ctspringantiquesshow.com

APRIL

The River Run 5k & 10k Races
Iron Horse Boulevard, Simsbury
simsburyriverrun.com

MAY

Shad Derby Festival
Various places
windsorshadderby.org

JUNE

Travelers Championship
TPC River Highlands, Cromwell
travelerschampionship.com

JULY

Greater Hartford Festival of Jazz
Bushnell Park, Hartford
hartfordjazz.org

AUGUST

Plainville Hot Air Balloon Festival
Norton Park
197 South Washington St., Plainville
plainvillefireco.com/Balloon_Festival.html

SEPTEMBER

Berlin Fair
430 Beckley Rd., East Berlin
(860) 828-0063
ctberlinfair.com

Farm Fest
Hilltop Farm,
1616 Mapleton Ave., Suffield
hilltopfarmsuffield.org/farmfest

Mum Festival
70 Memorial Blvd., Bristol
(860) 584-4718
bristolmumfestival.com

Old Wethersfield Arts and Crafts Fair
Cove Park, State St., Wethersfield
(860) 529-7656
wethersfieldhistory.org/visit/
wethersfield-arts-and-crafts-fair

Southington Apple Harvest Festival
75 Main St., Southington Town Green,
(860) 276-8461
southingtonahf.com

Suffield on the Green
Suffield Town Green
friendsofsuffield.org/suffieldonthegreen.
html

Wapping Fair
South Windsor Fairgrounds
75 Brookfield St., South Windsor
wappingfair.org

Wethersfield Cornfest
Broad Street Green, Wethersfield
(860) 721-6200
wethersfieldchamber.com/event/
the-cornfest

OCTOBER

Glastonbury Apple Harvest Festival
Riverfront Park
300 Welles St., Glastonbury
(860) 659-3587

Hartford Marathon
Begins at Bushnell Park
(860) 652-8866
hartfordmarathon.com

Max's 5th Annual HOPtoberfest
Rosedale Farms & Vineyards
25 East Weatogue St., Simsbury
rosedale1920.com/events/

Plainville PumpkinFest
1 Central Sq., Plainville
(860) 747-1965
plainvillepumpkinfest.com

NOVEMBER

Holiday Light Fantasia
Goodwin Park, Hartford
holidaylightfantasia.org
Runs Nov through Jan, proceeds to
charity

Manchester Road Race
Main St., Manchester
manchesterroadrace.com

DECEMBER

First Night Hartford
Bushnell Park, Hartford
firstnighthartford.org

Taking the family to see a major-league baseball game is expensive. But here in Connecticut, you can get all the authentic appeal of America's pastime without having to sell your Mickey Mantle rookie card. You can sit close to the action, and chances are good you'll be able to snag a foul ball or a player's autograph. Best of all, you might discover the next Barry Bonds or Derek Jeter before the rest of the world catches on. Check out the ***New Britain Bees*** (New Britain Stadium, Willow Brook Park, 230 John Karbonic Way; 860-826-BEES; nbbees.com). The Bees are members of the Atlantic League, and are not affiliated with any major league team. They play Apr through Sept and offer many kid-friendly activities, all at a fraction of the cost of a trip to New York or Boston.

Avery's Beverages (520 Corbin Ave.; 860-224-0830; averysoda.com) is another jewel in New Britain. In fact, it's the wonderful Aladdin's cave of jewel-colored soda and mysterious Rube Goldberg machinery some readers might remember from their childhoods. At Avery's they bottle soda the way it used to be done back in the day, wooden carrying cases and all. The family has been bottling soda in the same red barn since 1904. Sherman F. Avery used to deliver his soda all over New Britain and beyond in a horse-drawn wagon before he went modern in 1914 and purchased a delivery truck. Today, they still make deliveries to nearby towns. Or you can visit their store to sample that high-quality soda pop made from only the finest quality ingredients, including real cane sugar (no sugar substitutes here!), and naturally pure well water. You can even try your hand at making your own, but beware—some results from that endeavor include bottles of Dog Drool Soda, Toxic Slime, and Monster Mucus. Um, yuck? Perhaps it's safer to stick to some of Avery's original recipes of cola, lemon-lime, ginger ale, and root and birch beer. Whatever your taste, you'll find it bottled in glass to preserve that old-fashioned flavor. You can even have personalized labels printed on your soda, a great idea for weddings or other special occasions. Avery's has such a fascinating history, and if you have the time, call ahead to arrange a tour of the bottling works. You won't be disappointed.

As you drive down Route 9 between New Britain and Farmington, you'll pass a hauntingly familiar sculpture of American marines raising a flag. This is the *Iwo Jima Survivors' Memorial Park and Monument*. It is dedicated to 6,821 Americans who, during World War II, gave their lives in the desperate fight for the Pacific island of Iwo Jima, the place where it was said that "uncommon valor" was a "common virtue." The monument's sculpture re-creates the famous flag-raising by American troops atop Mount Suribachi. On special days, such as Veterans Day, the monument is decorated with an avenue of American flags. Open 24 hours daily.

Southington

If you have little ones with you, be sure to visit *Karabin Farms* (894 Andrew St.; 860-620-0194; karabinfarms.com). They've been in town since 1972, and what started out as a hobby for owners Michael and Diane Karabin has turned into a family-run, family fun place. As their children grew and went off to college, they came back, one by one, to be involved in the business in some way. Together they have planted over 2,000 fruit trees and 10,000 Christmas trees. They offer pick-your-own apples, peaches, pumpkins, and Christmas trees (they also offer pre-cut ones). There are hayrides to the fields, live animals to visit (including funky-looking Highland cattle), snacks to be had at the snack barn, as well as an entire treasure chest of things to be discovered in the store. Throughout the year, along with the fresh fruit and vegetables, you can also find homemade pies, local honey, maple syrup, jams, pickles, and soup mixes. They also offer humanely raised (right on the farm) meat. Seasonal flowers, including a huge variety of poinsettias at Christmas, as well as specialty soaps and candles. The farm is open daily Apr through Dec 23, 9 a.m. to 5 p.m.; Jan through Mar, Sat and Sun, 9 a.m. to 5 p.m.

Board & Brush (61 Center St.; 203-343-6445; boardandbrush.com/southington) is a do-it-yourself workshop where you can go by yourself or with a group of friends and create home decor projects from scratch. No experience, supplies, or tools are needed; they are all provided for you. You choose the design and an instructor walks you through the process. It's sort of a like a Paint Night, but with wood. Owners Scott and Lisa Selby decided to start their own Board & Brush (they are a franchise) when Scott was looking for a change from his HR career and Lisa was looking to go back to work after raising their two sons. The timing was perfect and they opened their doors on Center Street. While the bulk of their projects use wood, they also offer classes in glass, chalkboard, pillows, slate, and terra cotta. It's also BYOB, so make it a night. Visit the website today to see upcoming classes!

Plainville

Back in the eighteenth century, Route 10 was the major thoroughfare passing through *Plainville*. It was down this road that Rochambeau's French army marched on its way to join Washington and travel to Yorktown, and then win the decisive battle of the American Revolution and head back to Boston. The location of one of the French campgrounds is marked by a small plaque on Main Street (Route 10) after the intersection of Hatters Lane (on the right) and before Winchell Smith Dr. (on the left, if you're going north). The plaque reads: "In 1781 and 1782 Jean Baptiste Count de Rochambeau and his French troops marched by here enroute to and from Yorktown, Va."

No matter the century, traveling creates an appetite, and there's no better place to stop than *J. Timothy's Taverne* (143 New Britain Ave.; 960-747-6813; jtimothys.com), just as travelers have been doing for centuries. The restaurant is housed in a building built in 1789, President George Washington's first year in office. Back then, the tavern was owned and operated by John Cooke. Cooke's Tavern became a well-known stagecoach stop for travelers of the day. When the time came, John passed the business and building down to his son, George, who lived there for almost a century, still operating the tavern. Upon George's death in 1923, his niece, Nancy Kirkham, inherited the tavern. In 1934, the tavern was transformed into a full-service restaurant, which it has been ever since. Although the Cooke family sold the business to current owners Tim Adams and Jim Welch in 1979, they are proud to carry on the tradition.

Today, under the name J. Timothy's, the tavern offers six public dining rooms their infamous Dirt wings. Their wing sauce has been voted best in the country, with their buffalo wings taking second place, and they are proud of it! They even have directions on the website clarifying the correct method for ordering. They take their wings seriously. You've been warned. Open daily at 11:30 a.m. with closing times varying, but generally between 10 and midnight. Check the website for the latest news.

Bristol

If you're looking for some great family fun, head east from Plainville to Bristol's *Lake Compounce* (186 Enterprise Dr.; 860-583-3300; lakecompounce.com). Now the country's oldest amusement park, Lake Compounce has been serving

Going Up?

On your way to Lake Compounce, you may notice a tall, interesting-looking building jutting out of the trees. It looks a little like a transplanted skyscraper from the city. It is actually an elevator test tower. Located on the grounds of the Bristol Research Center, the tower is used by the Otis Quality Assurance Center. Topping out at 383 feet, the test tower is the tallest in North America.

up family fun and thrills since 1846 with its 427 acres, 20-acre lake, and myriad rides and attractions. There really is something for everyone, including a great portion of the park for the smaller children, with age-appropriate rides and shows. The more daring can choose from three coasters: the Zoomerang; Boulder Dash, voted number one wooden coaster in the world; and Phobia Phear Coaster, New England's first triple-launch coaster. If you're willing to get wet, there's Riptide Racer, Clipper Cove, Mammoth Falls, and much, much more, including Lights Out, which is a high-speed water slide in, you guessed it, the dark. For those of you who are looking for tamer options, check out the beautiful 1898 carousel. You'll find horses carved by Looff, Carmel, and Stein & Goldstein. There are forty-nine horses (twenty-seven jumpers and twenty-two standers), a goat, and two chariots. The original Wurlitzer organ still grinds out tunes for riders. Like we said, something for everyone. Open daily 11 a.m. to 8 p.m. Memorial Day through Labor Day and then sporadically from Labor Day until the end of Dec, during which the park offers some way-cool Halloween and holiday lights events. Be sure to check their website for details and admission costs.

Around the middle of the nineteenth century, Bristol was the center of clock- and watchmaking in the Northeast. At one time, the town supported 280 clockmakers, and in 1860, they turned out a total of 200,000 clocks. Today, the great clockworks are only a memory preserved in the town's **American Clock & Watch Museum** (100 Maple St.; 860-583-6070; clockandwatchmuseum.org). Within the walls of the 1801 Miles Lewis House and two modern additions, the museum manages to display a collection of more than 5,500 clocks and watches, including many made locally. This vast assemblage is organized by type and eras, so that as you move from room to room, you can observe how the styles of clock cases changed to match furniture styles. Tours are entirely self-guided and take a suggested hour and a half; the exhibits are well marked. Among the more interesting items are some oak clock cases from the 1920s and 1930s, which are exhibited together with the metal rollers that pressed the intricate designs into the wood. There are also lovely "tall" clocks, including some made by Eli Terry. There's even one clock whose workings are carved entirely from wood. The American Clock & Watch Museum is open 10 a.m. to 5 p.m. daily during Apr; Dec through March, Fri, Sat, and Sun, 10 a.m. to 5 p.m. Admission. Blue Star Museum.

Clocks and watches aren't the only items collected in Bristol. Housed in a restored turn-of-the-twentieth-century factory building, the **New England Carousel Museum** (95 Riverside Ave.; 860-585-5411; thecarouselmuseum. org) contains some of the best examples of antique carousel art in existence, hundreds of pieces in all. Featured items include a collection of band organs, the entire carousel from Santa's Land in Putnam, Vermont, and a gorgeous pair of 1915 carved chariots, each encrusted with 1,500 glass jewels. The museum also has two art galleries and a fine history exhibit. This was the first museum of its kind on the East Coast, and many preservationists still consider it the best.

The main museum occupies the building's ground floor. Wood carvers and painters perform restorations on the second floor, and if you happen to be there while they are working, you can go upstairs and watch. The second floor also contains the **Museum of Fire History**, which is worth a visit and is included in the admission price. Open year-round, Weds through Sat, 10 a.m. to 5 p.m.; Sun., noon to 5 p.m. Closed major holidays, but usually open for local school holidays. You can also reserve the museum for special events year-round, including themed birthday parties and weddings. Admission. Blue Star Museum.

One of the best attractions in Bristol is one you are unlikely to stumble across unless you're a native Nutmegger and you happen to be around at Halloween time (and happen to also read this book!). **Witch's Dungeon Classic Movie Museum** (98 Summer St.; 860-583-8306; preservehollywood. org) has been in operation for more than fifty years, and it all started with young Cortlandt Hull, who, as an ill child, spent time building model monster kits. As he grew up, he became fascinated with the theatrical transformations from human to monster. Soon Cortlandt grew bored with his models and hungered for more. He was disappointed with visits to different wax museums that just didn't do it for him, so he started creating his own full-size versions of his favorite monsters, and they seemed to take on a life of their own. It was a real family affair—Cortlandt's dad helped him with a building to house them in and built the backgrounds, his mom re-created many of the famous costumes for his creatures, his uncle acted as engineer—and the rest is history.

By the 1970s and 1980s, Cortlandt's skills had improved, and his "little" museum started to gain national attention from the likes of the *New York Times*, *National Geographic*, and *Ripley's Believe It or Not!* Members of the acting community took notice, too, and lent their support. Vincent Price, John Agar, and

Mark Hamill all did special recordings for the museum. People from all over the country have come to visit this Connecticut treasure. Cortlandt's beloved creatures are now sought after and travel the country to star in their own special displays. Cortlandt himself is well known as an artist. Who knew all this would come from his interest in monster models?!

Cortlandt moved his museum to a larger space within the **Bristol Historical Society**, and the museum is now wheelchair accessible. They are open the last weekend of Sept and through Oct, Fri through Sun, 7 to 10 p.m. Small admission charge, cash only, which goes to benefit the museum and the historical society.

Places to Stay in The Heartland

GLASTONBURY

Butternut Farm
1654 Main St.
(860) 633-7197
butternutfarmbandb.com
Moderate
So much more than just a bed-and-breakfast, Butternut Farm is a labor of love for innkeeper Don Reid

Connecticut River Valley Inn
2195 Main St.
(860) 633-7374
crvinn.com
Moderate to expensive
Beautiful any time of the year in the Connecticut River Valley

SIMSBURY

Simsbury 1820 House
731 Hopmeadow St.
(860) 658-7658
simsbury1820house.com
Moderate to expensive
Rambling 1820 house with comfortable accommodations

Linden House Bed and Breakfast
288/290 Hopmeadow St.
(860) 408-1321
lindenhousebb.com
Moderate
Located in the village of Weatogue in Simsbury, everything a New England getaway should be

Places to Eat in The Heartland

AVON

First & Last Tavern
26 W. Main St. (US 44)
(860) 676-2000
firstandlasttavern.com

Inexpensive to moderate
Comfortable pub-style place offering casual Italian fare. The focaccia is delicious.

COLLINSVILLE

Crown and Hammer Pub
3 Depot St.
(860) 693-9199
crownandhammer.com
Moderate to expensive
Great pub-style food, live entertainment, and beautiful views of the Farmington River and dam

LaSalle Market & Deli
104 Main St.
(860) 693-8010
lasallemarket.com
Inexpensive
Great location with live music

HARTFORD

Trumbull Kitchen
150 Trumbull St.
(860) 493-7412
maxrestaurantgroup.com
Moderate to expensive
Contemporary restaurant
for fusion cuisine;
reservations are a must

PLAINVILLE

Cottage Restaurant and Cafe
427 Farmington Ave.
(860) 793-8888
cottagerestaurantandcafe.
com
Moderate to expensive
Family-owned and
-operated restaurant
serving contemporary
American fare

SIMSBURY

Brookside Bagels
563 Hopmeadow St.
(860) 651-1492
Inexpensive
Incredibly fresh bagels
in interesting flavors,
awesome selection
of cream cheese and
lox, creative sandwich
combinations

The Litchfield Hills

West of Hartford is **Litchfield County**, an area largely synonymous with Connecticut's western uplands. Moving north and west through Litchfield, you get deeper into the **Litchfield Hills**, a forested spur of the Berkshires that typifies what comes to most people's minds when they think of New England.

Steepled white churches, romantic old inns, quaint antiques shops, and small establishments run by Yankee craftspeople still abound. In recent years, though, the Litchfield Hills have become home to many of the rich and famous. Their arrival has brought upscale shops and nouvelle restaurants that give the area a cosmopolitan flavor.

The southern portion of this hill mass merges into the region's "Alpine Lake" country, an area reminiscent of Switzerland, with cool forest-shrouded lakes and tranquil meadows. This region is home to some of the state's best inns. Cutting between the Litchfield Hills and New York's Taconic Mountains, from the extreme northwestern corner of Connecticut to Stratford on the coast, is the Housatonic River. In its northern reaches, the Housatonic is a wild freshet that is surely one of the prettiest rivers in New England. Litchfield County is bordered by Massachusetts on the north and New York on the west. To the south of the lake country are the populous counties of Fairfield and New Haven.

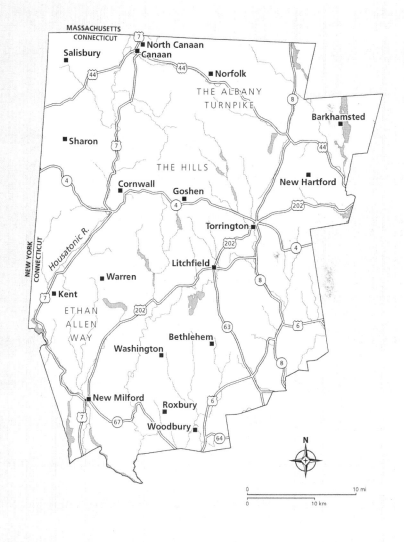

The Albany Turnpike

In the days before railroads and superhighways, Hartford and Albany, New York, were linked by a rutted roadway called the **Albany Turnpike**. This highway of sorts was the main route through the rugged northwestern uplands, and its location determined the patterns of settlement in this part of the state. Today, the successor to the old turnpike is Route 44, and any traveler through this part of Connecticut must pass over it.

New Hartford

One of the easternmost townships along the Litchfield portion of Route 44 is **New Hartford**, home to **Satan's Kingdom State Recreation Area**. The origin of this name has been the subject of debate for years, but it likely was named for the bandits who used to hide out in the rugged, wooded countryside that flanked the turnpike and offered a perfect hiding place from which to ambush and rob the Hartford–Albany stagecoaches. Across the street from the recreation area is Satan's Kingdom Road, marked by a street sign . . . most of the time. As you can imagine, this sign is a temptation for modern-day thieves and it routinely gets stolen. At one point, a new sign was put up but it didn't read "Satan's Kingdom Rd.", but "Statan's Kingdom Rd." Was this a typo or a deliberate attempt to dissuade would-be hooligans? Either way, the sign was soon stolen. So goes the cycle. Maybe they should just rename the road.

Within Satan's Kingdom you will find the popular **Farmington River Tubing** (92 Main St.; 860-693-6465; farmingtonrivertubing.com), which operates from Memorial Day through mid-September, outfitting people with life jackets and inflated inner tubes and sending them on down the river. Once you receive your equipment, you are literally on your own until you reach the outtake point two and a half miles downriver. The company will not help you if you fall out of your tube and they advise you not to stand up while in any of the three Class 1, 2, and 3 rapids you will encounter on your trip. They also recommend you do not leave the river until you finish the route. Tubing is not for everyone: Minimum age suggestion is ten, minimum height and weight is four feet and fifty pounds, but the company leaves it up to your discretion. They suggest you wear shoes, and we suggest you pick a pair that will stay on your feet. Local fishermen have complained about the number of shoes they have "fished" out of the river and the pollution just isn't good for anyone. Operation is weather permitting, so it's always best to call ahead before making the trip. Cash only.

Also located in New Hartford is the **Collinsville Antiques Co. of New Hartford** (283 Main St.; 860-379-2290; collinsvilleantiques.com). If you're wondering about the name (we were confused, too), it's because the company was formerly located in Collinsville, where it had operated since 1989. When new owners Doug and Cindy Szydlo purchased the business in 1995, they expanded it into the wonder it is today. Often voted Best Antiques Shop by the *Hartford Advocate* and *Hartford Magazine*, the shop outgrew its space in the old Collins Company. The town didn't want to lose the business, and it caused quite a stir, but it was time. In 2005, the company found its new home in New Hartford's Waring manufacturing building, but kept the name as a nod to its beginnings. Open daily, 10 a.m. to 5 p.m.

Barkhamsted

North of New Hartford, Route 44 loops through *Barkhamsted*. If you're here during the cooler months, say, February or March, a visit to the *Kasulaitis Farm and Sugarhouse* (69 Goose Green Rd.; 860-379-8787) to watch the process and buy some tasty maple products is a must. If you miss sugaring off, stop by anyway and watch the lambs frisk and frolic in the spring pasture. Such sights are good for the soul.

Something else that's good for the soul is watching New England's color change as she greets autumn in all her splendor. Barkhamsted's combination of sparse population, winding roads, heavy forest, and large lakes makes it one of the most dramatic parts of Connecticut for leaf peeping.

One of the best **fall foliage jaunts** through Barkhamsted starts north of the town at the junction of Routes 20 and 181 in Hartland. If you approach this intersection from the east on Route 20, you'll pass through West Hartland on the way. Don't let this confuse you; with typical Yankee contrariness, West Hartland is actually east of Hartland, so keep driving for another mile. At the intersection in Hartland, take Route 181 south. This road runs between the Barkhamsted Reservoir and the Farmington River, for much of the way under the limbs of the lovely **People's State Forest**.

At the tip of the reservoir, Route 181 meets Route 318. Take 318 east to the *Saville Dam*, which separates Barkhamsted and Compensating Reservoirs.

AUTHOR'S FAVORITES

Litchfield Distillery	The Daffodils at Laurel Ridge
Barbara Farnsworth, Booksellers	Saville Dam
White Flower Farm	

Barkhamsted Reservoir is the chief supplier of water for Hartford. The dam, named for Caleb Mills Saville, chief engineer, was built in 1940 and is 135 feet tall and 1,950 feet long. The dam really is beautiful at any time of the year with its castle-like structure and stone work. You can read more about the dam's history on the Connecticut history website (connecticuthistory.org). There's parking nearby and even on the dam itself; this is a popular spot to stop for pictures or a picnic.

From the dam, continue east to Route 219. From there you can drive south to pick up Route 44, return west for more leaf peeping, or loop up to Route 20 in Granby.

If after reaching Saville Dam you're still in the mood for more fall color, head back west on Route 318 for half-mile beyond the intersection of Route 181. Turn right on E. River Road. This will take you directly through **People's State Forest** along the banks of the West Branch of the Farmington, where even on the hottest day the tall trees and pines keep the forest shady and glade cool. This forest has a whole bunch of trails to explore, including the yellow Jessie Gerard Trail, on which you will find the site of a village that existed more than 270 years ago. Established in 1740 by Mary Barber and her husband, James Chaugham, this village was known as the Barkhamsted Lighthouse and became a regular stop for stagecoaches traveling through the area. Barber and her husband decided to move to this area of wilderness to escape her father, who was not happy that she, a white woman, married Chaugham, a Narragansett Indian. They, their children, and their children's children lived quite happily there for the next 120 years. Now a State Archaeological Preserve known as the **Lighthouse Archaeological Site**, the former village is not much more than a few cellar holes, but it is a stop on the **Connecticut Freedom Trail** and a continuing reminder of the ongoing fight for freedom from discrimination. The forest recreation area is open from 8 a.m. to sunset.

The nearby village of **Riverton**, was the former home of the Hitchcock chair, first produced in 1825. While other Connecticut entrepreneurs were experimenting with the use of interchangeable parts in the manufacture of rifles and clocks, **Lambert Hitchcock** set out in 1818 to mass-produce furniture in a little factory at the junction of the Farmington and Still Rivers. A decade later, Hitchcock was turning out 15,000 chairs each year, and his factory employed 100 people in the rapidly growing village of Hitchcocksville. The mass-produced Hitchcock chairs, selling for between 45 cents and $1.75, were an instant success. They were also extremely sturdy. Quality control consisted of dropping each assembled chair from a second-floor workshop into a waiting wagon; only those items that survived the drop unscathed were considered suf-ficiently sturdy to wear the Hitchcock label. Once the chairs were assembled, workers finished them by hand, often using multiple stencils that produced a colorful and distinctive look.

In the middle of the nineteenth century, Hitchcock's business foundered; in 1852, its owner died penniless. About the same time, the village that bore his name disappeared from the map. Tired of constantly being confused with nearby Hotchkissville, the residents of Hitchcocksville, in typically pragmatic Yankee fashion, changed the town's name to Riverton. Present-day Riverton is a sleepy, picturesque, quarter-mile-long village—little more than a quaint neighborhood tucked inside the larger town of Barkhamsted—where all three streets run alongside the Farmington River. Local stature and "image" were almost completely dependent on the venerable **Hitchcock Furniture Factory and Factory Store**, both of which ceased operations in April 2006. But Rick Swenson, owner of **Still River Antiques**, continued to sell fully restored Hitchcock furniture. In 2010, he and his business partner, Gary Hath, purchased the Hitchcock name, plans, and artwork in the hopes of continuing the legacy and "bringing Hitchcock furniture into the twenty-first century while maintaining the quality and integrity of Lambert Hitchcock's original dream." **The Hitchcock Chair Company**, (13 Riverton Rd.; 860-738-9958; hitchcockchair.com) is open Tues through Sat, 10 a.m. to 4 p.m. or by appointment.

Other village attractions are easily reachable. It's just a 5-minute walk along Route 20 from the local Grange Hall on the banks of Sandy Brook at the west end of town to the bridge spanning the Farmington River at the east end. But that stretch of road abounds with enticing stores and snack shops. You might, for example, wrap up your visit with a deli sandwich and Moxie from the **Riverton General Store** (2 Main St.; 860-379-0811; rivertonct.com). Open daily from 6 a.m. to 4 p.m., you can eat at their outdoor seating area or have a picnic along the river.

Or perhaps a stop at **Greenwood Glass** (3 Robertsville Rd.; 860-738-9469; petergreenwood.com) to see what Peter Greenwood is up to at his studio, where he teaches and practices the art of glass blowing. Located in an 1829 church, the studio is open Tues through Sat., 9 a.m. to 5 pm.; it's always good to call ahead and make sure he's going to be there, though.

If you or someone in your group likes fishing, then don't pass by **Uncle Aaron's Tackle Shack** (4 Robertsville Rd.; 860-307-7156; uncleaaronstackleshack. com), where you can pick up crawlers, worms, flies, or any other creepy crawly thing you'd need to land a prize fish. Uncle Aaron also has a collection of antique reels for you to check out. And any questions you have about fishing, Uncle Aaron is your guy. He'll make sure you have what you need.

Norfolk

Located at the junction of Route 44 and Routes 272 and 182 and with *Campbell Falls* and *Haystack Mountain State Park* just north of the town center, *Norfolk* is a crossroads of tourism in northwest Connecticut. It's the music, though, for which this town is known. Norfolk's love affair with music dates back to the 1890s when the **Litchfield County Choral Union** was founded by Ellen Battell and her husband Carl Stoeckel, whose father was the first professor at the Yale School of Music. The couple would hold concerts at their Litchfield Road mansion. In 1906, as the concerts (and the audiences) grew, the couple built a **Music Shed** in which to hold them. Musicians from around the world came here to play throughout the years. When Ellen died in 1939, her will stipulated that her estate and its facilities be used for Yale University's summer music school. Thus began an enduring tradition.

The first-rate acoustics of this Music Shed can still be enjoyed today at the annual *Norfolk Chamber Music Festival* (20 Litchfield Rd.; 860-542-3000; music.yale.edu/Norfolk), an event that is sort of like Tanglewood without the crowds. The concert schedule and participants vary from year to year but they never disappoint. There are Fri and Sat evening performances throughout June, July, and Aug.

The music legacy is not all Ellen Battell Stoeckel and her family left to the town of Norfolk. The shingle-sided, barrel-vaulted 1889 **Norfolk Library** was donated by Isabella Eldridge in honor of her parents, Reverend Joseph and Sarah Battell Eldridge. Isabella's sister, Urania Battell Humphrey donated the 1888 **Battell Memorial Chapel** in the Church of Christ Congregational on Litchfield Road. It features priceless Tiffany stained-glass windows depicting the four seasons that were later donated by Ellen Battell Stoeckel in 1929. Mary Eldridge commissioned the 1889 **Joseph Battell Fountain** on the green, designed by high-society architect Stanford White, in honor of her uncle Joseph. Mary Alice Bradford Eldridge paid for the 1892 **Norfolk Town Hall**. The Battell/Eldridge family's affluence is matched only by their generosity and love for their town.

Norfolk was also home to many less fortunate people, including **James Mars**, who was born into slavery in Canaan, Connecticut, in 1790. Mars and his family escaped captivity and hid for many months at the homes of abolitionists in Norfolk, Connecticut. At the age of twenty-one, he gained his freedom thanks to new state laws. He became a deacon of Talcott Street Congregational Church in Hartford and worked for continuing civil liberties. He write his autobiography, *The Life of James Mars*, in 1864 to educate people about the existence of slavery. *Puppetsweat Theater*, a performance group out of Wesleyan University that uses puppets, masks, shadow play, and dance to explore ideas of social responsibility and history, created a provocative multimedia presentation of his life based on his book and has shown it at the Ballard Institute in Storrs as well as other places.

Mars died in 1880 at the age of ninety. He is buried in the **Center Cemetery** (15 Old Colony Rd.; 860-542-1775) in Norfolk alongside his father, Jupiter Mars, who served in the American Revolution. Their stones are located to the rear and left of the first entrance into the cemetery. To the right of this entrance, near the wall next to Old Colony Road, is the grave of Alanson Freeman, who served in the all-black Connecticut 29th Regiment of the Civil War.

Heading north on Route 272, you'll come to **Campbell Falls State Park** (Old Spaulding Road.; 860-482-1817), where you can see the Whiting River boil over rocks in a narrow gorge. You'll need to take a short hike to reach the falls; just follow the sounds of rushing water. The water drops in two levels, with a small pool in between and one at the bottom. The first level is a good place for a picnic among the weathered rocks. Campbell Falls is off Norfolk Road, just south of Southfield, Massachusetts, just before Spaulding Road. If you are traveling from the other direction, it's about five miles north of Haystack Mountain, on Route 272 in Norfolk.

north canaantrivia

Milo Freeland is credited with being the first African American to volunteer for the Union army during the Civil War. Freeland died in 1883, while living in East Canaan. A stone was placed in the Hillside Cemetery on Route 44 in North Canaan in 1996 during a ceremony in his honor.

Canaan

Although the festival in nearby Norfolk tends to be better known, the **Music Mountain Chamber Music Festival** (225 Music Mountain Rd.; 860-824-7126; musicmountain.org) is the oldest continuous chamber music festival in the US. Held in the tiny village of **Falls Village** in **Canaan** from mid-June to mid-Sept, this music festival offers sixteen concerts each year. They are mainly held on Sunday afternoons, but Saturday evenings often bring jazz concerts and other special events. Music Mountain was founded in 1930 as the permanent home for the Gordon String Quartet, and they have been offering chamber music ever since.

Salisbury

Way up in the farthest northwest corner of Connecticut is **Mount Riga**, which is part of a system of peaks that marches north and west from Salisbury to the

salisburytrivia

New York and Massachusetts borders. For many years, the iron-rich depths of these mountains were mined and supplied our nation with much-needed tools and weapons. People were needed to work these mines, and many came. A community emerged, and its people became known as the "Raggies," perhaps because they lived on Mount Riga. It is said that many of these people were immigrants, possibly from Latvia. They didn't know the culture, didn't speak the language, and kept mainly to themselves. And of course, we know how people generally feel about other people they don't understand. New England Yankees didn't go up and say, "Hey, tell me about your culture; I'd like to understand." Not feeling particularly welcome, the Raggies lived quietly on the mountain well into the twentieth century, even after the iron forges cooled. Today, there are myriad sources of information on this group of people, as descendants have begun to speak out and preserve their rich history and heritage.

If you'd like to hike to the summit of Mount Riga for the amazing views and one curious sight (sound?), there are many well-marked hiking trails to choose from. Near the summit is **Crying Child Rock**, which people say makes a soft crying sound just like an infant whenever the wind is right. Sit for a spell and listen.

The Lakeville section of Salisbury is where you'll find **Lime Rock Park** (60 White Hollow Rd. [main entrance]; 860-435-5000; limerock.com), probably Connecticut's most famous racetrack for NASCAR speedsters. From time to time, you can see celebrities behind the wheel. Tom Brokaw and Tom Cruise have made appearances. For us regular people, it's a fun place to spend the day. Home to the **Grand-Am Championship Weekend** and the traditional Memorial Day weekend season opener, Lime Rock goes out of its way to please the fans. Always wanted to drive a race car? There are multiple ways you can get on the track. From individual options to group experiences, check out their website to see what might work best for you. They also hold special events, such as the Farm to Track Picnic & Pig Roast, Car Shows, Scout Days, and Fourth of July fireworks.

A more recent addition to the park is the ***Round Hill Highland Games*** (facebook.com/RoundHillHighlandGames) held in late June. The Round Hill Highland Games are the third oldest games of their kind in the country, taking their name from their previous location on Round Hill Road in Greenwich. The games originated there in 1923 and are happy to have found a new home in Salisbury. These games are Scottish and attract clans, athletes, bands, pipers, drummers, drum majors, and dancers come from all over the country to participate in heavyweight, piping and drumming, and children's Scottish sporting competitions, partake in heritage society gatherings, purchase Scottish food, drinks, merchandise, jewelry, and clothing. Did we mention there's an adult kilted mile run? The games are open to the public, and are held rain or shine. Proceeds from tickets go to the Round Hill organization, which works to preserve Scottish heritage.

In 1924 and 1925 John, Olaf, and Magnus Satre immigrated to Salisbury from their native Norway where they were well-known Nordic ski jumpers and alpine and cross-country skiers. The brothers, probably missing their sport or wanting to share their skills, established the ***Salisbury Outing Club***, teaching the art of skiing. They held their first competition in the winter of 1927. It drew more than 200 attendees and cemented their place in Salisbury. After a few successful years, the club had a rough time during the war years, but rose once again in 1945, this time named the ***Salisbury Winter Sports Association*** (SWSA) (80 Indian Cave Rd.; 860-850-0080; salisburyisjumping.com). Today, the SWSA continues what the Satre brothers started on the hill that bears their name. They "teach the skills necessary for their enjoyment and lifelong pursuit" of Nordic ski jumping and alpine and cross-country skiing. They first hosted the **Eastern National Ski Jumping Championships** in 1952, and continue to do so today. The association is an all-volunteer, nonprofit effort that works to foster a love of skiing and jumping, especially in the young (although you have to be at least six years old to start). They sponsor events throughout the year, including Friday Night Lights, a Target Ski Jumping competition that is followed by a Human Dog Sled Race, ski invitational, a Snowball Dance in February, a Junior Ski Jump Camp, a ski swap and sale, and more. Be sure to check out their website for dates and information.

Ethan Allen Way

Cornwall

Cornwall is one of those ubiquitous Connecticut towns with multiple villages with similar names. I swear, sometimes they just do it to confuse us. The town of Cornwall was incorporated in 1740, named after Cornwall, England.

Located on the east bank of the Housatonic River, the town's population is less than 1,500 people, divided among five village communities: Cornwall Bridge, Cornwall Village, Cornwall Hollow, East Cornwall, and West Cornwall. They don't even have enough students to have their own school system (they are part of Regional District 1 and share schools with Canaan, Kent, North Canaan, Salisbury, and Sharon), yet they have three post offices. It truly is a beautiful town, if not a little confusing to outsiders. The town's most famous attraction is the West Cornwall Covered Bridge, the largest and handsomest covered bridge in Connecticut.

cornwalltrivia

The West Cornwall Covered Bridge is featured in the opening scenes of the 1967 film Valley of the Dolls as representation of life in New England.

To find the **West Cornwall Covered Bridge**, (not to be confused with the Cornwall Bridge, also in Cornwall), you'll need to find Routes 7 and 128, which intersect right at the bridge. Route 128 then takes you over the bridge and turns into the Main Street of West Cornwall. There are lots of opportunities for picture taking around the bridge, just be careful of the traffic and be sure to park out of the way.

. Originally designed by Ithiel Town, the bridge has been in continuous service over the Housatonic River since 1864. This is an impressive feat, especially considering the dangers it has faced. For example, it survived the flooding from the Hurricane of 1938, and Hurricanes Connie and Diane in 1955. In 1961, it stayed intact despite the severe ice jam that needed to be dynamited. In 1945, a 20-ton oil truck fell through the bridge floor, yet it held fast. The bridge is 172 feet long and 15 feet wide and is one of only three remaining covered bridges in the state. Perhaps you'll cross it on your way to one of the post offices.

On the west side of US 7, a couple hundred yards south of the bridge, is something right out of an H. P. Lovecraft horror novel. There, jutting out from under a canopy of overhanging trees along the side of the road is a big rock painted to resemble a most lifelike giant frog whose leering mouth seems to be reaching for the occupants of the passenger side of the car. But don't worry, the story behind the painting of this rock is not menacing. It all started more than sixty years ago when Margaret (Marge) Grusauski Wilson was on her way home from high school and noticed that a highway worker had painted two white eyes on the rock. The crew had recently painted the lines on Route 7, and the worker must have had a sense of humor. Marge went home and told her brother, John, about the rock, and the two of them decided to "do it up good." They went back later and added long rows of white teeth, ears, eyes, and a nose, adding black details. They chose a small black rock for the "monster's" hat. They were almost happy with their work, but something wasn't quite right. The next evening, Marge had a new partner in "crime" when she and her best friend, Marietta Baird, found a flat rock, painted it red, and gave the monster his tongue. **Monster Rock** was

cornwalltrivia

Famous *Law and Order* prosecutor Sam Waterston and *Chicago Med* doctor Oliver Platt both live in West Cornwall. If you see them, though, act cool! Don't blow it for us.

complete. Throughout the next few years, Marge and her merry band of helpers maintained the painted rock and here and there added a few new details. But no one ever talked about it. No one knew who the culprits were. Marge eventually moved to Florida, where she still resides today. She held her silence for a very long time, and a few other people took credit for painting the rock. Marge said she didn't know who took over when she stopped, or how the rock came to be painted green, but she was tickled pink that something that started as a whim has continued for such a long time. She was amused to learn from friends who were on a leaf tour from New York City that the bus tour actually stopped at the rock. So, when you stop to take a picture, be sure to think well of Marge, her family, her friends, and her Monster Rock.

About a mile south of the covered bridge also on Route 7 is *Clarke Outdoors* (163 US 7; 860-672-6365; clarkeoutdoors.com), which offers kayaks, canoes, and rafts for those who want to try the river's whitewater. The staff here know what they are doing; a safety talk is given before each trip, and employees are happy to answer any questions you have. They offer guided and unguided tours on the Housatonic River, including a lovely trip under the covered bridge. Reservations for the guided rafting trips are a must. Tip: Prices are lower during the week. Shuttle service available. Be sure to check out the expressive anthropomorphic critters adorning Clarke's signs and vans. These are original **Sandra Boynton** paintings! They also have a retail store with a large selection of equipment, clothing, and books. Open Mar through Nov, Mon through Fri, 10 a.m. to 4 p.m.; Sat and Sun, 9 a.m. to 5 p.m.

Five miles south of the Cornwall Bridge (the bridge, not the village) in Cornwall Bridge (the village, not the bridge) is the *Cornwall Bridge Pottery Store* (69 Kent Road South; 860-946-9679; cbpots.com), where you can see beautiful pottery at its source. Artist and owner Todd Piker invites visitors to wander through the kiln yard, watch potters at their wheels, and ask questions. Piker is a fount of knowledge, as he's been making and selling world-class stoneware since 1972. Much of Piker's pottery features a celadon glaze made from slag recovered from a local riverbed, where it was deposited by the iron-works that used to dominate the area's economy. None of the glazes, however, contain lead. Most items are decorated with simple blue or brown brushwork designs with an Asian flavor. The firing is done in a thirty-five-foot wood-fired kiln and the flames give the finished pieces distinctive two-tone markings. The workshop is open for visits, but it's always best to call ahead for the best hours. If you're lucky, you'll find some seconds available for sale here.

If you happen to be in the area on a weekend any time from early Feb to late Mar, known as the sugaring season here in New England, a stop at *Young Love Maple* (104 Kent Rd. S.; younglovemaple.com) makes good sense. See the process of making maple syrup from scratch and pick up a bottle (or two) to enjoy throughout the year. They are only open weekends, through the season, and it's best to call ahead to be sure they are there.

If you happen to travel north along Route 7 and the Housatonic, be sure to stop at *Gold's Pines* (Route 128), a fifty-six-acre plot of white pine and hemlock trees that contains the **tallest tree in the state** (at least it was as of the end of March 2016). The little forest was started by **Theodore S. Gold** in 1870. It was acquired by the state in 1941 and became part of the *Housatonic State Forest*. Gold's original stand of trees is believed to be almost 200 years old. The tallest tree is a white pine that was 158 feet tall when last measured. Access to the stand is off Route 128; the tree can be found on the west side of the trail before the trail curves to the right and passes a group of trees with species signs.

On the "other" side of the bridge (but still in West Cornwall) is a rambling, high-ceilinged former Masonic hall inside of which you will find *Barbara Farnsworth, Bookseller* (407 Sharon Goshen Tpke [Rte. 128]; 860-672-6571; farnsworthbooks.com). This establishment, founded in 1978, is an almost-religious experience for bibliophiles and collectors of old prints and maps. Did we mention that writer **James Thurber** used to live in this building, as did poet **Mark van Doren** and his brother Carl? And that **Philip Roth** lived a few miles away until his death in the spring of 2018. That's a lot of literary talent.

Unfortunately, in the spring of 2017, Mrs. Farnsworth went on what she calls a medical sabbatical and closed the physical store. Every once in a while she is able to go down and open it up, but due to ongoing health issues and life circumstances, she has moved the majority of her business online. The website is nicely laid out and she is adding items all the time. We encourage you to take a look, there are literally tens of thousands of books, and she knows her stuff, so the descriptions are almost as fascinating as the books themselves. Follow Farnswoth Books on Facebook to find updates and times she is able to open the store.

Nearby, you'll find **The Wish House** (413 Sharon Goshen Tpke [Rte. 128]; 860-672-2969; wishhouse.com), a whimsical store with the patchwork bear out front. The items in this store are eclectic and artfully arranged. You'll find gifts, clothing, books, soaps, linens, and a little bit of everything here, including Josh Bach ties, Anokhi bathrobes, Cornwall-made syrup, and more. Open Tues through Sun, 11 a.m. to 5 p.m. This is also where the **Cornwall Farm Market** (860-672-2969) is held every Sat, mid-May through early Oct, 10 a.m. to 1 p.m., on the lawn.

If you're a fan of things that go bump in the night, here's a ghost story from the area for you. In the early 1740s, a man by the name of Thomas Griffis settled a few miles south of today's Cornwall Bridge village, in a place called Dark Entry Forest. The forest was located in the shadows of the mountains that surround the town. He was joined over the next few years by members of the Dudley family as well as other settlers and together they tried to subsist on the rocky land not particularly suitable for farming or livestock. Why they chose the spot they did is a mystery, but it seems an unfortunate choice. The settlement became known as **Dudleytown** and its citizens faced years of bad luck, illness, crop failures, and more. Whatever happened here centuries ago will likely never be known with any degree of certainty. The forest will hold her secrets.

Today, the forest where Dudleytown is located is privately owned and trespassers will be ticketed by police for even stepping on the land. To learn more about the Dudleytown curse, we recommend picking up a copy of *Cursed in New England* by Joseph A. Citro (Globe Pequot).

East of West Cornwall is **Mohawk Mountain State Park** (20 Mohawk Mountain Rd.; 860-491-3620). The big draw here is skiing, but if that's not your thing, avoid the crowds and take a scenic warm-weather 2.5-mile stroll to the top of the 1,683-foot-high **Mohawk Mountain** instead. The view from the top is absolutely breathtaking.

The Mohawk Trail runs through these woods and can actually be accessed on Dark Entry Road and can be hiked through to Cornwall Village (or vice versa). While the Connecticut Forest and Parks Association closes this part of the trail around Halloween (for obvious reasons), it is open the rest of the year. Perhaps this is the perfect hike on which to ponder the fate of Dudleytown.

cornwalltrivia

In 1948, Mohawk Ski Area in Cornwall became the first ski resort in the country to make artificial snow. The first (unsuccessful) attempt involved trucking in 700 tons of ice from Torrington.

Kent

Main Street (US 7) in the town of **Kent** is known as **Ethan Allen Way**, after the Connecticut hero who was born in the area. This street is lined for several blocks with restaurants, art galleries, antiques stores, craft shops, and the like. You'll also find interesting establishments on Maple and Railroad Streets. Businesses come and go fairly frequently, so if you want to know what's there currently, you'll just have to visit.

A mile and a half north of North Kent on US 7 is **Kent Falls State Park** (462 Kent Cornwall Rd. [Rte. 7]; 860-927-3238). The broad meadow and shaded picnic areas visible from the road are inviting enough, but you might be inclined to pass it by if you weren't specifically looking for a place to spread a picnic lunch. Don't. The best part of the park is a 250-foot waterfall that is easy to miss despite being one of the state's largest, especially when the foliage of high summer obscures it from view. If you like tramping through the woods, you can hike to the top of the falls, or if you prefer less demanding pleasures, you can simply sit out on the rocks in the middle of the falls and dangle your toes in the torrent. Even though the water may be a tad cool for toe-dangling come autumn, we highly recommend visiting the park after the leaves have

Tall Tales of Ethan Allen

Ethan Allen is a favorite Connecticut hero, hence many stories have been passed down about the man. Here are a few of our favorites:

Ethan Allen was a big guy (six feet, six inches tall) with a big thirst. According to one "tall" tale, on a hot August afternoon, Allen and his cousin Remember Baker, having overindulged, repaired to nearby shady woods to sleep it off. Baker was awakened by a strange noise, and he watched in horror as a rattlesnake bit his drink-befuddled cousin over and over. Before Baker could find a weapon to subdue the serpent, it moved away from Allen, gazed at Baker with a certain drunken stare, then wobbled its way into the bushes, where it collapsed in a stupor. Allen awoke refreshed from his nap, except for complaints about "these eternal, damnable, bloodsucking mosquitoes," which had disturbed his rest.

It stands to reason that Ethan Allen would marry a woman as formidable as himself. His wife, Fanny, was, by all accounts, his equal in temper and independence. The story is told that Allen's friends became concerned about his drinking and decided to frighten him into leading a more temperate life. They wrapped themselves in sheets and hid beneath the bridge that Allen passed on his way home from his favorite tavern. Making the requisite booing, moaning, and keening sounds, they jumped out at their friend, only to scare his horse into rearing. Despite his snozzled state, Allen managed to control his mount and greeted the "apparitions" by proclaiming, "If you are angels of light, I'm glad to meet you. And if you are devils, then come along home with me. I married your sister."

turned and the summer crowds have thinned. The park is open in the daily in the summer, 8 a.m. to 7 p.m. The rest of the year it closes at sunset.

About a mile north of Kent, you'll find a big maroon L-shaped barn set back a short distance from the west side of US 7. The ground on which it sits used to be the Kent town dump, but all that changed back in the 1970s. At that time, New Britain's Stanley Tool Company was looking for a site for a museum to house a collection of American tools and implements collected by noted artist and author **Eric Sloane**. Stanley wanted the state of Connecticut to run the place, but the state would accept ownership only if the museum's site was somehow historically significant. As it turned out, down at the foot of the hill behind the town dump in Kent were the ruins of an old blast furnace that produced pig iron during most of the nineteenth century. The presence of this jumble of stone made the dump suitably historical, so Stanley acquired the property and had Sloane design a building for his collection. Thus was born the Sloane-Stanley Museum, now known as the ***Eric Sloane Museum & Kent Iron Furnace*** (31 Kent-Cornwall Rd. [Rte. 7]; 860-927-3849).

This place is not so much a museum of artifacts as a gallery of art objects. The tools collected here, some of which date from the seventeenth century, probably do have some historical interest as a link with everyday life in America's past, but Sloane vehemently rejected the image of himself as what he called "a nurturer of nostalgia." The contents of this museum are oddly beautiful. Sloane personally arranged and lighted the displays, and the resulting jumble of wooden bowls and woven baskets, yokes and mallets and pitchforks, axes and scythes, and weathered sawhorses has an internal order that is both pleasing and restful. It's as if each arrangement were a small work of art in itself.

In addition to the fine tool collection, the museum also contains a re-creation of Sloane's studio with some of his works on display. And don't forget that historic blast furnace; it's the tumbled pile of rocks surrounded by the split-rail fence at the bottom of the hill behind the barn. Open May to June, Fri through Sun, 10 a.m. to 4 p.m.; June through Oct, Thurs through Sun, 10 a.m. to 4 p.m. Admission. Blue Star Museum.

Located just off US 7 about four miles south of Kent, ***Bull's Bridge*** is one of only a few remaining covered bridges in Connecticut and one of two that are still open to traffic (the other is in West Cornwall, also off US 7 a few miles north).

kenttrivia

Macedonia Brook State Park in Kent is the largest state park in Connecticut.

ethanallentrivia

Litchfield-born Ethan Allen is one of the most colorful personalities in American history. The guy was a crusty old coot. You probably learned in fifth-grade history that Allen ordered the British commander of Fort Ticonderoga to surrender by declaiming, "Surrender in the name of the great God Jehovah and the Continental Congress." What he really said was something like: "Come out of there, you goddamn old billy goat." Spin doctors, even then.

Bull's Bridge was built in 1842 and spans the Housatonic River between New York state and Connecticut on the river's eastern bank. George Washington didn't sleep here, but he did pass over the bridge, and he (or a member of his party) did manage to lose a horse in the Housatonic while so doing. If looking at the bridge gives you a sense of déjà vu, it's because it's probably been the source of more quaint New England covered-bridge photographs on postcards and calendar covers than any other bridge in this part of the world.

After you cross the bridge, about three miles up the road on the **Schaghticoke Indian Reservation**, you'll find an old cemetery with many timeworn headstones, including one commemorating the last resting place of a "Christian Indian Princess." This tombstone belongs to **Eunice Mauwee**, born in 1756, the granddaughter of Chief Gideon Mauwee, the first recorded Sachem of the present-day Schaghticokes. She died in 1860 at the age of 104. Amazing. As you explore other tombstones here, remember to show proper respect and not take rubbings without permission.

The Hills

Goshen

They say that at one time, travelers passing through the Bridgeport area during the spring were shocked to see elephants plowing nearby fields; they were rented to local farmers by circus impresario **P. T. Barnum**. These days if you see an elephant strolling through a field along Route 4 in **Goshen**, it won't be plowing it—the various circus animals on the property belong to **Commerford Zoo** (48 Torrington Rd.; 860-491-3421; commerfordzoo.com), which operates kids' fun fairs and petting zoos throughout New England. Commerford's animals have also been known to make an appearance at birthday parties and weddings, and have even been in a movie or commercial or two. You can't tour Commerford's, but at any given time, a fair number of the residents will be exercising and visible from the road.

Just before you get to the rotary in Goshen, you'll see several large, intriguing stone cairns, surrounded by stout stone fences. You've reached the home of the 116-acre *Action Wildlife Foundation* (337 Torrington Rd., Route 4 West; 860-482-4465; actionwildlifefoundation.com). This former dairy farm–turned–game park is home to many exotic creatures, zebras, Watusi cattle, water buffalo, a potbelly pig, llamas, bison, elk, Scottish cattle, boars, emu, and more. In fact, they have animals from six of the seven continents. There's a petting zoo with sheep and goats, maybe even a pig or a cow, depending on the day. There's a museum with recreated wildlife displays, an exhibit where you can touch all different kinds of fur and antlers. There is also an eighteen-acre drive-through safari where you can see different kinds of deer, emus, and other animals.

Hours can vary by season, so it's always good to check ahead, but generally they are open Sat and Sun, 10 a.m. to 4:30 p.m. during the spring months; Wed through Sun, 10:30 to 4:30 in the summer; Fri, 11 a.m. to 3 p.m. in the fall. If it rains, they close. Exhibits are handicap accessible. Admission.

Nodine's Smokehouse (39 North St.; 800-222-2059; nodinesmokehouse. com) is one of the best smokehouses in New England. It's also something of a Connecticut institution. Nodine's (it's pronounced no-DINES) carries many specialty items, ranging from smoked hams, turkeys, and chickens to the more exotic smoked pheasants, shrimp, and venison sausage. Nodine's more common meats can be enjoyed in made-to-order sandwiches. Open Mon through Sat, 9 a.m. to 5 p.m.; Sun, 10 a.m. to 4 p.m. If you see something you like but don't want to drag it along for the rest of your trip, never fear; they have a mail-order operation.

Torrington

No one driving past 192 Main St. in *Torrington* can possibly ignore the awe-inspiring symphony in Roman brick and rosy-red slate that occupies the property. At first, all you see is the big, round, three-story corner tower. Then the eye begins to jump from dormer to porch to porte cochere, taking in the Victorian carvings, the intricate sashes, the many small details that speak of another age, when decoration for its own sake was a common element of American home-building.

The magnificent, sixteen-room *Hotchkiss-Fyler House* is now the headquarters of the *Torrington Historical Society* (860-482-8260; torringtonhistoricalsociety.org). It still displays the original mahogany paneling, hand stenciling, and parquet floors that made it such an opulent example of Victorian excess when it was built by **Orsamus Roman Fyler** back in 1900. The original furnishings, on display here, are almost as extravagant as the house itself. Several of the rooms feature wonderful little collections of art objects, including gold Fabergé spoons, Sèvres porcelain, Victorian art glass, and Meissen porcelain figurines. The Hotchkiss-Fyler House is open mid-Apr through the end of Oct, Wed through Sat from noon to 4 p.m. An adjacent museum devoted to local history is open mid-April through Oct, Tues through Sat, 10 a.m. to 4 p.m. Admission.

One of the nicest places to take a leisurely fall hike is located in *Burr Pond State Park* (385 Burr Mountain Rd.; 860-482-1817). The circuit around the eighty-eight-acre pond in the park is a pleasant walk. There's history in the park, too: It was the site of Gail Borden's first American condensed-milk factory. In 1856, Borden, who was from Torrington, created a way to preserve milk by condensing it; his creation was called the "milk that won the Civil War." A bronze tablet marks the place where the factory once stood before being destroyed by fire. Some of the trails are perfect for little ones or those not up to a strenuous hike. The 438-acre park also offers swimming, fishing, swimming, boating, and picnicking.

torrington trivia

Torrington was once known by the rather odd moniker of "Mast Swamp."

Torrington is also the birthplace of notorious abolitionist **John Brown**. While he wasn't successful in his attempt to free the slaves at Harpers Ferry, and paid for his efforts with his life, Brown certainly left his mark on our state's and nation's history. The house where he was born on May 9, 1800, was destroyed by fire in 1918, but the site is marked with a stone wall and a small memorial. To find it, follow Route 4 west from Torrington center toward Goshen. Take a right onto University Drive. Follow for about 1 mile before turning left onto John Brown Road. The site is about a half mile down the road on the right.

Litchfield

The stark white Congregational church with the towering spire situated on the north side of the *Litchfield Green* is quite possibly the most photographed church in New England. While the world has certainly changed since the green was laid out in the 1770s, there's still an old-time, upscale feel here.

The heart of historic Litchfield consists of a block or two of North Street, a few blocks of South Street (Route 63), and a few blocks of West Street immediately off the green. There's plenty of on-street parking, so you can leave your car and take your time to enjoy the history and shopping to be found.

While you can't visit the following privately owned homes, you can stroll by and take a minute to appreciate them. Standing on the green, facing north, look for East Street, on which you'll find *Dr. Reuben Smith's 1781 Apothecary Shop* (9 East St.), the earliest commercial building in the state (this building used to exist next to Dr. Smith's North Street residence, but was moved to its present location in 1812 and is now occupied by a doctor's office).

Now turn east and walk toward South Street (Route 202), where you will find the renovated 1812 **Litchfield County Jail** (7 North St.) standing on the corner but looking much different than its past life. This is the oldest public building in town and served as a holding place for prisoners of the War of 1812, making it one of the oldest penal facilities in the state. It served as a jail until the early 1990s, then as a rehabilitation center until 2010. It stood vacant for a while and was offered to the town at no cost, but it was determined to be too big of a project for them to maintain. In the late summer of 2014, a private real estate developer purchased the building for $130,000 and began renovations, not really knowing what they were going to end up with but having a vision of a multi-use venue, with retail, office, and living spaces. The renovations were carefully overseen by the Litchfield Planning and Zoning Commission to ensure that the historic character of the building was maintained. Pictures of this renovation can be found at facebook.com/7northstreet, and they're pretty cool. By July 2017, things were looking good, but all the spaces had yet to be filled. Each tenant had to be carefully screened and the zoning process navigated. Today, you'll find **The Bakehouse of Litchfield** (7 North St.; 860-361-6423; thebakehousect.com), sharing space with other businesses in the renovated building. Reuse at its best! And since you're there, this bakery is a good place to stop and grab some delicious bread or other portable food to bring with you if you're going to make a stop at the Litchfield Distillery (see below). You'll want some cushion in your stomach if you're going to taste their samples!

Head down the road to the 1816 **First National Bank of Litchfield** (13 North St.). This building has housed a bank since it was built and is the oldest continuously operating business in Litchfield and the oldest nationally chartered bank in the state.

Next up is the 1760 home of **Benjamin Tallmadge** (47 North Street). Once an aide to George Washington, Tallmadge purchased the house after taking a liking to the area when the army had passed through. Tallmadge and his family lived there until his death in 1835. It was purchased and sold a few times before coming back into the family when Tallmadge's granddaughter, Julia Tallmadge Noyes, and her husband bought the house. They eventually passed it to their daughter, Emily Noyes Vanderpoel, who used it as a summer residence until her death in 1939. The house passed through a few owners during the twentieth century. In 2009, the house was up for sale again and languished on the market for a couple of years. Around 2011, there was hope that the Litchfield Historical Society could purchase it, but it proved too big a project for them. The house had been through foreclosure and had undoubtedly seen better days. But by the end of 2011, the house was scooped up by restorers extraordinaire Louise Arroyo and Thomas Callahan. These two men have been busy in Connecticut, purchasing and restoring historically significant houses, mainly in the northwest region of the state. In 2014, the 6,840-square-foot home that currently sits on just under one acre sold for close to a million dollars and is currently off the market. Another treasure saved.

A bit farther up North Street, across from each other, you have the *1760 Sheldon Tavern* (73 North St.), where George Washington really did sleep (he visited town five times), and *Dr. Reuben Smith's house* (of apothecary fame, remember the shop used to be here, next to his house before it was moved). This house is notable for having been built in 1770 by the famed builder of churches, **Giles Kilborn**, who lived in nearby Bantam and also built the West Church there.

If you'd like to learn more about the architecture and history of houses in this area (and there are a lot of eighteenth- and nineteenth-century homes here) visit historicbuildingsct.com/towns/Litchfield and browse to your heart's content. As we said earlier, though, these buildings are all privately owned and only some are occasionally open to the public, so please be respectful!

A building you *can* visit is back past the green on South Street. The *Litchfield History Museum* (7 South St.; 860-567-4501; litchfieldhistoricalsociety.org) is located in the Noyes Memorial Building and allows you to trace the history of Litchfield through a variety of exhibits. There's a really nice collection of historic items from the town and surrounding areas, including information on the 1792 Pierce Academy and its founder Sarah Pierce. The groundbreaking academy was the first in the country for girls. Pierce established her innovative program in the family home on North Street in 1792, and it ran successfully until 1833. Today, there is only a marker to indicate the site; the house currently at 133 North Street was built on the site of the former academy. The museum does a good job of displaying what a typical day for the girls there would have been like.

The museum is open mid-Apr through the end of Nov, Tues through Sat, 11 a.m. to 5 p.m.; Sun, 1 to 5 p.m. Admission is free. The lower level of the building is home to the *Helga J. Ingraham Memorial Library*, which is open to researchers year-round Tues through Fri, 10 a.m. to noon, and 1 to 4 p.m.

When you're done here, head to the *Tapping Reeve House & Litchfield Law School*, located a block south of the museum at 82 South St. Founded in 1773, this was America's first law school. Tour the school that trained political conspirator and former vice president **Aaron Burr**. Of course, it also schooled the likes of **John C. Calhoun** and some 130 other congressmen and senators, not to mention three Supreme Court justices, six cabinet members, and a dozen governors. Today, the Reeve House exhibits tell the story of students who attended the school. As part of the Litchfield Historical Society, the Tapping Reeve House & Litchfield Law School is also open mid-Apr through the end of Nov, Tues through Sat, 11 a.m. to 5 p.m.; Sun, 1 to 5 p.m. Admission is free.

Visitors can also explore the grounds of the house, known as **Tapping Reeve Meadow**, year-round, dusk to dawn. The grounds have been landscaped with plants and elements that would have been found in this area from the eighteenth through the twentieth centuries. You'll find a small orchard, a chestnut grove, a children's garden, and education pavilion all accented with stonewalls and period fencing. Programs and events are often held here throughout the year. Visit litchfieldhistoricalsociety.org/calendar-list for the latest offerings.

Now that you've done your homework and taxed your brain with all these names and dates, take a little adult time, get back in your car, and head to the *Litchfield Distillery* (569 Bantam Rd.; 860-361-6503; litchfielddistillery.com) where you can learn all about the process of distilling spirits and just how much goes into what they call the "Farm to Bottle to Farm process." It is incredibly illuminating to see the science behind creating these delicious concoctions and how the two brothers who own the distillery, David and Jack Baker, truly embody the "spirit of hard work." One of the brothers will take you on a tour through the process, which ends with a tasting of their bourbons and vodkas (and their maple syrup if you're lucky!).

The distillery is generally open daily from 11 a.m. to 6 p.m., with tours taking place on the hour. If you walk in between tours and they're not busy, they will take you right away. If you want to be sure you'll be accommodated at a specific time, call ahead or visit their website or Facebook page and make a reservation. You must be 21 or older to take part in the tasting, although those younger than that can accompany you. Tours are free (for now).

If you prefer wine to bourbon and vodka, visit the *Haight-Brown Vineyard* (29 Chestnut Hill Rd.; 860-567-4045; haightvineyards.com), owned by Litchfield native Amy Senew and her husband Jacques Muratori, who met while both working in software but yearning for something more. Muratori is originally from South Africa, where their winemaker, Charl van Schalkwyk, hails from. The vineyard was established in 1975 by Sherman Haight, who had the winery building constructed a year later, making Haight-Brown the first winery established in the state. Haight sold the winery to Senew in 2007 and she promised to uphold his traditions, which she has. Today, the winery owns or leases twenty acres on which they grow their grapes to produce Chardonnay, white, red, and Riesling wines, as well as deliciousness such as Morning Harvest, Apple Crannie, Strawberry Bliss, and Honey Nut Apple wines.

They offer special events, classes, and live music throughout the year. There are tastings that include chocolate and/or cheese, depending on your desire. They sell food on the premises and there is beautiful outdoor seating on their patio weather permitting. Outside food can be brought in for the picnic grove and lower patio. They are open year-round, Mon through Thurs, noon to 5 p.m.; Fri and Sun, noon to 6 p.m.; Sat, noon to 6:30 p.m.

Once you're done imbibing and you have your bottle safely tucked into the trunk of your car for later, head out to walk it all off at the ***White Memorial Foundation and Conservation Center*** (80 Whitehall Rd.; 860-567-0857; whitememorialcc.org). These 4,000 acres constitute one of Connecticut's largest nature centers and wildlife sanctuaries. This privately owned facility administered by the nonprofit **White Memorial Foundation** contains bird-feeding stations, numerous picnic areas, camps, several campgrounds, bird-watching platforms, forty miles of riding and hiking trails (including some on boardwalks through expansive wetlands and one for the blind with Braille signs), more than seventy acres of open water, and more than half of the Bantam Lake shoreline, a marina, and event facilities for rent. The property is open year-round for fishing, canoeing, cross-country skiing, and similar activities.

As one might hope of a conservation center, the White Memorial Foundation has continually taken steps to reduce its carbon imprint on the earth. They have installed solar panels on the activity center that now supply just under thirty percent of the museum's annual electricity requirements. They added a geothermal heat pump system in 2010, which reduced their heating and cooling costs by about thirty percent. A year later, they installed a wind turbine to supplement their energy needs. They welcome questions about how these green initiatives have worked for them and if they would work for you as well.

The Conservation Center's Nature Museum features fluorescent rocks, a working honeybee hive, and a variety of exhibits, including some stunning nature dioramas, as well as live animals. They also offer scavenger hunts (both indoors and outdoors) to keep little ones busy. There is a gift shop, as well, should you wish to peruse. The center and shop are open year-round, Mon through Sat, 9 a.m. to 5 p.m.; Sun, noon to 5 p.m. Admission for non-members, free for members. Admission for children younger than twelve (accompanied by an adult) is free for seventeen weeks of the year. This is made possible through member donations and is continually growing.

Not exhausted yet? Head south on Route 63 to ***White Flower Farm*** (167 Litchfield Road, Morris; 860-567-8789; whiteflowerfarm.com), a family-owned and -operated mail-order nursery that has been in business since 1950. One of the best things about this company is that it wasn't started by a master gardener or farmer. It was started by two writers from New York City, who purchased land in Litchfield with a barn on it that they converted to their house in 1930. As they say, one thing led to another, and the pair found themselves planting seeds, creating gardens, growing vegetables and wanting to share them with others. The converted barn still stands on the north side of Esther's Road along with the Moon Garden the couple created with all white flowers and from which the company gets its name.

The folks at White Flower Farm love their property so much that they've created a walking tour (self-guided) that begins with the original house and takes you through seven display gardens and ends at their retail store. You'll see amazing blooms and plantings and will surely get ideas for your own home. They also offer a variety of talks and events throughout the year, a full list of which is on their website.

A more recent addition to the farm is the herd of Angus cattle. You can go to the farm and pick your own steer from the herd if you wish, or if you'd rather, you can just put in an order for the cuts you wish. The cows are normally committed to well in advance, so you may have a bit of a wait. The process and prices are outlined on their website with the promise that all the animals are humanely and naturally raised without chemicals or cruelty.

White Flower Farm is open daily 9 a.m. to 5 p.m. during the growing season, which is generally mid-Mar through Nov. It's always best to call ahead and be sure they are open.

North of White Flower Farm, back toward the green but to the east on Route 118 (East Street), just past the East Cemetery is the **Lourdes in Litchfield Shrine** (83 Montfort Rd.; 860-567-1041; shrinect.org). For thirty-two years, Montfort Missionaries have operated this thirty-five-acre shrine, which features a replica of the famous grotto at Lourdes, France. An outdoor Stations of the Cross path winds its way to a spectacular crucifixion scene at the top of the hill. The grounds are open year-round sunrise to sunset daily, and include a picnic area and gift shop. In addition, outdoor services are conducted, weather permitting, throughout the pilgrimage season (May 1 to mid-Oct), Tues through Sun, 11:30 a.m. If the weather does not cooperate, Mass is held in the chapel. There is a series of special blessings throughout the year, including an Anointing of the Sick, a Blessing of Animals, a Living Rosary, a Living Nativity, and more. They also offer a summer book reading and lecture series. Check their website for the latest information.

Wisdom House Retreat & Conference Center (229 E. Litchfield Rd.; 860-567-3163; wisdomhouse.org), formerly a convent for the Sisters of Wisdom, is now the site of Connecticut's only outdoor labyrinth. Don't arrive thinking you'll find a high, boxwood maze like those in England or in Colonial

Williamsburg. The low circular path is a symbol older than time and one that transcends religions. Walking the spiral path helps you meditate and heighten your awareness. You'll find a helpful pamphlet at Wisdom House suggesting different meditative approaches to walking the labyrinth. Whichever approach you take, it's a peaceful way to get in touch with your inner self, find some peace in the silence, and shed the cares of twenty-first-century life. Many visitors use the labyrinth for silent meditation, so it probably isn't a place to visit if you are accompanied by rowdy children or a particularly talkative friend. The center offers all sorts of services on the seventy-acre site, including an outdoor swimming pool, overnight accommodations for 140, conferences, and more. Visit their website for the most up-to-date information.

South of Wisdom House Retreat & Conference Center is **Topsmead State Forest** (Buell Road; 860-567-5694), an estate-turned-park that looks as if it belongs in the British midlands. When Waterbury heiress **Edith Morton Chase** came home from a European tour enchanted with English manor houses, she was determined to build herself an authentic Cotswold cottage, complete with leaded-glass casement windows, hand-hewn beams, and buttery stucco exteriors. She found the right location in Litchfield. The Cotswold cottage of her dreams was designed by architect **Richard Dana**, who shared Miss Edith's love for English cottage architecture.

Topsmead, however, was more than a building. It was also a vast garden and a working farm. Miss Edith was as fond of English country gardens as of English architecture, and she surrounded her home with formal manicured gardens and cutting gardens full of the flowers most beloved by English gardeners: roses, sweet William, and phlox. Even in her late seventies, she reputedly walked a daily mile around these gardens, inspecting, issuing orders, and sipping from an ever-present glass of skim milk.

When Miss Edith died in 1972, she left her 511-acre estate to the State of Connecticut so that everyone could enjoy a touch of England in Litchfield. Topsmead State Forest is open all year for picnicking, sledding, cross-country skiing, and hiking; there's even a letterbox or two. You can tour the house on the second and fourth weekends of each month from June to Oct, noon to 5 p.m. (the last weekend of Oct, it closes at 4 p.m.).

Fifty years after his father sold off the last cow from their family's dairy operation, John Morosani of **Laurel Ridge Grass Fed Beef**, had reinstated the cattle on his family's 700-acre farm and developed a thriving business. However, according to Morosani and his business partner, Jim Abbott, this wasn't their original intent. They decided to bring cattle back to the land to help maintain the overgrown fields. They thought they'd raise a few cows, use the meat themselves, and call it a day. But the more they learned about the business, and the more local residents heard about them, well, growth was natural. By starting off slow with seven calves in the spring of 2003, and applying for various government grants to help, Morosani and Abbott built Laurel Ridge (66 Wigwam Rd.; 860-567-8122; lrgfb.com) into the successful business it is today.

Laurel Ridge's cattle are entirely pasture fed with their diets not supplemented by "anything but a salt lick." The farm also offers pastured pork, humanely raised on high-quality pig feed and foraged food. Laurel Ridge meat is in such demand now that Morosani and Abbott have a hard time keeping up. They sell their products at various farm markets, farm stands, and stores throughout the area; check their website for details.

Now, you might think that Laurel Ridge would be most famous for its beef, but it's not. It's really the flowers. Daffodils, in fact—thousands of them. It all started back in 1941 with Remy and Virginia Morosani when they first moved to Litchfield and purchased seventeen acres of land. The couple was purveying their property and decided that one pasture was just too rocky to be of much use as a crop field, so they planted 10,000 daffodil bulbs. Do you know what daffodil bulbs do every year? They multiply. Like rabbits. The Morosanis were diligent in digging up their multiplied flower bulbs and replanting them every fall for more than twenty years. By then, the daffodils had become something of a local legend and people came from miles away to see their beauty. The Morosanis started the **Laurel Ridge Foundation** to be managed and supported by their descendants to ensure the daffodils would be cared for. Lucky for John, hay season for his cows is winding down when the major work for the daffodils begins. To find the daffodils, head south on Wigwam Road for about a half mile. There are walking trails and myriad photo ops when the flowers are in bloom (April and May), just please be respectful of the No Parking signs and do not block private drives. For more information on when to visit, please go to litchfielddaffodils.com.

On Route 209, in southwest Litchfield, you'll find the ***Bantam Cinema*** (115 Bantam Lake Rd.; 860-567-1916 or 860-567-0006 for show times; bantamcinema.com), just south of Route 202. The Bantam Cinema is an old-fashioned movie theater that screens those offbeat, independent, or imported films that never seem to get much play at suburban theaters. Even though the screening rooms and sound systems are modern, it's a wonderfully intimate and kind of old-fashioned way to see a film. The cinema is the "oldest continuously operated movie house" in the state. It opened in 1927 and showed silent movies. It then went through a variety of owners until Lisa Hedley purchased it in 1990 and started the "Meet the Film Maker" series. She would invite writers, actors, producers, and directors to come speak about their work.

The cinema saw some big names, likely due to its proximity to New York and the fact that more than a few Hollywood names live or lived in the area. In any event, the likes of Arthur Miller, Maureen Stapleton, Liza Minelli, and Mia Farrow all appeared. New owners took over in 2007, but the lecture series continued, bringing Rebecca Miller, Joan Rivers, and Daniel Day-Lewis, who came to speak about his part in *Lincoln*. Check the cinema's website for upcoming events. In the meantime, taken in a film and enjoy the atmosphere. You can even get organic popcorn with real butter.

And since you are in the area, it would be a mistake to bypass the **Bantam Bread Company** (853 Bantam Rd.; 860-567-2737; bantambread.com). This is the type of hearth-baked bread that people line up for in New York and Los Angeles. Holiday Bread is a popular (and vegan) option made with organic white and whole rye flours and seasoned with "cranberries, raisins, pecans, sourdough, rye chops, caraway seeds, and sea salt." Other offerings include a semolina batard, a sunflower and flax seed loaf, a Calamata olive sourdough, and more. If you're looking for something a bit sweeter, there is a whole array of cakes, tarts, cookies, and biscuits. Try a few Dirt Bombs, nutmeg-scented muffins dipped in butter and rolled in cinnamon sugar. Heaven.

The owners are big proponents of supporting local artisans as well and offer an ever-changing variety of local goods. Some of these include delicious-smelling **Goatboy Soaps** (New Milford), **Winding Drive Jellies and Jams** (Woodbury), greeting cards by local artists, seasonal fruits and vegetables from local farms, oils and vinegars from local importers, regional cheeses and butters, the list goes on and on. The bread is fresh and delicious, and doesn't stay on the shelves for long. Open Wed through Sat, 8:30 a.m. to 5:30 p.m.; Sun, 8:30 a.m. to 4 p.m. Closed Mon and Tues.

If you're looking for something sweeter, don't pass **Love Heart's Bakery and Cafe** (583B Bantam Rd.; 860-361-6526; loveheartsbakery.homestead. com), where you'll find a cozy little place that serves up deliciousness. Named after owner Allison Barker-Croce's daughter, the bakery half offers a wonderful assortment of cookies, brownies, baklava, cakes (chocolate, fruit, carrot, cheese), pies, and tarts. On the café side you can choose from soups, salads, and/or sandwiches and wraps on fresh-made breads. You never know what is going to be on the menu, so stop in often.

Bethlehem

For most of the year, **Bethlehem** (on Route 61 north of Woodbury) is just another quiet, pretty New England country town. During the Christmas holiday season, however, all that changes, and for a few brief weeks, Bethlehem bustles with activity.

ANNUAL EVENTS IN THE LITCHFIELD HILLS

APRIL

Riverton Fishing Derby
Farmington River between Hogback
Dam and Pipeline Pool
(860) 379-0811
rivertonct.com

MAY

**Annual Sports Car Championships &
Royals Car Show**
Lime Rock Park
467 Lime Rock Rd., Lakeville
(800) 435-5000
limerock.com

JULY

Litchfield Jazz Festival
116 Old Middle St., Goshen
(860) 361-6285
litchfieldjazz.com

AUGUST

Bridgewater Country Fair
100 Main St. South, Bridgewater
(860) 354-1509
bridgewaterfair.com

**Sharon on the Green Arts and Crafts
Fair**
63 Main St., Sharon
(860) 364-1400

Terryville Lions Country Fair
171 Townhill Rd., Terryville
(860) 582-0709
terryvillefair.org

SEPTEMBER

Bethlehem Fair
384 Main St. North, Bethlehem
(203) 266-5350
bethlehemfair.com

Colebrook Fair
562 Colebrook Rd., Colebrook
colebrookfair.weebly.com

Goshen Fair
116 Old Middle St., Goshen
(860) 491-3655
goshenfair.org

OCTOBER

Harvest Bounty Brew Fest
421 Bantam Rd., Litchfield
(800) 801-FEST
beerfests.com/events/
harvest-bounty-brew-fest/

Harwinton Fair
150 Locust Rd., Harwinton
(860) 307-1925
harwintonfair.com

Riverton Fair
16 Main St., Riverton
(860) 379-0060
rivertonfair.org

DECEMBER

Christmas in Riverton
rivertonct.com

The reason, of course, is the name. The local post office doubles its staff each December to accommodate the thousands of folks who want a Bethlehem postmark on their Christmas cards. If you're going to be passing through during early December, bring yours along and they'll be glad to add them to the bin. The ***Bethlehem Christmas Town Festival*** in mid-December also draws a lot of people to listen to the music, ride hay wagons, and look at holiday arts and crafts and a small festival of lights—a far cry, you will agree, from the days when the Puritans who wrote the colony's stringent blue laws prescribed a 5-shilling fine for "Christmas Keeping." For details call the town clerk's office during the morning at (203) 266-5557.

South of Bethlehem, about one and a half miles down Flanders Road (off Route 61), is the **Abbey of Regina Laudis** (273 Flanders Rd.; 203-266-7727; abbeyofreginalaudis.org), which operates the Monastic Art Shop, offering items handcrafted on the premises by Benedictine nuns. Among crafts represented are printing, potting, and blacksmithing. You can also buy beauty products, honey, herbs, and postcards showing the abbey grounds. The abbey's holiday decorations include a nativity scene composed of eighteenth-century Neapolitan figures. Open by appointment. Call ahead or visit their website for hours and information on special events.

Woodbury

Situated in the south-central part of Litchfield County on US 6, **Woodbury** was one of the first towns established in inland Connecticut. During the early eighteenth century, it was home to **Moll Cramer**, the best known of Connecticut's witches. Known as the "Witch of Woodbury," Cramer resided in a hut she built on **Good Hill** and supported herself by begging. Good Hill got its name from the fact that while Moll lived there, storms and high winds never seemed to cross Woodbury. After Cramer disappeared from Good Hill without a trace, Woodbury was hit by a series of destructive storms. Even today, old-timers speak of needing a "Moll Cramer storm" after a summer dry spell. If you enter Woodbury from Roxbury on Route 317 (Good Hill Road), you'll pass over the crest of the hill near the township line.

Today, US 6 runs through the center of Woodbury past rows of eighteenth- and nineteenth-century houses, many of which have been converted into antiques and gift shops. In fact, in this neck of the woods, Woodbury's Main Street is nicknamed "**Antique Avenue**." Some travel guides create the impression that unless you roll up in a chauffeured Rolls, you won't get very good treatment at many of the antiques shops in Woodbury. Not so! Even if you show up in faded jeans and scuffed-up sneakers, you can look forward to being treated with great kindness and helpfulness.

It's a pleasure just to walk through **Mill House Antiques & Gardens** (1068 Main St. North [US 6]; 203-263-3446; millhouseantiquesandgardens.com), a restored mill house with imaginative displays of top-quality English and French furniture. Mill House also offers extraordinary gardens full of antique urns and statues. They promise you'll really feel as if you're strolling through Europe. Open Mon through Sat, 10 a.m. to 5 p.m.; Sun, noon to 5 p.m.

For a taste of the Woodbury that antiquers rarely see, visit the **Canfield Corner Pharmacy** (2 N. Main St.; 203-263-2595). It has an old-fashioned soda fountain and is crammed from floor to rafters with every nostrum and homemaker's convenience on the market. Travel back in time when you step through the doors and "walk on wooden floors older than you!" How can you resist? Open Mon through Fri, 9 a.m. to 6 p.m.; Sat, 9 a.m. to 3 p.m.

Founded in 2008 by husband and wife team of Fran Adams and Ron Pinto **Winding Drive Gourmet Specialties** (744 Main St. South; 203-263-6961; windingdrive.com) serves up the most delicious and unique jams, jellies, and marmalades. Driven by what is in season and in the kitchen, Fran combines flavors in all the right ways. What makes it all the more amazing is that she is a self-taught cook, learning through trial and error. She only started making the jams and jellies so her husband could have something to sell at local farmers markets after he lost his job earlier in 2008. When they saw how well the creations sold, they decided to take it full-time and open their own place. We're so glad they did. The couple uses locally grown food, doesn't overload the jams and jellies with sugar, and they never use preservatives. You can find Winding Drive Gourmet Specialties at select retailers and farmers markets throughout the state. Check their website for a list.

Although they are not antiques, the pewter plates, mugs, lamps, and other accessories at the **Woodbury Pewter Factory Store** (860 Main St. South; 800-648-2014; woodburypewter.com) look as authentic as any antique you would buy in Woodbury. Woodbury Pewter has been around since 1952, when it was a tiny shop tucked into a blacksmith's shop. Today, it's a modern retail operation that features not only its own products but also the pewter work and jewelry of pewterers from across America. Open Mon through Sat 9 a.m. to 5 p.m.; Sun 11 a.m. to 5 p.m. Woodbury Pewter also holds several very good sales throughout the year.

A glebe is the parcel of land granted to a clergyman during his tenure of office. The gambrel-roofed **1740 Glebe House** (49 Hollow Rd.; 203-263-2855; theglebehouse.org), off US 6 in the center of town, has always had ecclesiastical connections. Mere weeks after the start of the American Revolution, a group of clergy secretly assembled in the house to elect the first American bishop of the Episcopal Church, the **Reverend Dr. Samuel Seabury**. His election broke the American connection with the Church of England and laid the foundation for the separation of church and state in America. Today, the old farmhouse is used as a museum and kept much as it was. The original paneling remains, and the rooms are stuffed with period furnishings collected locally. Open May through Oct, Wed through Sun, 1 to 4 p.m. (other times by appointment). Admission.

Roxbury

The town of **Roxbury** was home to **Alexander Calder**, twentieth-century sculptor, from 1933 until his death in 1976. Calder has many ties to our state. He is the creator of the city's *Stegosaurus* (see page 16). He was also a favorite of Wadsworth Atheneum director **Chick Austin**, who purchased and exhibited his work. He spent two weeks in 1925 sketching scenes from Bridgeport's Ringling Bros. and Barnum & Bailey Circus, which greatly influenced his life's work.

Calder moved to Roxbury with his wife Louisa James (grandniece of Henry James) when they purchased an old farmhouse in town, painted it flat black, and converted an old ice house into a studio. They had two daughters, Sandy and Mary, The Calders spent the next years summering in Roxbury and renting studio space in New York in the winter months. Calder met with great success, becoming one of the world's most acclaimed artists. Calder died in New York on November 11, 1976, at the age of seventy-eight.

In a *New York Times* article from the day after he died, journalist John Russell writes, "The last weeks of Alexander Calder's life were spent in New York City, at the home of his daughter Mary Howar, in an atmosphere of universal jubilation. No one who was there will ever forget the party which was given for him last month at the Whitney Museum by Howard and Jean Lipman. His show had just opened to enormous acclaim; people had come from far and wide; Calder danced; Mrs. Calder called for her favorite samba; Georgia O'Keeffe and Norman Mailer and Louise Nevelson and John Cage and Merce Cunningham were on hand to greet one of the people who has best deserved the name of 'American.' He loved it, and we loved him, and we shall go on doing it for ever and ever."

Calder's home can still be seen at 306 Painter Hill Road, but it is privately owned so please be respectful.

Washington

Lake Waramaug State Park (30 Lake Waramaug Rd.; 860-868-2592) offers seasonal camping, fishing, swimming, car-top boating, and picnicking. With its surrounding forests and hills, the lake is often likened to Switzerland's Lake Lucerne, and the inns that ring its waters reflect the same alpine charm. The lake is named for **Chief Waramaug**, whose Wyantenock tribe hunted and wintered in the area. One of the best ways to see the area, especially during leaf-peeping season, is to take the almost-one-mile drive around the lake. The burning autumn colors of the surrounding hardwoods, reflected by the cool, crystal-clear lake, make this a picture-postcard setting.

The Legend of Chief Waramaug and His Great Lodge

About the time settlers first arrived in northwestern Connecticut, the Native Americans who lived along the banks of the Housatonic River were led by a great leader, **Chief Waramaug**. Waramaug lived in a lodge high above the west bank of the Housatonic, not far from the beautiful alpine lake that bears his name. The lodge was so majestic that it was called Waramaug's Palace and, in its time, was without a doubt the most elegant dwelling in Connecticut. According to legend, Waramaug's longhouse was twenty feet wide by one hundred feet long. Native American artists from all over New England worked ceaselessly for months to create Waramaug's Palace. Using bark gathered from all over New England, they intricately painted the bark with sumptuous colors distilled from herbs and flowers. Although much of the decoration came from Waramaug's own people and from the Iroquois from nearby New York, the Hurons, the Delaware, and even the fearsome Mohawks all sent their greatest artisans to decorate Waramaug's great lodge.

The interior was as magnificent as the outside. Waramaug's council chamber was decorated with portraits of the great chief, his family, and the elders and wise men of the tribe. Other rooms were alive with pictures of the animals who shared the forests with Waramaug and his people. According to legend, Chief Waramaug died peacefully in his great lodge and was buried nearby. For years after his death, passing warriors would add a stone to his gravesite as a gesture of respect for the great leader.

The crossroads village of **New Preston** at the southeast tip of Lake Waramaug contains several shops that are well worth a stop, especially if you like antiques. **Dawn Hill Antiques** (11 Main St.; 860-868-0066; dawnhillantiques. com) specializes in eighteenth- and nineteenth-century Swedish furnishings. Open Wed through Mon, 11 a.m. to 5 p.m. **J. Seitz & Co.** (9 E. Shore Rd.; 860-868-0119; jseitz.com) handles both Southwestern antiques and reproductions, as well as other home furnishings and decor, apparel and accessories for both men and women, jewelry, and gifts. If you're lucky, you'll find yourself in town during the semiannual tent sale. Open Mon and Wed through Sat, 10 a.m. to 5:30 p.m.; Sun, 11 a.m. to 5 p.m. **Privet House** (13 E. Shore Rd.; 860-868-1800; privethouse.com) offers jewelry, table- and kitchenware, soaps, cream, candles, and more. Their website says they are an "An Emporium of Home Goods, Antiques, and Curiosities." Their items certain are original. Open Wed through Mon, 11 a.m. to 5:30 p.m. Closed Tues.

Southeast of New Preston off Route 199 is the ***Institute for American Indian Studies*** (38 Curtis Rd.; 860-868-0518; iaismuseum.org). Splendid Indian craft exhibits and authentic re-creations of Indian dwellings are among the features of this museum. The institute attempts, fairly successfully, to cover 10,000 years of Native American life; displays include a seventeenth-century Algonquian village and garden, a furnished longhouse, a simulated archaeological site, a prehistoric rock shelter, and a variety of nature trails. There's also a museum shop. The institute holds several special events throughout the year. The museum is open Wed through Sat 10 a.m. to 5 p.m.; Sun and noon to 5 p.m. Be sure to keep a sharp eye out for signs directing you to the museum; they are easy to miss.

Warren

The Hopkins Inn (22 Hopkins Rd.; 860-868-7295; thehopkinsinn.com) in ***Warren***, overlooking the northern shore of Lake Waramaug, has welcomed travelers since 1847, and they are good at what they do. The food here is so stellar that people tend to recommend the inn solely for its cuisine and forget that it is a warm and comfortable hostelry in its own right, with twelve guest rooms and two private apartments at reasonable rates. The outdoor patio, open for dining spring through fall, provides a spectacular view of the lake. The cuisine is contemporary Austrian, complete with rich desserts. The inn is open year-round; the restaurant is open from late Mar through Jan 1. When the restaurant is closed, the inn operates as a bed-and-breakfast.

There's no connection between the inn and the ***Hopkins Vineyard*** (25 Hopkins Rd.; 860-868-7954; hopkinsvineyard.com). But the dairy farm–turned–winery and the inn do share a name and spectacular views of Lake Waramaug and the surrounding countryside. The Hopkins family has farmed the land around the lake since the late 1700s but didn't plant its first grapevine until 1979. The vineyard produces a variety of wines, including a pretty good sparkling wine made in the traditional Champagne method. Try their off-dry cider as an ingredient for autumn recipes or as a celebratory drink before Thanksgiving. You'll find tastings, sales, and a gift shop in the winery's bright red barn. The winery also hosts special events throughout the year. Hours can vary, so it's best to check the website or call before planning your trip.

Places to Stay in the Litchfield Hills

Places to Eat in the Litchfield Hills

NORFOLK

Manor House
69 Maple Ave.
(860) 542-5690
manorhouse-norfolk.com
Expensive
Beautiful Victorian B&B in the heart of Norfolk

WASHINGTON

Grace Mayflower Inn & Spa
118 Woodbury Rd.
(Route 47)
(860) 868-9466
gracehotels.com/mayflower
Expensive
Located less than two hours from New York in the middle of beautiful Washington, the Mayflower offers five-star accommodations

WOODBURY

Curtis House
506 Main St.
(203) 263-2101
curtishouseinn.com
Inexpensive to moderate
Connecticut's oldest inn, in operation since 1754 in one way or another. Be sure to ask the owners about the secret entrance, rumored to have been used by the Freemasons once upon a time.

BARKHAMSTEAD

Log House Restaurant
110 New Hartford Rd.
(860) 379-8937
theloghouserestaurant.com
Moderate
Family-owned and -operated since 1973

NEW PRESTON

Nine Main Bakery & Deli
9 Main St.
(860) 868-1879
Moderate
Offers bakery items, specialty sandwiches, and salads

NORFOLK

Wood Creek Bar & Grill
14 Greenwoods Rd. W
(860) 542-1200
woodcreekbarandgrill.com
Moderate

RIVERTON

Sweet Pea's
6 Riverton Rd.
(860) 379-7020
sweetpeasrestaurant.com
Moderate to expensive
Located in an antiques-filled, Victorian house, offers New American cuisine featuring in-season ingredients, children's menu, complimentary wine tasting, and outdoor dining.

WOODBURY

Curtis House
506 Main St.
(203) 263-2101
curtishouseinn.com
Moderate to expensive
This beautiful country inn serves typical Yankee fare, including chowders, potpies, steak, seafood, and wonderful desserts. Traditional pub fare is also served.

Gateway to New England

For most of America, Connecticut's southwestern shore is truly the Gateway to New England, the place where mid-Atlantic names, customs, and speech patterns begin to drop away and we Yankees start to quietly assert our personality. Most visitors to New England form their first impressions of our region from what they see in the busy towns and cities of Fairfield and New Haven Counties.

Geographically, the Gateway country is really just one long, lightly wooded coastal plain, with elevations ranging from sea level along the shore to eight hundred feet inland. The coastline of this low-lying plain is broken by many small bays and inlets and by the mouths of five rivers: the Mianus, Saugatuck, Mill, Housatonic, and Quinnipiac. A few miles inland, numerous lakes and ponds dot the countryside. The neighboring Long Island Sound helps temper the climate, making for pleasant summers and relatively mild winters, with plenty of rain and moderate snowfall.

The Gold Coast

Greenwich

The southernmost of Fairfield County's towns, *Greenwich* is only twenty-eight miles from Times Square, and many of its residents commute daily to jobs in the banks, brokerage houses, and corporate headquarters of Manhattan. As do thousands of others in the southwestern towns. The wealth they bring back to the state combined with that generated by the dozens of corporations that have headquarters here has helped earn this area the nickname of the Gold Coast. As you move north and east, the tony quality of the Gold Coast gives way to the working-class atmosphere of cities such as Bridgeport and Norwalk. This transition is complete by the time you cross the line into New Haven County, the bridge between the commuter towns of the southwest and the outlying communities of metro Hartford. New Haven is a mixture of town and gown, famed as the site of Yale University, but also revered by the cognoscenti as the home of Louis' Lunch, birthplace of the American hamburger. Across the Quinnipiac River from New Haven, population density begins to fall away quickly as one moves east, and the eastern townships of New Haven County are really more typical of the shore than of the populous southwestern part of the state.

greenwichtrivia

In 1640, European settlers gave Native Americans twenty-five coats in exchange for the land now occupied by the prosperous town of Greenwich.

As its mission statement proclaims, Greenwich's *Bruce Museum* (1 Museum Dr.; 203-869-0376; brucemuseum.org) "bridges the arts and sciences for people of all ages and cultures to foster learning and to preserve the past for the future."

Sounds uplifting, to be sure. Fortunately, it's also fun. For big people, the collection includes works by some of Connecticut's famed impressionists,

AUTHOR'S FAVORITES

Stamford Cone

Center Church on the Green

Discovery Museum and Planetarium

Tidal Marsh Trail

United House Wrecking Inc.

including **Childe Hassam**, plus a wealth of art honoring diverse cultures. For the youngsters, there are scads of well-thought-out interactive exhibits. There are also temporary exhibits throughout the year. Open 10 a.m. to 5 p.m. Tues through Sun. Admission; free on Tues. Blue Star Museum.

Little Bethel A.M.E. Church (44 Lake Ave.; 203-661-3099) and *First Baptist Church* (10 Northfield St.; 203-869-7988; firstbaptistgreenwich.com) are the first and second African-American churches, respectively, to be established in Greenwich. Before the nineteenth century, the African-American community really had no defined nucleus; they were not allowed such freedom. But as slaves began to gain their freedom, this started to change. Neighborhoods began to appear, and many turned to religion for comfort and community. Little Bethel A.M.E. Church was established in 1883, while First Baptist came along in 1909, although the first official prayer meeting of the congregation occurred in 1897. Both churches are now listed on both the **Connecticut Freedom Trail** and the **National Register of Historic Places**.

When the *Merritt Parkway* was opened in 1938, it was praised for its beauty and efficiency. Today, it is acclaimed as a scenic alternative to the newer, grittier, and truck-laden I-95. The Merritt, which is on the National Register of Historic Places, runs thirty-seven miles, from Greenwich on the state line to Milford's border at the Housatonic River. At that point it becomes the Wilbur Cross Parkway, and the scenery and architecture become less distinguished.

Credit for the Merritt's unique charms goes especially to its landscape architect, **Weld Thayer Chase**, and to **George Dunkelberger**, designer of the sixty-eight distinctive bridges. Watch closely and you will see the Connecticut state seal, an owl, a blue-and-white Yale textbook, and a pair of Nike's wings on the many Art Deco spans that cross the parkway. The grassy median that separates the Merritt's north- and southbound lanes is also a delight, with its varied landscape of trees and shrubs. Two bonuses: The Merritt is toll-free, and trucks are not allowed. One drawback: The Merritt is a two-lane highway, so if there are traffic issues, there's not a lot of room to maneuver; be prepared to wait.

Stamford

As you leave Greenwich and enter *Stamford*, watch for the *Stamford Cone* on the corner of N. State Street and Washington Boulevard in its own little park-like area. Stop for a visit and you'll feel like you're standing inside a giant kaleidoscope. This forty-five-foot-tall structure is made up of 204 panels of glorious stained glass. There's something magical about standing inside and watching the play of light and color. The cone is open to the public from 9 a.m. to 4 p.m. After dark, the cone is lit inside until dawn.

Be sure to stop in at ***United House Wrecking Inc.*** (535 Hope St.; 203-348-5371; unitedhousewrecking.com). Just look for a rambling collection of buildings surrounded by a chain-link fence and guarded by a bunch of stone yard animals and lots of other junk . . . er, treasures.

Inside are more than two and a half acres of every type of antique something or other you can (or can't) imagine. The main display area contains antique furniture, some salvaged from Gold Coast mansions, some from manor houses in England and France; others are quality reproductions. While they are no longer in the demolition business, the owners travel the world to bring back a wide variety of unusual architectural items. There's so much that they organize it in sections: tables here, cabinets there, chairs over yonder; there are doors, fireplace mantels, patio furniture, weathervanes, fountains, gates. If you need it, you're likely to find it throughout their 43,000 square feet of retail space. The establishment's discovery by both Oprah Winfrey and Martha Stewart has caused the size of weekend crowds to balloon. If you really want to browse, go during off-peak hours. Open 10:30 a.m. to 6:30 p.m., Mon through Sat; 10:30 a.m. to 5 p.m., Sun.

Jackie Robinson Park (Richmond Hill Ave and W. Main St,), on the city's west side, is dedicated to the baseball Hall of Famer who broke the color barrier on April 15, 1947, when he became the first African American to play major league baseball. Within the park is a bronze statue of the man who called Stamford his home for nearly twenty years. The statue declares Courage, Confidence, and Perseverance—words to live by.

The ***Stamford Museum and Nature Center*** (39 Scofieldtown Rd.; 203-322-1646; stamfordmuseum.org) is something of a hybrid, with plenty to appeal to a variety of tastes. For many visitors, the animals on the small working farm are the main attraction. Wheelchair-accessible paths wind gently around pastures and barns with cows, oxen, sheep, goats, pigs, llamas, alpacas, horses, donkeys, and barnyard fowl. One of the neatest exhibits includes a microscope/television system for viewing the mysteries of pond life. The nature center's 118-acre woodland site also includes galleries for interactive exhibits, a planetarium, picnic tables on a meadow overlooking the pond, a state-of-the-art observatory with research telescope, two stores, and a vast hardwood forest with miles of hiking trails.

Norwalk

During the 1930s, unemployed artists were commissioned under the **Works Progress Administration** (WPA) to paint murals, many portraying the art of everyday life in America, in public buildings. Most of the structures that once housed these underappreciated masterpieces have fallen victim to the wrecking ball, but some of Connecticut's Depression-era buildings, especially post offices, still display these modern wonders. *Norwalk*, however, has retained and restored one of the largest collections of Depression-era murals in the US. Maintained by the *Norwalk Transit District* (275 Wilson Ave.; 203-852-0000; norwalktransit.com), these murals were originally painted on the walls of the old high school. When that building was torn down, the art was carefully preserved, restored, and rehung in municipal buildings throughout the city. You'll find them at the city hall, community college, Maritime Aquarium at Norwalk, the public library, and of course, the transit district.

If you're looking for some on-the-water time, the *Small Boat Shop* (144 Water St.; 203-854-5223; thesmallboatshop.com) offers guided tours of the beautiful and privately owned Norwalk Islands. You must make reservations in advance; the tours carry a fairly hefty per-person price tag.

SoNo, shorthand for *South Norwalk*, was once an all-too-common decaying inner-city neighborhood, but that all started to change in 1949 when a man named **Roger Wilcox** and his family built a community. This community, they decreed, would be "a different type of community with a completely democratic character, [with] no discrimination because of race, color, creed or politics." This was a new idea in 1949; it pleased some folks and greatly displeased others. But the community has survived and is officially on the **National Register of Historic Places**, as well as gaining a mention on the Connecticut Freedom Trail. The community known as **Village Creek Historic District** includes Dock Road, Outer Road, and Split Rock Road. Today, the area around Washington and S. Main Streets has pulled itself up by the bootstraps to become a home to artists and artisans, much like Manhattan's trendy SoHo. This restored waterfront is now home to dozens of galleries, specialty shops, and restaurants.

The centerpiece of the SoNo revival is the *Maritime Aquarium at Norwalk* (10 N. Water St.; 203-852-0700; maritimeaquarium.org). At the center, part museum, part aquarium, and part theater, what ties it together is life on (and by) the sea. The building also contains restaurants and a nice gift shop. Open daily 10 a.m. to 5 p.m. (until 6 during July and Aug). Closed Thanksgiving and Christmas. Admission.

The *SoNo Switch Tower Museum* (77 Washington St.; 203-246-6958; westctnrhs.org/tower.htm) is an interesting part of the district's thriving cultural scene. Run by the Western Connecticut chapter of the **National Railroad Historical Society**, the museum was originally the switch tower in the timing building. Now it is a participatory museum. Some memorabilia is on display, but the main attraction is standing above the tracks and watching the trains roar by beneath you. Visitors can also pull the levers that move the switches and

norwalktrivia

At one time, Norwalk was the oyster capital of Connecticut. Severe pollution changed all that for a while. Today, thanks to tough environmental legislation that is cleaning up Long Island Sound, Connecticut is once again one of the country's top oyster producers. And the new home base for Connecticut's oystering industry is, once again, Norwalk.

signals on the main line. The museum is open May through Oct, Sat and Sun, noon to 5 p.m. Admission is free, but donations are appreciated.

Just a short ferry ride off Norwalk, the historic *Sheffield Island Lighthouse* (132 Water St.; 203-838-9444; seaport. org) is a pretty cool place to spend a hot summer day. Sheffield is the outermost of Norwalk's thirteen islands and offers scenic views of both Long Island Sound and the Norwalk River. The passenger ferry leaves for the island from Seaport Dock (corner of N. Water and Washington Streets in South Norwalk) twice a day on weekdays and three times on weekends. Weekend and holiday service starts Memorial Day weekend; daily service runs from late June through Labor Day. Dates and times are posted on the website. On the round-trip cruise, the ferry's crew offers lively commentary on Norwalk's oystering past and the island's sometimes racy history and folklore. Island clambakes are held Thurs evening throughout the summer. There are also Haunted Lighthouse and Christmas in July weekends. Whenever they choose to go, visitors can tour the lighthouse, picnic, or walk to the trail of the McKinney Wildlife Refuge. Fee for ferry ride and clambake. The light, which is now on the National Register of Historic Places, was constructed in 1868 and was an active working light until 1902.

Westport

Downtown *Westport*, with its collection of boutique shops, has its own charm, although the streets and stores can get crowded on peak shopping days. The shops come and go, so just park and go where your fancy takes you.

One of the best reasons for visiting Westport even on the busiest days is a place called *Coffee An'* (343 Main St.; 203-227-3808), a world-class doughnut shop. The doughnuts are made from scratch, and they keep coming fresh out of the oven all day. They also serve breakfast, salads, and sandwiches. Open Mon through Fri, 6:30 a.m. to 3:30 p.m.; Sat, 6:30 a.m. to 3 p.m.; Sun, 7:30 a.m. to 1 p.m.

One of the oldest nature centers in Connecticut is a good place to walk off doughnuts from Coffee An'. *Earthplace* (10 Woodside Ln.; 203-557-4400; earthplace.org) offers two and a half miles of trails (open dawn to dusk) and an excellent display of native plants on this seventy-four-acre sanctuary. On weekends, the hands-on aquarium exposes kids to marine life, and the Discovery

Room has many hands-on natural-history activities, puzzles, artifacts, and scientific equipment to use. Since 2005, the exhibit hall has featured activities for kids. There is also an animal rehabilitation center where injured and abandoned animals are cared for. The center also has a wheelchair-accessible trail. The center is open Mon through Sat, 9 a.m. to 5 p.m.; Sun, 1 to 4 p.m. Admission.

In 1802 **Henry Munroe** purchased eight acres of land in Westport. Four years later, he and his wife, Lyzette, moved from Fairfield into their new house in Westport. While this is a significant accomplishment for the times, it is even more significant considering the Munroes were African American. Theirs is one of the few houses in the area known to be built by a free black man in the nineteenth century. The house and barn still stand today and are a stop on **Connecticut's Freedom Trail**, but are privately owned and not open to the public. While you cannot visit their home, you can visit their final resting place in *Green Farms Burying Ground* (Sherwood Island Connector and Green Farms Road) in Westport. This cemetery holds some beautiful headstones that are a window into the past. You'll find the Munroes in the far southwest corner.

Fairfield

The *Connecticut Audubon Birdcraft Museum* (314 Unquowa Rd.; 203-259-0416; ctaudubon.org/birdcraft-museum) is housed in the first privately owned songbird sanctuary in America. It was established in 1914 by **Mable Osgood Wright**, a pioneer in the American conservation movement and founder of the **Connecticut Audubon Society**. Recognized as a National Historic Landmark in 1993, the Birdcraft Museum underwent interior and exterior structural renovations back in 2014 and the redesign of interactive exhibits and refurbished dioramas is ongoing. While the museum will be closed during renovations, the sanctuary will remain open daily, year-round, dawn to dusk.

fairfieldtrivia

Wiffle ball was invented by David N. Mullaney of Fairfield in 1954. By the way, "wiffle" comes from the sandlot baseball term "whiff" (strike), which is what you usually do when you try to hit that crazy plastic ball with all those holes.

Bridgeport Area

Bridgeport

Phineas Taylor (P. T.) Barnum is quite possibly the country's most famous entertainment entrepreneur. Born in 1810, in an era when entertainment was pretty much divided along class lines between the cultural and the popular, Barnum revolutionized showbiz by presenting entertainment designed to appeal to people of all classes. Over time, his name came to be linked with three things: showmanship, the circus, and a legendary quote that he never said, "There's a sucker born every minute."

Barnum also served as the mayor of Bridgeport in 1875, and today that city is repaying him by working hard to rebuild the museum that honors his work and memory. The ***Barnum Museum*** (820 Main St.; 203-331-1104; barnum-museum.org) has met with disaster after disaster. An F1 tornado blew through the city in 2010, hitting the museum and causing serious structural damage along with damaging many of the precious artifacts. In 2011 and 2012, Hurricane Irene and Superstorm Sandy caused additional damage to the museum. The first priority of the museum staff was to save and restore as many artifacts as possible. Once that was done, they turned to the job of stabilizing the museum's building, which is a jewel on its own.

Recovery efforts are still ongoing and day-to-day operations and programming at the museum has been understandably curtailed, but you can still see some of the exhibits. Their gallery has been temporarily moved to the **People's United Bank Gallery** located behind the museum. The staff has gathered artifacts that belonged to Barnum along with pieces of historic Bridgeport. The Wonders of Barnum exhibit features curiosities from his life in show business. The museum is open year-round Thurs and Fri, 11 a.m. to 3 p.m.; during summer they also open on weekends. With all the changes, though, it's always advised to check the website before traveling and see what is what. Admission is free, but donations are welcome. Alas, the show must go on.

bridgeporttrivia

Famous last words: On his deathbed, P. T. Barnum is reported to have said, "How were the receipts today at Madison Square Garden?"

Bridgeport has another museum that is definitely worth a visit. Someone once described the ***Discovery Museum and Planetarium*** (4450 Park Ave.; 203-372-3521; discoverymuseum.org) as "more fun than a basket of puppies." It is indeed a splendid place for kids of all ages.

This 20,000-square-foot museum offers permanent and changing exhibits throughout the year. While some museums are "don't touch" places, the Discovery is a "please touch" place. You can make a variety of delightful things happen by simply pulling a lever, turning a crank, or pushing a button. At the Dare to Discover exhibit you can design a structure then see how earthquake vibrations impact it. And the Everbrite exhibit will summon your inner child. Inspired by the eighties, phenomenon the Lite-Brite, this massive exhibit features 464 adjustable LED dials that rotate through the color spectrum. Visitors

One to Watch

When sisters Mary and Eliza Freeman purchased neighboring lots in Bridgeport to build their homes, they did not intend for those houses to serve as a symbol of American freedom more than 150 years later. They could not have known that the community would come together to save their homes with the wish to create an important cultural exhibit that would teach future generations the history of African Americans in our state, help revitalize the surrounding community, and serve as a role model to other communities.

The Mary & Eliza Freeman Center for History and Community (freemancenterbpt. com) is still in the planning stages, but is already facing serious challenges. The Main Street houses that belonged to Mary and Eliza have fallen into such a state of disrepair that they are in danger of being demolished. Luckily, the houses were recently placed on the National Trust for Historic Preservation's list of America's 11 Most Endangered Historic Places.

The houses, along with the **Walters Memorial A.M.E. Zion Church** (12 Gregory St.), are all that remain of a free black community referred to as Little Liberia that thrived in the nineteenth century. The women's history is as amazing as the homes they built. Neither sister ever married, and they were successful at a time when being a woman and being black were not in their favor. For a bit, they both lived in New York City and amassed huge real estate portfolios. At the time of her death in 1862 at the age of fifty-seven, Eliza had $3,000 in real estate. Mary subsequently grew that investment to more than $30,000, possibly up to $50,000, an amount second only to P. T. Barnum.

At the time of publication, the efforts to preserve these significant spaces continue. Maisa L. Tisdale, head of the Mary and Eliza Freeman Center, estimates it will take $1.6 million to restore the homes and even more to create a museum. We have no doubt Connecticut will rally and save this treasure.

Mary and Eliza, we are rooting for you!

are invited to create designs, patterns, pictures, or simply explore. Sounds like an enlightening experience. Be sure to check out the Discover Museum's gift shop; it's thoughtfully stocked with lots of low-priced goodies. The museum is open year-round Mon through Sun, 10 a.m. to 5 p.m., although hours may shorten in the colder months. Admission.

The Henry B. duPont III Planetarium offers shows starting at 1 p.m. (for children 7 and under) and 3 p.m. (for 8 and older). There are more shows on the weekend, so check the website or call for details. Planetarium admission is included in the general admission.

Connecticut's Beardsley Zoo (1875 Noble Ave.; 203-394-6565; beardsleyzoo.org) claims its mission is "acquainting a diverse public to the

bridgeporttrivia

A fun-loving bunch of students, who have remained nameless, are sometimes credited for inventing the game of Frisbee by tossing back and forth empty pie tins from Mrs. Frisbie's Bridgeport bakery.

delicate balance that exists between living things and their environment." They do that through a variety of exhibits and educational programs. The facility includes a picnic area, snack bar, and gift shop. It is open daily from 9 a.m. to 4 p.m. Admission.

A relic from a different era in our history, the *Famous 50's Diner* (472 Huntington Tpke; 203-572-0777; famous50sdiner.net) is a destination in itself. When you walk in the door, it's like you literally walked back in time. Memorabilia from the sock-hop era line the walls, furniture is reminiscent of the times, and the food, well, it's diner delicious and reasonably priced. Even the friendly staff is outfitted with Pink Ladies T-shirts. To you from me, Pinky Lee. Open daily, 7 a.m. to 3 a.m.

Trumbull

Trumbull resident **Nero Hawley's** life is chronicled in the book *From Valley Forge to Freedom: A Story of a Black Patriot*, published in 1975. He was one of the many slaves who fought in the Revolutionary War for freedoms they could only imagine they would eventually enjoy. Hawley did gain his freedom at the end of the war and lived to be 75 years old. He is buried in **Riverside Cemetery**, a short walk from Daniel's Farm Road near Route 127 in Trumbull. You'll find his final resting place in the center of the far end of the small graveyard.

Shelton

The Jones family believes if you are good to the land, the land will be good to you. In fact, those words have been passed down for generations by **Phillip James Jones**, founder of *Jones Family Farms* (606 Walnut Tree Hill Rd.; 203-929-8425; jonesfamilyfarms.com) in *Shelton*. And that was 150 years ago, so they must be doing something right. The family currently farms four hundred acres and offers pick-your-own opportunities throughout the year—pumpkins in the fall, strawberries and blueberries in the summer, Christmas trees in the winter. The family also owns and operates *Jones Winery*, and its wine is consistently voted Best Connecticut Wine by *Connecticut Magazine*. A more recent addition to the farm is *The Harvest Kitchen* where they offer small farmhouse cooking classes to teach visitors how to take farm-fresh food and turn it into a healthy, delicious meal.

Special events are offered throughout the year. The farm is generally open Mon through Sat, 9 a.m. to 5 p.m.; Sun, 8 a.m. to noon, with longer or shorter hours depending on the season. The winery is open Fri, Sat, and Sun, 11 a.m. to 5:30 p.m., with expanded hours in the warmer months. Everything is weather-dependent, so be sure to call or check their website before traveling.

Derby

The majestic and ornate **Sterling Opera House** (4 Elizabeth St.) across from the green was the first building in the state to be added to the National Register of Historic Places and now this beautiful Victorian building designed by **H. Edwards Ficken**, co-designer of New York's Carnegie Hall, is in dire need of restoration.

In its heyday, the building acted as the town hall, police department, and grand stage all in one. It saw the likes of Harry Houdini, Amelia Earhart, John Philip Sousa, Donald O'Connor, John and Ethel Barrymore, George Burns, Gracie Allen, Milton Berle, Bob Home, and Bing Crosby. But in 1945, that all came to an end and the curtain fell for the last time on this grand lady.

Today, the peeling paint, broken windows, and scattered debris all lend fodder to the idea that the building is haunted. Reports of shadowy figures, orbs of light and objects moving on their own get passed from person to person. Some report seeing a little boy playing with a soccer ball who seemingly disappears, some speculate that the spirit of Charles Sterling, the piano maker from Derby for whom the structure is named, may walk the halls.

The building's exterior was recently restored and some funds have been secured to continue on the inside with hopes of possibly returning the building to its former use as a town hall. While the opera house is currently closed to the public, keep an eye on it for ghostly occupants and possible renovations.

Stratford

Do you have a future pilot in the family? Then the **National Helicopter Museum** (2480 Main St.; 203-375-8857; nationalhelicoptermuseum.org), located in Stratford Eastbound Railroad Station, should be on your itinerary. Here your budding aviator can learn all about how these whirlybirds were developed. There are pieces designed by Stratford's own **Dr. Anselm Franz**, inventor of the

connecticutfree domtrailtrivia

Stratford resident Asa Seymour Curtis was a farmer with a huge heart. His home at 2016 Elm St. was a known stop on the Underground Railroad. Mr. Curtis is buried in Union Cemetery (23 Temple Court) in Stratford. See the rest of his story at ctfreedomtrail.org.

gas turbine engine in the 1950s. **Igor Sikorsky's** career is chronicled and a model of his first craft is on display. From the dragonfly and hummingbird to today's incredible flying machines, it's all here. Open the end of May through mid-Oct, Wed through Sun, 1 to 4 p.m. or by appointment.

Milford

Milford bills itself as the "little city with a big heart." With a population of more than 54,000, Milford has a rich and varied history along with a vibrant beach community. Originally purchased from Paugusset Chief Ansantawae, Milford became home to settlers beginning in 1639. Pirates are said to have roamed the area's waters and rumor is that **buried treasure** is hidden on a small island off the shores of *Silver Sands Beach*. In Revolutionary times, the city hosted George Washington as he made his way across the area. The city saw the ravages of the Civil War and helped slaves to freedom on their way through the Underground Railroad.

Fans of military history should visit the *Soldiers Monument* in Milford Cemetery (Prospect Street), which honors forty-six soldiers who contracted smallpox and were abandoned by a British ship on a Milford beach. One of the doctors who volunteered to try to help the men contracted the disease himself and is buried with them in the common grave. *The First Baptist Church* (28 North St.; 203-878-1178) contains a memorial marker honoring six African Americans who fought in the American Revolution.

Milford also has beautiful beaches. *Silver Sands State Park* (203-735-4311) is located off Route 1 and offers free parking (hard to find in this area!). There is a long wooden boardwalk to be enjoyed, and at low tide you can sometimes walk all the way out to **Charles Island** (remember, hidden treasure). Silver Sands and *Walnut Beach* (113 E Broadway) offer the longest stretch of beach in the city. The Walnut Beach community sponsors some cool events over the summer, including a free concert series sponsored by the local Rotary Club. Held on Sundays during July and August at 4 p.m. at the Devon Rotary Pavilion at Walnut Beach, the concerts feature local performers of all genres. Visit the Walnut Beach Association's website (walnutbeachassociation.com/summerconcertseries.html) for the latest.

New Haven Area

New Haven

New Haven's *Yale University* (24 Hillhouse Ave; 203-432-4771; yale.edu) is one of those American treasures that can be measured only in terms of firsts, bests, and similar benchmarks. In 1861, it granted the first doctor of philosophy degree in the US. In 1869, its School of Fine Arts, the first in the country, opened its doors. Yale numbers among its graduates men of the caliber of **Eli Whitney** and **Noah Webster** and since 1789, almost 10 percent of major US diplomatic appointees have been Yale grads.

Yale boasts some of the most interesting architecture in the country, and if you have a chance to simply walk through campus, I urge you to do so. Start at **Phelps Gate** on College Street. Beyond the gate is the *Old Campus*, ringed with Gothic buildings. *Dwight Hall* introduced Yale to this type of architecture in 1842. Built as the college library for the then mind-boggling sum of $33,253, it was a strange marriage of spare New England Puritanism with opulent overindulgence. It boasts thirty-two carved heads of man and beast mounted on turrets on its ninety-foot tower. Over the next seventy years, other architects designed additional Gothic buildings for the Old Campus. Bingham and Vanderbilt Halls on Chapel Street and the bridge over High Street all have their own menagerie of mythological beasts.

Yale graduate **James Gamble Rogers's** 221-foot 1921 *Harkness Tower* on High Street honors people and events associated with Yale history, including university founder **Eli Yale** and graduates Samuel F. B. Morse, Eli Whitney, John C. Calhoun, Noah Webster, Nathan Hale, and eighteenth-century fire-and-brimstone preacher Jonathan Edwards. James Fenimore Cooper also attended, but was asked to leave after two years.

Higher on the tower are figures from ancient history, such as Phidias, Homer, Aristotle, and Euclid. Rogers also designed the *Sterling Memorial Library*, the Sterling Law complex, and the Hall of Graduate Studies. The library's decorative sculpture has a surprisingly whimsical theme, with its bookworm perched above the Wall Street entrance. The *Sterling Law School* complex is a veritable jungle of legal symbols, including Minerva and her owl. A feisty bulldog serves as the school mascot. Free student-guided tours of Yale are available through the *Yale Visitor Center* (149 Elm St.; 203-432-2302; yale. edu/visitor/tours.html). Tours run Mon through Fri at 10:30 a.m. and 2 p.m., and on weekends at 1:30 p.m.

Yale University's *Beinecke Rare Book and Manuscript Library* (121 Wall St.; 203-432-2977; beinecke.library.yale.edu) is like no other building you've ever seen. To protect the fragile documents inside from sun damage, it was built without windows. Instead, the exterior walls are made of wafer-thin marble slabs. When the sun shines, the building's interior has a cloudy amber glow. The library, which is open to the public, has five major collections. The permanent exhibit on the mezzanine features the **Gutenberg Bible**. Printed in about 1455 in Mainz, Germany, it is regarded as the first book printed from movable type in the Western world. *Audubon's Birds of America* is also on display. This is a great place to visit, but maybe not one for toddlers or younger children. Open Mon, 10 a.m. to 7 p.m.; Tues through Thurs, 9 a.m. to 7 p.m.; Fri, 9 a.m. to 5 p.m.; Sat, noon to 5 p.m.; Sun, noon to 4 p.m.

They call it *The Tomb* (64 High St.), and the name fits. If you walk down High Street between Chapel and Elm Streets in downtown New Haven, you will come across a spooky stone edifice with no windows. This is the headquarters of **Skull and Bones**, the infamous secret society at Yale University. Its alumni include George H. W. Bush and his son George W., plus a host of CIA agents and big-shot dignitaries. Skull and Bones had an unwanted national spotlight shined upon its Greco-Egyptian facade during the 2004 presidential campaign, which featured the eerie coincidence of two "Bonesmen" (Bush the younger and US senator John Kerry) running against each other. Neither of them would discuss his membership in this elite group that supposedly practices secret rituals involving coffins. According to folklore, Geronimo's skull is inside the building. If you're contemplating trying to get inside, forget about it. Just walk on and wonder.

Yale is also home to several of America's finest museums. A showcase for British art and life, the *Yale Center for British Art* (1080 Chapel St.; 877-BRIT-ART; britishart.yale.edu) was built around the extensive collection of *Paul Mellon*, a 1929 Yale graduate who spent forty years amassing works by a host of British artists. Mellon's holdings have been expanded since the center opened in 1977, and the building now houses the largest collection of British art outside of Great Britain. It also houses a 13,000-volume research library. Open Tues through Sat, 10 a.m. to 5 p.m.; Sun, noon to 5 p.m.

On the opposite corner of Chapel and York Streets is the *Yale University Art Gallery* (1111 Chapel St.; 203-432-0600; artgallery.yale.edu). Founded in 1832, this is the oldest university art museum in the US, and its collection spans various eras, cultures, and art styles. The museum has gone through many changes and expansions over its long history. The museum's most recent expansion promises to enhance visitors' experience and learning. With more than 200,000 objects on display, how can a visit not be enlightening? There's also a sculpture garden, with works by Moore, Nevelson, and others, that makes an awfully nice setting in which to dream away a spring afternoon. Open Tues through Fri, 10 a.m. to 5 p.m.; Thurs (Sept through June), 10 a.m. to 8 p.m.; Sat and Sun, 11 a.m. to 5 p.m.

yaletrivia

The *Yale Bowl*, completed in 1914, was the first enclosed football stadium in the US, and while it wasn't quite the Final Four, the first intercollegiate basketball game was played in New Haven in 1896.

The *Yale Peabody Museum of Natural History* (170 Whitney Ave.; 203-432-5050; peabody.yale.edu), at the intersection of Whitney Avenue and Sachem Street, is the largest natural history museum in New England. Big deal, you say. Ah, but all children and those adults who are truly tuned in to "kid kool" know that "natural history" is just an adult euphemism for what it's really all about: dinosaurs. The big guys. T-Rex, Raptor Red, and their buddies.

The Peabody has the largest collection of mounted dinosaurs in the world, including the sixty-seven-foot Apatosaurus. It also boasts the original **Age of Reptiles** mural by Pulitzer Prize–winner **Rudolph Zallinger**. Sure, it has been reproduced countless times in books from coast to coast, but it's the biggest mural of its kind in the world, and nothing beats the overwhelming experience of standing in front of the real thing.

The Peabody is open Tues through Sat, 10 a.m. to 5 p.m.; Sun, noon to 5 p.m. Admission. Blue Star Museum. There's loads of great info about visiting the museum on their website, including information on how to get in free, so be sure to check it out.

But there's much more to New Haven than Yale University. For starters, there's the crypt under *Center Church on the Green* (250 Temple St.; 203-787-0121; centerchurchonthegreen.org). For tourists who are truly committed to getting off the beaten path, this attraction is hard to beat. It's not so much creepy as it is historic.

The graves in this crypt are believed to be unique to America. Nowhere else, historians say, was a church built over a colonial graveyard, a decision that helped protect the graves from the elements. The original graveyard dates to the 1600s. Here lie the remains of up to 1,700 early New Havenites, including Benedict Arnold's first wife and the family of President Rutherford B. Hayes, and Yale's founder, Rev. James Pierpont, among others. Headstones and tomb "tables" abound in the cold, subterranean expanse. The crypt's visiting hours are Apr through Oct, Sat, 11 a.m. to 1 p.m. The tours are free, but donations are accepted to help preserve the crypt and its remarkable contents. The church is also on the **Connecticut Freedom Trail** for its role in supporting the Mende African *Amistad* captives.

The remaining area of the graveyard became the *New Haven Green*. Instead of moving all the bodies, it is said, residents simply built up the ground

newhaventrivia

You probably know that Connecticut inventors produced the submarine and anesthesia, but did you know that the Nutmeg State was also quite possibly the birthplace of the lollipop? Some sources credit New Haven resident George Smith with the creation in 1908. The name (maybe) is a nod to the famous racehorse of the time, Lolly Pop. Who knew?

over them and moved the headstones to an existing cemetery. The bodies were left in peace until 2012, when Hurricane Sandy visited Connecticut. The winds took down a tree that had been planted hundreds of years ago on the green. When it toppled, its roots pulled out of the ground, bringing with it a human skeleton. The skeleton is believed to belong to one of the original residents of the graveyard.

Connecticut pizza lovers claim that **Frank Pepe Pizzeria Napoletana** (157 Wooster St.; 203-865-5762; pepespizzeria.com) in New Haven makes the best clam pizza in the Western world. There is some reason to accept that claim. Pepe's special white clam pizza, prepared by hand on the premises, like everything else here, is topped with fresh littlenecks, olive oil, garlic, oregano, and Romano cheese. For other types of pies, if you want cheese, you have to ask for it; otherwise, you get a marvelous pie crust topped with tomato sauce. The splendiferous pies are baked in a coal-fired oven to emerge as flat, crisp circles of dough with a firm, chewy crust.

Pepe's in New Haven is open Sun through Thurs, 10:30 a.m. to 10 p.m.; Fri and Sat, 10:30 a.m. to 11 p.m. (Pepe's also has other locations in Connecticut

The Boulevard for Bargains

You'll sometimes hear Nutmeggers whisper, "Oh, I got it at the Boulevard." There will usually be some winking and smiling going on during said conversation. That's because the **Boulevard** (500 Ella T. Grasso Blvd.; 203-772-1447; fleact.com) is a year-round flea market where bargains abound. We caution you, however, to go with your eyes open. While you will find great deals, you will also find cheap knockoffs. Most of the time people are good with that as long as the knockoff is well made, but you need to know what you are looking for so you don't get bamboozled. Do your research. The vendors here are hard core. They don't bargain much, but we, of course, encourage you to try—you never know. Bring cash; that's all they deal with. If you don't see it, ask. You may or may not get an honest answer. We suspect the Boulevard has been raided a time or two, so any truly name-brand merchandise is often sold quickly and quietly. For a while North Face jackets and UGG boots were hot items, but you might also find MAC makeup, Tiffany jewelry, Gucci, Louis Vuitton, Kate Spade, cowboy boots, hats, gloves, Coach scarves, dollar items, jeans, shoes, phone cases, and oh so much more.

In season you'll often find fresh vegetables. You just never know. There are a few food vendors, too. Bathrooms are sketchy. The flea market is held on an open field, and there is limited paved parking; the rest is on bumpy ground. They open at 7 a.m., but if you get there too early, they'll still be setting up. It gets busy fast, too. If you see something you like, we recommend you don't wait. If you do, it may be gone when you go back. There are, however, several vendors who sell the same or similar items, so be sure to look around, too. Open year-round, Sat and Sun, 7 a.m. to 4 p.m.

as well as in New York, Massachusetts, and Rhode Island; check the website for details.) If you can't handle the line at Pepe's (and there will be one), you can always try **Sally's** (237 Wooster St.; 203-624-5271; sallysapizza.com), but chances are there might be one there, too. You can't go wrong at either place; Sally's rivals Pepe's in the quality of pizza it serves. Open Wed through Sun, 3 to 10 p.m.

The **Five-Mile Point Light** (1 Lighthouse Rd.; 203-946-8005), located at the eastern point of New Haven Harbor, was built in 1847. The sixty-five-foot-high stone lighthouse was functional until it was taken out of service in 1877. Now it dominates **Lighthouse Point Park** (2 Lighthouse Rd.; 203-946-8019; newhavenct.gov). The park includes lots of nature trails, a bird sanctuary, a splashpad, and a 1916 carousel that is one of the largest in America (fifty-two feet in diameter) and holds seventy-two figures: sixty-nine horses, one camel, and two dragons. The parking fee is steep if you're not a resident, and there's a small admission for the carousel. Carousel rides are available noon to 4 p.m. weekends and holidays from Memorial Day through Labor Day.

newhaventrivia

New Haven is affectionately called the "Elm City" because of the stately elm trees that dotted the New Haven Green and Yale University in the late eighteenth century, creating a leafy canopy over the downtown area. Gradually these majestic trees succumbed to Dutch elm disease, but in recent years many have been replaced with a hardier species of elm.

New Haven is justifiably proud of its role in liberating the captives aboard the ship **Amistad**. In 1839, a group of Africans who had been kidnapped from their homes in Sierra Leone by slave traders mutinied and took over the ship. But they were seized by naval authorities and taken to New Haven for trial.

After being imprisoned in a jail on the New Haven Green, where abolitionists took up their cause, the prisoners were acquitted, first in Connecticut courts and then by the US Supreme Court. This amazing and courageous saga received wide attention when Steven Spielberg's movie *Amistad* was released in 1997. Three years later, a reproduction of the *Amistad* was completed in Mystic and arrived at its home port of New Haven in July 2000. The storied ship is available for tours when it is docked at Long Wharf, alongside **New Haven Harbor** (389 Long Wharf Dr.). But during many times of the year, it's on tour at other ports or in winter storage. Today, the *Amistad* is managed by **Discovering Amistad** (129 Church St.; Ste. 321; 203-498-8222; discoveringamistad.org). They treat the ship very much like a floating classroom, bring it and their programs to ports all over the state. Check the website to see where she'll be visiting next.

newhaventrivia

Famous New Haven inventions include the meat grinder, the corkscrew, and Isaac Strouse's misogynistic little torture device: the corset.

You can also visit the **Amistad Memorial** (165 Church St.) and read about Joseph Cinque (also known as Sengbe Pieh), one of the passengers on the ship. The eleven-foot bronze statue was created by Ed Hamilton and was dedicated in 1992. It stands in the location of the New Haven jail at the time of the trials.

East Haven

The *Shore Line Trolley Museum* (17 River St.; 203-467-6927; shorelinetrolley. com) in *East Haven* maintains nearly 100 vintage trolleys and other vehicles. For detailed descriptions of which ones are on display, visit their website; it's a wealth of information. There are also some interpretive displays, including hands-on exhibits and audio-video displays at the museum. We suspect, though, that most people will be drawn by the trolley rides. The museum offers three-mile round-trip rides in vintage trolley cars on the Branford Electric Railway, the nation's oldest operating suburban transportation line. Hard-core trolley freaks are also welcome to hang around the car barn watching the restoration process. You can picnic on the grounds, and there's also a gift shop. Your ticket entitles you to ride all day on all trolley cars, which depart from the station building every hour on the half hour beginning at 10:30 a.m., with the last departure at 4:30 p.m.

Hamden

Traveling north from New Haven, you'll come to suburban *Hamden*. The town's *Eli Whitney Museum* (915 Whitney Ave.; 203-777-1833; eliwhitney. org) includes displays tracing two centuries of industrial growth on the site plus various technology-oriented interactive hands-on exhibits. The museum is mainly devoted, however, to the achievements of Eli Whitney, one of the towering figures of the Industrial Revolution. Whitney was a local firearms manufacturer who pioneered the use of interchangeable parts. He also changed the course of American history by inventing the cotton gin, a device that became the foundation of the Southern plantation economy, spurred the spread of slavery, and contributed mightily to the political crisis that ended in America's Civil War. You'll find a waterfall, a covered bridge, and walking trails behind the museum. Open Sat and Sun, 11 a.m. to 4 p.m.

Hamden also contains some great picnic spots, most of them located within the confines of *Sleeping Giant State Park* (200 Mt. Carmel Ave., Route

10; 203-287-5658). According to legend, the basalt mountain where the park is sited is actually an evil giant by the name of Hobbomock, who was put to sleep to prevent him from doing harm to local residents. When you approach it from the north, the chain of high, wooded hills that make up the park really does resemble a sleeping giant. Today, people climb all over the giant. Many of Sleeping Giant's trails lead to gentle or moderate hikes, so even if you're out of shape you can still get in a good walk. All told, the park's 13,000-plus acres include more than twenty-eight miles of trails, some with spectacular views. There are parking fees for weekends and holidays Memorial Day through the end of Oct. The park is open 8 a.m. to sunset. In Spring 2018, the park was devastated by a tornado that tore through parts of the state. There was so much damage that the park was forever changed. The state closed the park and worked to clean up the damage and reroute and remark the trails, as many were unidentifiable. The Sleeping Giant Park Association keeps its Facebook page updated with the latest news and trail openings.

After your hike, visit **Wentworth Homemade Ice Cream Company** (3697 Whitney Ave., Route 10; 203-281-7429; wentworthicecream.com). Located just down the road from the Sleeping Giant State Park entrance, Wentworth's occupies a yellow-sided house on your right as you're leaving Hamden. Wentworth's makes all of its own ice cream on-site. Incredibly dense and not too sweet, Wentworth's products seem to capture the essence of each of the dozens of flavors in the ever-changing repertoire. Almond amaretto (one of many "adult" flavors that use real liquor) will win you over even if you don't care for sweet liqueurs. The best flavor of all, though, is the peach, a gift of ambrosia lovingly crafted from fresh, tree-ripened fruit. For kids, there are silly flavors such as Cookie Monster, neon-blue vanilla with cookie bits. There's even Canine Crunch for your fur-children. Wentworth's is open Mon through Thurs, 11 a.m. to 9:30 p.m.; Fri and Sat, 11 a.m. to 10 p.m.

North Haven

As you drive down Universal Drive in North Haven, you have no idea what's lurking behind the big box stores and myriad restaurants in the North Haven Commons shopping center. Maybe you saw the brown signs on the roads hinting at its existence, but you didn't truly know. But follow Universal Drive North all the way back, past all the turns, past Target, out the way back of the parking lot and you see it. The sign that directs you to the **Tidal Marsh Trail**. Created and maintained by **The North Haven Trail Association**, a nonprofit volunteer organization, this trail takes you on a lovely adventure along the Quinnipiac River, through abandoned rail yards and sandy-bottomed forests. You can walk right up to the sandy edge of the river and watch as crabs skitter off into the tall reeds. You can watch overhead and see osprey, heron, and other shore birds swoop along the water, and, if you're lucky, you might glimpse a bald eagle majestically standing watch. You can also see the Sleeping Giant snoozing in the distance.

The trail isn't long, only about two miles out and back. You'll pass abandoned railroad tracks being reclaimed by the forest, wildflowers, and a fair amount of evidence of late night visits of the more nefarious kind than yours. Just past the end of the trail, over the two graffiti-covered tunnels, you will find the abandoned **Cedar Hill Rail Yard**, one of the largest rail yards ever built in the US. Cedar Hill, built in the early 1920s, was once a major part of the east coast network of railways. The yard once held a reported 15,000 cars at one time, but all that is left of the former giant are rusted rails, crumbling buildings, and unsafe structures. We don't recommend poking around; instead, stick to the trail that meanders along the riverbanks.

South-Central Connecticut

Cheshire

The *Farmington Canal Greenway* is a Connecticut attraction that is quite literally off the beaten path. It's also a marvelous example of recycling on a grand scale. In the early 1800s, New Haven was a thriving port city, but there was a problem: The goods that arrived by boat couldn't be transported easily to the north. So in 1828, a canal, engineered by Eli Whitney and others, was built. It ran a total of eighty-three miles, from the harbor through Hamden, *Cheshire*, Plainville, and Farmington, and up to Northampton, Massachusetts. The Farmington Canal became the economic lifeline of central Connecticut. But just twenty years later, it was replaced by a railroad that ran adjacent to the canal.

The railroad operated until 1982, when floods washed out a portion of the line. For years the railroad beds lay abandoned and neglected. At best, they became overgrown with grass and weeds. At worst, sections became eyesores, piling up with fast-food packaging, soda cans, old tires, and discarded shopping carts. But as the national rails-to-trails movement gained momentum, a grassroots effort emerged in southern Connecticut to restore this historic rail-canal corridor for recreational use. The result is a linear park for walkers, joggers, cyclists, and cross-country skiers that starts in southern Hamden and runs into Cheshire with entrances in Hamden at *Brooksvale Park* (524 Brooksvale Ave.; 203-287-2669) and on Todd Street (350 feet west of the intersection with Route 10) and in Cheshire at Cornwall Avenue (0.6 mile west of the Cornwall Street and Route 10 intersection) and N. Brooksvale Road (1 mile west of the intersection with Route 10). Parking is available at each trail entry point. The trail is also wheelchair accessible and has benches every so often for resting. One more thing, if you're walking or have younger children, be aware of the sometimes numerous bicyclists and roller bladers on the trail. Most will shout an "On your left" or "On your right" before they come up behind you, so don't be alarmed, but be aware. The trail is open year-round dawn to dusk.

On Route 42, you'll find a restored section of the canal at **Lock 12 Historical Park** (487 N. Brooksvale Rd.; 203-272-2743). In addition to the canal, the grounds contain a museum, a lockkeeper's house, a helicoidal bridge, and a picnic area. The park is open year-round, dawn to dusk. The museum is open by appointment only.

At **Roaring Brook Falls** (203-272-2689; cheshirelandtrust.org), just off Roaring Brook Road (west of the junction of Route 70 and I-84), you'll find a wonderful hiking trail and overlook—the perfect place for a spring or fall picnic—and the foundation of an old mill to explore. But the draw here is Connecticut's highest single-drop waterfall. The Cheshire Land Trust's website makes the distinction between Roaring Brook Falls's single-foot drop and Kent Falls's 250-foot drop of multiple cascades.

Your kids might think that animation starts with *The Simpsons* and ends with *SpongeBob*, but a visit to the **Barker Character, Comic, and Cartoon Museum** (1188 Highland Ave., Route 10; 203-272-2357; barkermuseum.com) will widen their (and your) horizons. Herb and Gloria Barker, the museum's guiding lights, are longtime collectors of 'toon memorabilia, and they've packed a lot of history into this jewel-box museum. You'll find, among other things, many cartoon cells on view, a collection of lunch boxes and pull toys featuring cartoon characters from days gone by, and McDonald's Happy Meal toys, once giveaways, now pricey collectibles. Animators and illustrators such as George Wildman of Popeye fame often visit the museum for talks and special events. The museum is open Wed through Sat, noon to 4 p.m., with extended hours the end of June through Aug from 11 a.m. to 5 p.m. Admission. Blue Star Museum.

Named one of the Top Boutique Décor Shops in Connecticut by CBS Connecticut, **The Posh Pear** (830 S. Main St. [Rte. 10]; 860-863-5898; theposhpearct.com) offers the best of old and new with jewelry, local goods, gift items, DIY supplies, and more. They even offer workshops to create your own masterpiece. Open Tues through Fri, 11 a.m. to 5 p.m.; Sat 10 a.m. to 4 p.m.; Sun and Mon, "by chance."

Naugatuck

Established in 1790, **Gunntown Cemetery** (Gunntown Rd.) is home to members of both sides of the American Revolution. But even though relatives bid their loved ones goodbye with hopes they would rest in peace, there isn't a lot of peace to be found within this cemetery. There have been various claims of people hearing music coming from within its walls, some claim they have heard children laughing or have seen a young boy playing by the far wall and then disappearing. There are stories of a man riding a horse through the grounds or a man walking with a lantern and leading his horse. Multiple ghost hunters have visited, with varying degrees of success in communicating with the beyond. Orbs and mists have been captured on camera. Connecticut demonologists Ed and Lorraine Warren even declared the cemetery haunted. We leave it up to you to translate your experience here at Gunntown. As always, please be respectful of the surroundings. Also, parking is on a narrow road and cars go whipping by; you don't want to join the spirits who roam the grounds.

Waterbury

waterburytrivia

In 1790, the Grilley brothers of Waterbury made Connecticut's first buttons.

waterburytrivia

Preserving food in tin cans was a great idea, but getting the food out of those tins needed another. So when in 1858 Ezra J. Warner of Waterbury found a way to quickly open tins, tummies all across America thanked him.

Unfortunately, his invention looked more like something from a slasher movie than the latest housewife's helper. You stuck a rather intimidatingly big, curved blade into the tin and rammed it around. Since the opener tended to open the user as well as the tin, someone else invented the less dangerous cutting-wheel can opener a decade later.

Ten miles or so northwest of Cheshire is the city of **Waterbury**. The brass industry moved into the city in the mid-1800s, and the Brass Capital of the World, as it was then known, was built largely on wealth derived from brass manufacturing. In the years since, the industry has moved elsewhere, but its architectural legacy remains. During the heyday of brass, Waterbury residents erected hundreds of rambling Victorian mansions and imposing public buildings. Entire neighborhoods of these buildings are preserved almost intact, and as part of an ongoing renaissance program, other neighborhoods have been restored to their former glory. As a result, much of modern-day Waterbury is a living museum of nineteenth- and early twentieth-century architecture.

If you're interested in architecture, you'll want to visit the **Hillside Historic District**, once home to Waterbury's captains of industry. Now listed on the National Register of Historic Places, the district includes 310 structures dating from the nineteenth and early twentieth centuries. The center of Waterbury's restoration program, however, is the tree-lined city green, one of the most beautiful greens in any northeastern city. Within a few blocks of the green, you'll find scores of lovingly restored structures. Among the more interesting are a marvelously misplaced railroad station modeled on the Palazzo Pubblico in Siena, Italy. There are also five municipal buildings designed by prominent American architect **Cass Gilbert**.

The modernized and expanded **Masonic Hall** on the northwest corner of Waterbury's green houses the *Mattatuck Museum* (144 W. Main St.; 203-753-0381; mattatuckmuseum.org). This establishment is an oddly satisfying combination of industrial museum and art gallery. The gallery portion includes items spanning three centuries and is devoted to the works of American masters who have an association with Connecticut. The museum portion contains displays of household items and furnishings dating from 1713 to 1940 as well as exhibits dealing with local history, especially the history of the region's industrial development. Its holdings include collections of nineteenth-century furniture, novelty clocks and watches, early cameras, and Art Deco tableware. The most curious item is Charles Goodyear's rubber desk. The museum is open Tues through Sat, 10 a.m. to 5 p.m.; it is also open Sun noon to 5 p.m. (except during July and Aug). There is a gift shop and cafe on-site.

Souvenir hunters should check out what used to be the **Howland-Hughes Department Store**, a downtown stalwart built in 1890 and renowned throughout the state as the oldest freestanding department store in Connecticut. Today it operates as *The Connecticut Store* (140 Bank St.; 203-753-4121; shop. ctstore.com), well-named because the management focuses on inventory that consists exclusively of made-in-Connecticut merchandise.

It's your chance to browse for Woodbury pewter, wristwatches, and buttons produced right here in Waterbury, Bovano enamelware from Cheshire, Liberty candles from Bolton, Allyn neckwear from Stamford, and Lego building blocks from Enfield—plus made-in-Shelton Wiffle balls, made-in-Orange Pez candy dispensers, and made-in-Norwich Thermos bottles. Also in stock are clothing, housewares, games, puzzles, and wood carvings. This one-of-a-kind place has weathervanes, too, custom-crafted in Meriden. The store is open Tues through Fri, 10 a.m. to 3 p.m.

Meriden

Way before there were golden arches on every street corner, the central Connecticut towns of *Meriden* and Middletown had developed a local specialty called the "steamed cheeseburger." Steaming the burgers makes them incredibly juicy and reduces the sharp Wisconsin cheddar to just the right degree of molten wonderfulness. Locals know to order theirs in the form of a "trilby" (a regional term for anything served up with mustard and onions). You have your choices in the area for steamed cheeseburgers. Perhaps the most well-known is **Ted's Restaurant** (1046 Broad St.; 203-237-6660; tedsrestaurant. com), where they've been serving, and we kid you not, world-famous steamed cheeseburgers since 1959. And it's been run by the family since Ted opened it. His son, Paul, took over when his dad passed away, and now Paul's nephew Bill Foreman operates the restaurant. Bill knows his stuff and has been able to open additional locations in Cromwell (43 Berlin Rd.; 860-635-8337) and New Haven (344 Washington Ave.; 203-234-8337). Stop by any of them for this Connecticut must. Open Sun through Wed, 11 a.m. to 9 p.m.; Thurs through Sat, 11 a.m. to 10 p.m.

There's also **The Original Lunchbox** (620 E. Main St.; 203-238-0313; thelunchboxct.com), which offers their steamed deliciousness with a variety of toppings, and breakfast all day as well. Open Mon through Sat, 7 a.m. to 3 p.m.

Then there's **K LaMay's** (690 East Main St.; 203-237-8326; klamayssteamedcheeseburgers.com), where Kevin LaMay whips up steamed cheeseburgers just like he learned to do at Ted's. That's right, he used to work there and has now struck out on his own, with his own, secret recipe for some serious delicious burgers. He started out serving hot sandwiches from a back room in a Meriden pub called Garryowen's. His creations were so well-received, he moved his operation into his current location and has been there ever since. K. LaMay's is open Mon through Sat, 10:30 a.m. to 8 p.m.; Sun, 11 a.m. to 3 p.m. LaMay also serves his style of steamed cheeseburger at the Double Play Café in Wallingford (320 Main Street; 203-265-2599).

Next door to Kevin's restaurant is **Les's Dairy Bar** (654 E. Main St.) where you can get a cool treat to wash down that burger. Choose from flavors such as tiramisu, white cake batter, and cheesecake, as well as Italian ice in flavors such as lemon or blood orange and frozen yogurt. Les's has been an institution since it opened in 1950, and for many people in town, the fun just doesn't start until Les's is open. Open daily from sometime in Mar to early Oct (depending on the weather), 11:30 a.m. to 10 p.m.

Another interesting eatery in the area is **Huxley's Bookmark Café** (1376 East Main St.; 203-237-4087; huxleysbookmarkcafe.com). Named for English author Aldous Huxley, Huxley's has been in the Klonaras family since 1999 when Gregory Klonaras purchased it. Now his son Dimitrios runs the café alongside his dad and mom, Stella. There's definitely a literary theme. The walls are lined with shelves filled with books of all tastes. The painting that hangs on the wall depicts Aldous Huxley in much the same setting. Huxley is the author of a book called *The Doors of Perception,* which is famous not for its literary acclaim but because it's where The Doors took their name. Their book theme carries through to the menu where they offer a Poetic Breakfast and a Literary Lunch. If you're in a hurry, call ahead and they'll have your meal ready for you. Open Sat and Sun, 6:30 a.m. to 2 p.m.; Mon through Fri, 6:30 a.m. to 2:30 p.m.

Call ahead to Huxley's and order a breakfast sandwich and home fries to go, then head over to **Black Pond State Park** (1690 East Main Street, Middlefield) on the town line, where you can enjoy your breakfast while soaking in the quietude of Black Pond and the surrounding forest. No one is usually there very early in the morning unless they are fishing, and it's always fun to watch the fishermen ply the waters as the steam rises on a cool morning. Ahh, perfection. Enjoy.

Wallingford

Another option for that Connecticut original—steamed cheeseburgers—is the next town over from Meriden. In **Wallingford** you can try **American Steamed Cheeseburgers** (92 Quinnipiac St.; 203-294-8888; americansteamedcheeseburgers .com). Tucked behind the Wallingford Train Station, this establishment has been churning out delicious food since 2013 with owner Jayson Anthony Paul at the helm. You can get veggie burgers, salmon sandwiches, and even an egg and cheese sandwich. If you dare, you can get The Bimmer, which is two double cheeseburgers, two steaks, and extra, extra cheese. You can even get a hot dog on a cheeseburger! Open Mon through Thurs, 11 a.m. to midnight; Fri and Sat, 11 a.m. to 2 a.m.; Sun, 11 a.m. to 10 p.m.

Wherever you choose to eat, be careful what you say when talking to other Nutmeggers about steamed cheeseburgers. People are about as loyal to their burger joint as they are to their baseball team and will argue until the cows come home on whose is better.

Tucked away on the back roads of Wallingford is **Beaumont Farm** (945 E. Center St.), a very cool place to visit at any time of the year but especially cool around the holidays when owner Billy Beaumont creates the farm's annual holiday display. Past years have featured characters in scenes from *Frozen, Santa Claus is Comin' to Town*, and more. The tradition goes back many years and is an anticipated holiday treat for many locals. The display can be found at the intersection of East Center Street and South Airline Road from mid-December through mid-January, but that's not written in stone. The farm itself is open year-round, offering fresh fruit and vegetables, flowers, pumpkins, and more. Mon through Sat, 9 a.m. to 7 p.m., Sun to 6 p.m.

If consignment shops are your thing, don't miss **Cindy's Unique Shop** (32 N. Colony St.; 203-269-9341; cindysuniqueshop.com), where you will find all sorts of treasures. There's the usual brand-name items at greatly reduced prices

Trail of Terror

If you're anywhere in the state of Connecticut on a weekend in October and you like to be scared—set your sights for *Wallingford's Trail of Terror* (60 N. Plains Hwy.; 833-600-0054; trailofterror.com). While this wonderful New England town is filled with spooky extravaganzas at this time of the year, this Trail of Terror is *really* scary. (This is *not* a children's activity.)

You travel outdoors through more than thirty "very interactive" fright scenes. Some you'll recognize and love. Some, not so much. *But* it's all for a good cause! This is a volunteer-run operation and they donate all the proceeds to charity. Over the years, the trail has donated $700,000 to the local Red Cross chapter. They also support the Community Revitalization Efforts of Wallingford and other local charities (a complete list is on their website).

The attraction is very popular and they limit the number of tickets each night to make sure everyone has time to complete the trail. If you don't plan ahead, they may sell out before you arrive! Luckily, there are a few ways you can go about gaining entrance. If you're feeling lucky, head on over and wait in line for a $15 general admission ticket. You can also go to their website and purchase a $20 Timed Ticket ($18 if you purchase it before Sept 1). This works much like the Disney Fast Pass. You will be given a time and date at which you are to arrive at the trail for your turn. Not much waiting. There are also group discounts.

The trail is weather dependent and will close for heavy rain and/or wind. They keep their Facebook page and Twitter up to date, so it's best to watch there if you're thinking of heading out. The trail opens Fri, Sat, and Sun at 7 p.m. Last entry is 11 p.m. on Fri and Sat); 10 p.m. on Sun.

Parking can be a little difficult. You can pay $8 to park in the Polish National Alliance parking lot, but everything else is at your own risk. Please respect the No Parking signs, cars *will* be towed. Happy scaring!

(Vera Bradley, Longenberger, etc.), but you'll also find refinished farmhouse furniture, handmade wooden signs, jewelry, glassware, holiday decorations (seasonally), and more. Cindy even posts pictures on her Facebook page every week so you can see all the cool new things that have arrived. She'll save things for you if you see it and must have it, but only for a limited time. She also offers great discounts and is always willing to work with her customers. Open Tues through Sat, 10 a.m. to 5 p.m.; Sun, 11 a.m. to 4 p.m.

Next to Cindy's is **Redscroll Records** (24 N. Colony St.; 203-265-7013; redscrossrecords.com). What started as a record label and morphed into a record store is owned by Joshua Carlson and Rick Sinkiewicz. They carry records, CDs, tapes, books, magazines, accessories, and more. They "specialize, but are not limited to, music that is generally off the mainstream radar (underground)." They

OTHER ATTRACTIONS WORTH SEEING

Bovano,
830 S. Main St., Cheshire
(888) 816-9766
bovano.com
Gift shop includes Bovano enamelware

Lockwood-Mathews Mansion Museum
Mathews Park,
295 West Ave., Norwalk
(203) 838-9799
lockwoodmathewsmansion.com

Meeker's Hardware
90 White St., Danbury
(203) 748-8017

Railroad Museum of New England
242 E. Main St., Thomaston
(860) 283-7245
rmne.org

St. James Church
25 West St., Danbury
(203) 748-3561
saintjamesdanbury.org
Established in 1762, used as storage during the Revolutionary War

St. Peter Church
104 Main and Center Streets, Danbury
(203) 743-2707
stpeterdanb.org
Established in 1851, third oldest parish in the diocese

Stepping Stones Museum for Children
Mathews Park,
303 West Ave., Norwalk
(203) 899-0606
steppingstonesmuseum.org
Focusing on the arts, science and technology, and culture and heritage

also buy, sell, and trade, which gives them a nice selection of both new and used items. They are not particularly interested in "most 78s, anything classical, show tunes, crooners," but other than that they are happy to take a look at what you have. They said there's no need for an appointment and there are no set hours to bring your stuff in. "Any time we're open you can come on by." Open Tues through Sat., noon to 8 p.m.; Sun and Mon, noon to 6 p.m.

How about eating or having a drink in a restaurant that used to be a library? You can, at *The Library Wine Bar and Bistro* (60 North Main St.; 203-678-4656; thelibrarywinebar.com). Formerly Wallingford's town library, this 1889 beautiful building has numerous floors and incredible acoustics. It wasn't always this beautiful; in fact, the Gouveia family put a lot of time and effort into bringing this beauty back to her glamorous self. The food they serve is just as beautiful, which makes the entire thing an amazing experience. The bar and patio are open for happy hour Sun through Thurs, 3 to 6:30 p.m.; Fri, 3 to 7:30 p.m. Dinner is served Mon through Thurs and Sun, 4 to 9 p.m. (bar stays open until 10); Fri and Sat, 4 to 10 p.m. (bar until 11). Sunday brunch is served from 10 a.m. to 2 p.m.

And if you like their restaurant, you're going to love their winery with its beautiful stone house, stunning views, and lip-smacking wine. *Gouveia Vineyards* (1339 Whirlwind Hill Rd.; 203-265-5526; gouveiavineyards.com) sits on 140 acres of beauty. Seriously, the views from up there are incredible and worth the trip alone. Joe Gouveia purchased the Wallingford property in 1999; the tasting room followed in 2004. The winery has seen many special occasions since then and has really become a destination. Set among rambling farmland, the vineyard produces 90,000 bottles of wine a year, such as Chardonnay Oak, Seyval Blanc, Whirlwind Rose, Stone House White, Cabernet Franc, and more. Wine tastings are available and you'll receive four preselected wines and one of your choice, and you get an etched souvenir wine glass to keep. Definitely come for the wine, stay for the views. Open Jan 2 through Feb 28, Thurs and Fri, 11 a.m. to 8 p.m.; Sat and Sun, 11 a.m. to 6 p.m.; Mar 1 through Dec 31, Mon through Fri, 11 a.m. to 8 p.m.; Sat and Sun, 11 a.m. to 6 p.m.

Maybe beer is more your taste than wine. If so, head to *Cliffside Brewing* (16B Center St.; cliffsidebrewing.com), where owner David Durant creates magic. He started homebrewing in 2012 and felt it was time to bring his beer to the public. He and his team share their passion for small-batch brewing with his customers. He also offers other local beers on a rotating basis. Children are welcome, but Fido isn't allowed in due to health codes. Service dogs, of course, are welcome. They offer free popcorn and $1 bags of chips to keep the hunger at bay. If you want more than snacks, there are local restaurants who will deliver to the brewery for you. They also offer special events throughout the year, including trivia night and wing night. Watch their website for times and dates. Open Thurs and Fri, 5 to 9 p.m.; Sat, 1 to 9 p.m., Sun, 1 to 8 p.m.

Danbury Area

Weston

Weston is an especially pretty town smack-dab in the middle of Fairfield County, thanks to tough zoning regulations and restrictions on development. According to folklore, old Mr. Scratch himself left some hoofprints on the rocks thereabouts. Lucifer's purported stomping grounds are now the site of the *Lucius Pond Ordway/Devil's Den Preserve* (203-226-4991) on Pent Road (take Godfrey Road, which is off either Route 53 or 57, to Pent Road). Owned by the Nature Conservancy, Devil's Den consists of more than 1,756 acres with twenty miles of hiking trails. This is a great place to scout out examples of rare or unusual plant species, including hog peanut and Indian cucumber root. Or you can just have a pleasant hike. If you plan to do so, be sure for your own safety that you pick up a map at the Pent Road entrance and sign in. Special programs and guided walks are held on some weekends, with attendance by reservation only. The park is open from dawn to dusk daily. There are no restrooms, and dogs and bicycles are not allowed.

Wilton

When **J. Alden Weir** saw his first impressionist painting in a Paris gallery, it gave him a headache, but by 1881 the American artist was honing his own distinctively impressionistic style. Today, his Wilton home, **Weir Farm** (735 Nod Hill Rd.; 203-834-1896; nps.gov/wefa/index.htm), is a National Historic Site. Weir designed his farm as he would a painting, mixing and matching visual elements until everything was perfect.

The farm, which he called "the Land of Nod," provided inspiration for his own paintings of late nineteenth-century family life and for the works of fellow artists **Childe Hassam**, John Twachtman, and John Singer Sargent. The self-guided *Painting Sites Trail* is a living landscape. It's well marked to highlight a series of views from Weir's paintings, including Weir Pond, which he built with the prize money from his 1895 painting *The Truants*. Admission is free, as are ranger-led tours. The grounds are open year-round dawn to dusk; the visitor center is open May through Oct, Wed through Sat, 10 a.m. to 4 p.m.; Dec through Mar, Sat and Sun, 10 a.m. to 4 p.m. Tours of the house are offered May to Oct, Wed through Sun, 11 a.m., 1, 2, and 3 p.m. Limited to twelve people, first come, first served.

Ridgefield

Nearby *Ridgefield* was the site of a minor 1777 skirmish known as (what else?) the **Battle of Ridgefield**, in which Benedict Arnold led the colonists against General William Tryon's British. The historic 1733 **Keeler Tavern** still carries a legacy of the battle in the form of a British cannonball embedded in the wall. Now the *Keeler Tavern Museum* (132 Main St.; 203-438-5485; keelertavernmuseum.org), the inn has been restored and furnished with authentic eighteenth-century furniture, appointments, and artifacts. There's also a pretty cool gift shop. Guides in colonial dress conduct 45-minute tours of the tavern Feb through Dec. Open Wed, Sat, and Sun, 1 to 4 p.m. (last tour is at 3:30 p.m.). The museum and gift shop close for the month of January. Admission. There is a garden that bursts with color in the spring, summer, and fall, and is free and open to visitors from dawn to dusk.

A short distance down Main Street is the *Aldrich Contemporary Art Museum* (258 Main St.; 203-438-4519; aldrichart.org), the only large museum in our state dedicated to contemporary art. Before its 2004 reopening, the museum underwent a huge renovation. Formerly housed in a historic building known as "Old Hundred" (due to its 100-year history in the town), the museum received a facelift that charged architect Mark Hay with "the challenge of expanding a contemporary art museum located in a historic district with colonial roots." He did a fine job. This private facility is definitely contemporary and includes a screening room, performance area, education center, project space with twenty-two-foot-high ceilings, and more. This close to New York, it tends to get works from the best of America's young artists. Often the artists represented are relative unknowns whose first important exposure comes at the Aldrich.

You can tour the museum and its grounds on your own if you wish, but there are also guided tours for a per-person fee or a curator-led tour for about double the price per person. These guides know their stuff and can make your visit a true experience. You can also purchase some cool add-ons to your tours and make a day of it. For example, you can have a farm-to-museum packed lunch brought to you, or have the museum lay out a traditional tea service for you and your guests with sandwiches and pastries to boot, or enjoy a glass of champagne and a cheese plate before or after your late afternoon tour.

Behind the museum is a broad green lawn dotted with several dozen pieces of modern sculpture. Most are massive, towering over the art aficionados in their midst. All are imbued with a special strangeness that comes partly from their staid colonial surroundings. Scattered about this sculpture garden are wrought-iron tables and chairs where visitors can sit and relax.

The Aldrich is open Wed through Mon, noon to 5 p.m. The garden is always open, even when the museum is closed. Admission, but military families, teachers, and children twelve and under are admitted free. There is also free admission on the third Saturday of each month.

The Aldridge Museum orders its farm-to-museum lunch and its cheeses from *No. 109 Cheese & Wine* (109 Danbury Rd.; 203-438-5757; 109cheeseandwine. com), where the husband and wife owners Monica and Todd Brown combine the best of all worlds—cheese and fresh, gourmet snacks in one of their small shops and wine and craft beer in the other. The Browns carefully choose their stock so that they easily pair with each other and they often have guest pourers come in and share their wares. The two work well together, with Monica offering private pairing classes and tastings and Todd spearheading the picnic basket program, offering packaged meals much as he does for the Aldrich. Open Tues through Thurs, 10 a.m. to 6 p.m.; Fri and Sat, 9 a.m. to 6 p.m.; Sun, 10 a.m. to 4 p.m. They also own a shop in Kent (14 N. Main St.; 860-592-0366).

Redding

When Washington's Northern Army went into winter quarters at the end of November 1778, it was dispersed in an arc from New Jersey to Connecticut to ring the British garrison in New York. Three of the army's brigades had their winter encampment at *Redding*, where they were strategically positioned to defend the region from British raiders. Their commander was Major General Israel ("Old Put") Putnam, a larger-than-life hero, who is often called

ANNUAL EVENTS IN GATEWAY TO NEW ENGLAND

MAY

Dogwood Festival
Greenfield Hill Congregational Church
1045 Old Academy Rd., Fairfield
(203) 259-5596
greenfieldhillchurch.com

JUNE

International Festival of Arts and Ideas
New Haven
(888) ARTIDEA (278-4332)
artidea.org

AUGUST

Milford Oyster Festival
downtown Milford
milfordoysterfestival.org

New Haven Open at Yale
Connecticut Tennis Center at Yale
New Haven
(855) 464-8366
newhavenopen.com

SoNo Arts Celebration
Washington and S. Main St., Norwalk
sonoartsfest.com
(203) 866-7916

Good Vibes Only Festival
McLevy Green
102 Bank St., Bridgeport
infobridgeport.com/event/
good-vibes-only-festival-on-mclevy-green

SEPTEMBER

New England Chowdafest
17 Cedar Crest Pl., Norwalk
(203) 216-8452
chowdafest.org

Fall Festival and Hawk Watch
Audubon Center
613 Riversville Rd., Greenwich
(203) 869-5272
greenwich.audubon.org

Connecticut Folk Festival and Green Expo
Edgerton Park
75 Cliff St., New Haven
ctfolk.com

Greenwich Wine + Food Festival
100 Arch St., Greenwich
serendipitysocial.com/
greenwich-wine-food

Norwalk Oyster Festival
42 Seaview Ave., Norwalk
seaport.org/Oyster-Festival
(203) 838-9444

North Haven Fair
290 Washington Ave., North Haven
(203) 239-3700
northhaven-fair.com

Orange Country Fair
525 Orange Center Rd., Orange
(203) 430-6044
orangectfair.com

West Haven Apple Fest
West Haven Green
1 Church St., West Haven
westhavenapplefest.com

Wolcott Country Fair
245 Wolcott Rd., Wolcott
(203) 879-5466
wolcottfair.com

OCTOBER

Pumpkins on the Pier
Walnut Beach
113 Bdwy., Milford
boysandgirlsclubofmilford.com/
pumpkinsonthepier

Scare Fair
Weston Historical Society
104 Weston Rd., Weston
westonhistoricalsociety.org

DECEMBER

Brookfield Craft Center Holiday Exhibition
and Sale
Rte 25, Brookfield
(203) 775-4526
brookfieldcraft.org/holidays

Fantasy of Lights
Lighthouse Point Park,
2 Lighthouse Rd., New Haven
(203) 777-2000
goodwillsne.org

Connecticut's Paul Bunyan. There is a memorial to Old Put on Hartford's Bushnell Park and more about the man in that section of the book.

That winter was relatively mild, but the harvest had been poor, and supplies were scarce. The men, many of whom had been through the hell of Valley Forge the previous year, began to mutter about a similar privation winter in Connecticut. Then in December the state experienced one of the worst winter storms in New England history. Two days after it ended, the men of one brigade mutinied and prepared to march on the colonial assembly in Hartford to demand overdue supplies and wages. Putnam was able to break up the protest only with the greatest of difficulty. Thus began the winter encampment at Redding that came to be known as Connecticut's Valley Forge.

The original encampment is now the site of **Putnam Memorial State Park** (499 Black Rock Tpke.; 203-938-2357; putnampark.org), Connecticut's oldest state park, at the junction of Routes 58 and 107 in Redding. These days the twelve-man huts are just piles of stone where their chimneys stood, and the old magazine is only a stone-lined pit. The officers' barracks have been rebuilt, though, and there is a museum containing exhibits dealing with the Redding encampment. There's also a great statue by the front gate showing Old Put riding his horse down a flight of stairs to escape capture during a British raid in February 1779. Open daily, 8 a.m. to sunset.

Bethel

The **Bethel Cinema** (269 Greenwood Ave.; 203-778-2100; bethelcinema.com) screens art and independent films, attracting a large audience wanting more than the latest blockbuster sequel. The two-screen theater is known for showing films long before the rest of the world hops on the bandwagon. Generally two films are shown during a run, and mainstream movies are shown as well. The matinees are kind to tight budgets, and local restaurants offer discount deals. The theater publishes a newsletter with information about upcoming features and film-related lectures.

Readers of a certain age might have spent their teen years hanging out at drive-in restaurants where the uniformed carhops roller-skated out to your car and delivered the food on steel trays that clipped to the window (others may have heard stories from parents and grandparents). At the **Sycamore** (282 Greenwood Ave.; 203-748-2716; sycamoredrivein.com), those readers can relive those memories (or introduce them to younger generations). In continuous operation since 1948, the Sycamore is an old-fashioned drive-in restaurant that has been become a Bethel landmark. Carhop service is available spring, summer, and fall. Just pull in and flash your lights. It's not all atmosphere, either. The burgers are juicy and tasty. The brewed-there root beer (the recipe for which is a deep, dark secret) can taste sweet and full or sparkly and dry, depending on its age. The malts are made with real malt powder. The Sycamore hosts Cruise Nights throughout the summer, but you might see a vintage car pull in at any time (with Sunday often having a regular traffic in these vehicles). Open Mon through Thurs, 6:30 a.m. to 8:30 p.m.; Fri, 6:30 a.m. to 9 p.m.; Sat, 7 a.m. to 9 p.m.; Sun, 7 a.m. to 7:30 p.m.

Danbury

There was a time when a good hat was an essential wardrobe item, and you weren't really dressed without a good topper. In those days, Connecticut was hatmaker to America, and **Danbury** was the center of the hatmaking business. Today the glory days of hatmaking are remembered along with other Danbury history in the **Danbury Museum and Historical Society** (43 Main St.; 203-743-5200; danburymuseum.org). There are actually several buildings at this address, and exhibits are scattered among them. The oldest building, the Rider House, was saved from demolition in 1941, thanks to the efforts of Danbury's citizens, and is now part of the museum. Exhibits deal with early American life, the Revolutionary War, and the history of Danbury. Another highlight is the recording studio of opera singer Marian Anderson, who was a Danbury native and the first African American to perform at the Metropolitan Opera in New York. One year before she and her husband purchased this house in Danbury in 1940, Anderson performed her famous concert on the steps of the Lincoln Memorial after being denied permission to sing at Constitution Hall. An astounding 75,000 people watched. The studio is a stop on the Connecticut Freedom Trail and houses many artifacts from her career and life. Museum hours are Tues through Sat, 10 a.m. to 4 p.m. (summer and spring); Fri and Sat, 10 a.m. to 4 p.m. (fall and winter). Tours are offered from 10 a.m. to 3 p.m. on days they are open.

Danbury is also home to the natural beauty that is **Tarrywile Park** (70 Southern Blvd.; 203-744-3130; danbury-ct.gov). This 722-acre town-owned park offers twenty-one miles of hiking trails through meadows and forest, along streams and ponds, up steep climbs among granite outcroppings. There are picnic areas, too, for those less inclined to hike (or for refueling after). Don't be surprised if you see a bunch of kids running in groups, several high schools in the area use the park for cross-country meets. The park is open from dawn until dusk.

Within the Tarrywile Park are two beautiful structures, one in its heyday, the *Tarrywile Mansion*, and one that has seen better days, Hearthstone Castle. Both are listed on the National Register for Historic Preservation, but only the mansion is in current use. Surrounded by beautiful gardens, an orchard, and manicured lawns, the mansion is a popular spot for weddings and other social events. There's even a children's garden on the front lawn for the littles to explore. In 1910, Charles Darling Parks bought Tarrywile Mansion from Dr. William C. Wiles and had a modern (for the time) dairy operation there. Mr. Parks was a very successful businessman as president of C.D. Parks Company and held many interests in Danbury.

Hearthstone Castle (tarrywile.com/hearthstone-castle) is currently fighting for its life as once again people are working wonders to save a piece of our state's history. Studies are being done on how the structure, if saved, could be best utilized. Grants have been secured in the hopes of going forward with a restoration.

Originally designed as a summer estate for Danbury native Elias Starr Sanford and his wife Emma, the magnificent three-story, sixteen-room mansion was designed by Ernest G.W. Dietrich; it took four years to complete, from the fall of 1895 until the summer of 1899. And in all its beauty, it reportedly never won the heart of Mrs. Sanford. The family owned it for only five years before selling it to Victor Buck, who later sold it to Charles Darling Parks who owned the neighboring Tarrywile Mansion. Parks wanted the castle as a wedding gift for his oldest daughter, Irene Parks, who had just married Louis Chadwick Rathmell. Irene lived at Hearthstone until her death in 1982, at which time the property went to Richard and Constance Jennings, who lived there until the spring of 1987. In 1987, the entire Tarrywile Estate was purchased by the town and the two buildings placed on the register. Today, the castle lies in ruins behind fences to keep trespassers out. It has escaped the wrecking ball on numerous occasions and only the future can tell what will happen.

Of course, ghostly tales will be associated with such a sight. It truly is something to see the skeleton of such grandeur being reclaimed by nature. There are myriad pictures of the ruins online and in some you can definitely see mists, whether they be from shadows or otherworldly. People have reported hearing noises, seeing shadowy figures in the castle and surrounding woods, a ghost dog and unafraid deer have also been reported. But, alas, who really knows. Visitors are not allowed past the fences for any reason. If you want to get involved, see how you can contribute the campaign to save this wonderful piece of history.

Adults commuting into Manhattan may think of trains as something to be endured, but some of us will always see trains as romantic and vaguely magical. At the **Danbury Railway Museum** (120 White St.; 203-778-8337; danburyrailwaymuseum.org), housed in a restored 1903 train station and adjoining a six-acre rail yard at Danbury's Union Station, a group of dedicated volunteers is doing its part to keep that magic alive. They've transformed the old station into a museum of train paraphernalia and restored trains.

The museum holds some neat events, such as Easter, Christmas, and Halloween trips, and rides in the rail yard, including the opportunity to experience the turntable. Near the front of the museum is a small but interesting gift shop. If Union Station looks familiar, it should. Alfred Hitchcock used it in *Strangers on a Train* as the setting for his own cameo appearance. Open June to Aug, Mon through Fri, 10 a.m. to 4 p.m.; Sat, 10 a.m. to 5 p.m.; Sun, noon to 5 p.m.; Sept to May, Wed through Sat, 10 a.m. to 4 p.m.; Sun, noon to 4 p.m. Admission.

castletrivia

The castle is so named possibly because of the eight stone fireplaces it contains.

All the rock used to build the castle was quarried on site.

All the interior woodwork was imported from Italy.

The wrought iron chandeliers, lamps, and wall sconces were made by Cephas B. Rogers Company in Danbury.

There was reportedly a secret passage from the castle's kitchen to its study.

danburytrivia

Zadoc Benedict founded the nation's first hat factory in Danbury in 1780. It produced a dizzying three hats a day! By the mid-1800s, the Hat City led the world in hat production, and by 1949 more than 66 percent of the nation's hats carried a "made in Connecticut" label. From 1949 to 1977, Connecticut honored the hat industry with Hat Day, and both houses of Connecticut's legislature would be filled with examples of the hatmaker's art, from tough-guy fedoras to Miss Porter's–perfect pillboxes.

Brookfield

Looking for a one-of-a-kind gift for that special someone? Head to the **Brookfield Craft Center** (286 Whisconier Rd.; 203-775-4526; brookfieldcraft.org) north of

Danbury on Route 25, which houses a school of contemporary arts and crafts within six colonial buildings (including a 1780 gristmill) set on the banks of Still River. The associated arts-and-crafts gallery and retail shop offers unique hand-crafted items from the artists themselves. From woodcrafts to fused glass to jewelry to pottery and cloth, you're sure to find something you just have to have, and that no one else will! Open Tues through Fri, noon to 5 p.m.; Sat, 11 a.m. to 5 p.m.; Sun, noon to 4 p.m. Closed major holidays.

You don't have to travel to Napa for amazing wine. Brookfield's **DiGrazia Vineyards** (131 Tower Rd.; 203-775-1616; digraziavineyards.com) delivers on the goods. Family-owned and -operated since 1978, DiGrazia offers a wide variety of flavors. Some of their offerings include pomegranate and Connecticut-grown pear wines, Yankee Frost, Wild Blue Too, and Paragran. Tastings of six wines of your choice are available. Make your selection and enjoy it with your picnic lunch at their outdoor seating area (don't worry, there's room inside, too, if you'd rather). Open Thurs through Mon, 11 a.m. to 5 p.m.

Newtown

East of Danbury is **Newtown,** where the **Second Company of the Governor's Horse Guards** (4 Wildlife Dr.; 203-426-9046; thehorseguard.org) practice, usually in full uniform. A horse guard practice is something no horse- or animal-loving kid can resist. Chartered in 1808, the Second Company of the Governor's Horse Guards was used mainly to escort the governor and distinguished visitors on ceremonial occasions. It is one of the oldest cavalry units in continuous service in the country. Today, the troop is an all-volunteer cavalry militia designated by the governor to serve the people of southwestern Connecticut. The troop's horses, which are donated, are a variety of breeds. Weekly practice drills take place Nov to Apr, Sun at 10 a.m., and Apr to Nov, Thurs at 7 p.m. You can also see them at their July horse show and Fall Open House. Check their website for details and call or e-mail ahead and let them know you're coming if you want to watch.

Monroe

Connecticut's most famous ghost, the "**White Lady**," is said to haunt the **Stepney Cemetery** (Pepper Street) in Monroe and the **Union Cemetery** (Sport Hill Road) down the road in nearby Easton. Visitors to the cemeteries report that the apparition wears a white nightgown with a bonnet. Others say they've seen not only the White Lady but also shadowy specters who try to grab her. The late Ed Warren of Monroe, a legendary ghostbuster who, incidentally, is also buried in Stepney Cemetery, believed her name was Mrs. Knot, and her husband was murdered near Easton in the 1940s. Mrs. Knot is said to have met the same fate as her husband shortly after his unfortunate demise. As with any cemetery, visit with respect and only during its operating hours.

Southbury

Not so long ago, your chances of seeing eagles hunting and soaring in the wild were somewhere between slim and none. Today, thanks to the Endangered Species Act, the American eagle population is itself soaring, and we need to continue to protect them. One way we can do that is to draw awareness and education the public about these majestic birds. In winter, Connecticut bald eagles find the **Southbury** area much to their taste. In fact, it's such a popular place that their eagle buddies from as far away as Canada and Maine flock there, too. The **Shepaug Dam Bald Eagle Observation Area** (2150 River Rd.; 203-267-4666; shepaugeagles.info) is a wonderful place to watch for these majestic birds. Supported by First Light Power Resources, this observation area is staffed by knowledgeable guides to coach you in observing these beautiful birds—some of whom have a wingspan of seven feet—while they fish, hunt, and soar. To use a worn-out phrase, they take your breath away. Eagle observations are held mid-Dec through mid-Mar on Wed, Sat, and Sun, 9 a.m. to 1 p.m., although the season can vary. Please check the website for current conditions. It also has a page with essential tips for planning your visit and a place to make the required online reservations.

By the way, bald eagles aren't really bald. In truth, they have a glorious head of white feathers. The bald part comes from the word *piebald*, which means "white."

When you have your fill of the eagles (is that even possible?), you'll want to bring your camera with you to **Southford Falls** (175 Quaker Farms Rd.; 203-264-5169), where you'll find the lovely cascade of Eight Mile Brook as it rushes to meet the Housatonic River. The park also includes the remains of the Diamond Match factory, which was destroyed by fire in 1923. The ruins include an old steam engine foundation, a grinding stone, and some of the sluice pipe. The little covered bridge, built by carpenter Ed Palmer with the help of author/artist **Eric Sloane**, is based on an eighteenth-century arch design. There are picnic tables by the bridge, just the place for a romantic spring picnic, or you can perch on a rock by the falls and spend some time just listening to the water or reading. The park also includes

southbury trivia

Kettletown State Park in Southbury gets its name from the story that settlers paid the Native Americans, who originally lived on the spot, one brass kettle for the land.

a lookout tower, great for viewing fall foliage. Southford Falls State Park is located just south of Southbury on Route 188, south of I-84.

Oxford

Rich Farm Ice Cream Shop (691 Oxford Rd.; 203-881-1040; richfarmicecream. com) on Route 67 has been serving up delicious, creamy concoctions made with milk from Dave and Dawn Rich's own herd of Holsteins since 1994, but the farm has been in Dave's family for five generations. In summer, the place is packed, and you might wait in line a good fifteen to twenty minutes. You won't be bored because this is a real farm with real farm looks and real farm smells. At haying time during the summer, just a whiff of the fresh-cut hay distills summer. As for the ice cream, you can choose from among twenty-five everyday flavors with additional seasonal favorites, such as pumpkin, and kid flavors, such as Cookie Monster. Or keep things simple and stick with a good old-fashioned chocolate cone. The shop also makes ice cream cakes and seasonal treats, such as ice cream Yule logs. They also now serve lunch Mon through Fri. Bring cash—they don't accept plastic—and please leave Fido in the car so he doesn't scare the cows. Open daily Apr through Oct, 11:30 a.m. to 9 p.m.

Places to Stay in Gateway to New England

Places to Eat in Gateway to New England

GREENWICH

Homestead Inn
420 Field Point Rd.
(203) 869-7500
homesteadinn.com
Very expensive
Four-star luxury hotel in ritzy Greenwich offering eighteen rooms and suites with amazing furniture

DANBURY

Goulash Place
42 Highland Ave.
(203) 744-1971
Moderate
Located in a mostly residential neighborhood, Hungarian food at its best

MILFORD

Rainbow Gardens Restaurant and Bar
117 N. Broad St.
(203) 878-2500
rainbowgardens.org
Moderate to expensive
New American cuisine served in a lovingly restored Victorian on the Milford Green

NEW HAVEN

Claire's Corner Copia
1000 Chapel St.
(203) 562-3888
clairescornercopia.com
Moderate
Vegetarian, organic, sustainable, kosher, and gluten-free

Marjolaine Pastry Shop
961 State St.
(203) 789-8589
marjolainepastry.com
Inexpensive
Great place to stop to
satisfy your sweet tooth

NEWTOWN

King's Breakfast & Lunch
271 S. Main St.
(203) 426-6881
Inexpensive
This is your quintessential
food joint with lots of
options and good food

STAMFORD

Long Ridge Tavern
2635 Long Ridge Rd.
(203) 329-7818
longridgetavern.com
Moderate to expensive
New American cuisine
served in a historic tavern

Coast & Country

Connecticut has 253 miles of shoreline, all of it bordering the Long Island Sound. This coastline was settled shortly after the first towns were built in the Connecticut River Valley. Today the southwestern portion of the state's coastal plain has been largely urbanized, while much of the eastern portion has been given over to tourism. It is the less densely populated portion of this coastline (between New Haven and Rhode Island) that most people envision as the Connecticut shore. Home to clam shacks and posh inns, popular sandy beaches and lonely old lighthouses, modern submarines and ancient whalers, riverboats and coastal mail packets, the Connecticut shore reflects the romance of the sea like few other places on Earth.

Even if you're not a big fan of the sea, this part of Connecticut has much to offer. The inland portion of the coastal plain and the lower reaches of the Thames and Connecticut Rivers, in fact all of New London and Middlesex Counties and the easternmost part of New Haven County, are all part of what we call "the Shoreline." Here you'll find attractions as disparate as the glorious wedding-cake architecture of the Goodspeed Opera House and the Gothic extravagance of Gillette Castle, or the famous hunt breakfasts at the Griswold Inn and the renowned hot dogs at Higgies in Higganum.

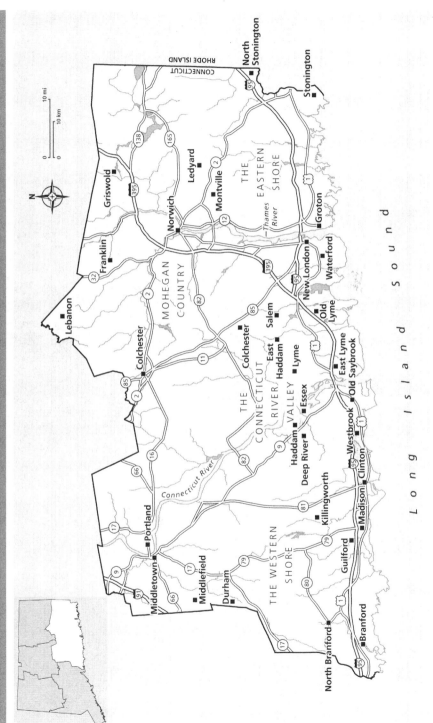

The Western Shore

Branford

According to legend, **Captain William Kidd** was a black-hearted pirate and bloody-handed murderer who savagely preyed upon America's eastern coast. Well, not exactly. As a matter of public record, the real Captain Kidd was a Scottish-born merchant transplanted to America who was commissioned in 1695 to hunt down the pirate Thomas Tew (of Newport) in the Indian Ocean. While pursuing Tew, Kidd stretched the limits of his commission, which embarrassed his prominent British backers (including the Crown). When he returned home, Kidd was seized and, after a rigged trial in which evidence of his innocence was suppressed, convicted of murder and piracy and hanged in 1701.

Whether your view of Captain Kidd leans toward the mythical or the historical, it's hard to resist the tantalizing legends of pirate gold and buried treasure. Many of these tales are linked to Connecticut's **Thimble Islands**, just off the coast of **Branford's Stony Creek**, and local residents have long nurtured the Kidd mythology.

The Thimble Islands were discovered in 1614 by Adrien Block, but were known to Native Americans before that as "the beautiful sea rocks," or *Kuttomquosh*. That's pretty much what people thought of the islands, too, that they were not much more than pretty rocks from which to harvest seaweed, fish, or oysters. In fact, not knowing quite what to do with them in the late eighteenth century, the town of Branford deeded them to residents who could prove they were descendants of the original town settlers. So, the islands hung around being pretty rocks for a few decades before a man by the name of William Bryan decided to build a hotel on his island. And what legend helped sell those rooms and attract tourists? You got it, Captain Kidd. Things sort of took on a life of their own and the islands became a hot tourist destination.

After the Civil War, summer homes, private residences, and more hotels were built on the islands. Boating companies adjusted their routes to include stops on the islands, and life was good until September 21, 1938, when the

Hurricane of '38 hit the area without warning. The timing of the storm was such that Long Island Sound saw waves as high as forty feet. The Thimble Islands were severely damaged, entire houses swept out to sea, seven residents lost their lives. Followed closely by the Great Depression, the storm was the beginning of permanent change for the archipelago. They would never be the same bustling tourist attraction they were.

Today, twenty-three of the 365 "islands" (some are merely rocks jutting out of the water) are inhabited, only six have electricity. Their rich history has been preserved, however, and stories abound. Including some of the famous residents who have called them home, **P. T. Barnum**, William Taft, Gary Trudeau and his wife Jane Pauley, and, lately, a woman by the name of Christine Svenningsen who now owns numerous islands. Stony Creek residents are keeping a close eye on Mrs. Svenningsen as she buys up and apparently lovingly restores property on the islands. No one is quite sure what her plans are, but as the purchases add up, residents are getting nervous. All eyes will surely be on the real estate pages.

For a closer look at the islands, hop aboard a Thimble Island Cruise. Take your pick of several different-sized boats run by the three companies who cooperatively run the tours. There's the forty-foot *Volsunga IV*, captained by Anna Milne (4 Indian Point Rd.; 203-481-3345; thimbleislands.com). Captain Milne just recently earned her captain's license, but she's no stranger to the seas; salt water runs in her veins. Anna took over captain duties from her dad, the well-known Captain Bob Milne after he suffered life-changing injuries in a motorcycle accident in 2015. Anna proceeded to earn her captain's license, raise money to purchase the business, and learn what she needed to know. She wasn't alone, though. Shortly after her father's accident, Captain Mike Infantino called Anna and told her that she didn't need to worry; he and his employees would keep the *Volsunga IV* up and running while the family figured out what they were going to do. And they did. Throughout that entire summer, Captain Mike, his sons, and fellow captains David Atkinson, Bob Lilquist, and Bill Smith along with volunteers all pitched in and kept the Thimble Island Cruises and *Volsunga IV* operating. They regularly moved employees from their own boats to Anna's in order to keep things running smoothly. That's just how the Branford and Stony Creek folks roll.

Today you'll find Anna confidently captaining her boat, giving tours and a running commentary to make her father proud. Forty-five minute tours are offered Tues through Sun (closed Mon) and generally leave the dock on the hour. You'll need cash or a check to purchase your tickets though; no plastic is accepted. They generally operate early May through Oct, weather permitting, but check the website for the latest days and times.

Captain Mike Infantino runs his own business with the forty-four-foot *Sea Mist* (30 Indian Point Road; 203-488-8905; thimbleislandcruise.com) along with his sons Justin and Bryan. They offer a variety of tours showcasing the region's geography and wildlife, with lively stories about the area in which they grew up. Their Thimble Island tours run from May through Oct (weather permitting). Cash or check; they don't accept credit cards, either.

Your third option for cruising the islands is with Captain Dave Kusterer on his twenty-six-foot boat *The Islander*. Captain Dave's family has owned a home on Kidd Island since 1903, so he knows what he's talking about. He claims on his website that his smaller vessel can reach places the larger boats cannot. Carrying only fourteen passengers at a time, *The Islander* is a more intimate option that offers 45-minute tours from mid-June to mid-Sept.

These are the three main boating companies who operate cruises of the Thimble Island. You really can't go wrong with any of them, the rates are competitive, within a dollar or two of each other, and they all know their stuff. One note: All the islands are privately held. Unless you're an invited guest, don't plan on getting off the boat to explore; uninvited guests are understandably not welcome.

thimbleislandstrivia

While some of the Thimble Islands are admittedly not more than a rock occasionally peaking above the water's surface, the name comes not from their small size, but from a type of wild blackberry—thimbleberries—that once grew there.

Whichever cruise you choose, be sure to ask about the wealthy widow Svenningsen and see what she's been up to, although you may or may not receive an answer.

The Thimble Islands are not Stony Creek's only claim to fame. The **Stony Creek Quarry** (99 Quarry Rd; 203-488-4283; stonycreekquarry.com) has also made its mark in American history. You could say it made several. Most notably in New York City where the quarry's pink granite can be found in the pedestal of the Statue of Liberty (not the base upon which she stands, but the granite holding the pedestal itself), in parts of Grand Central Station, Jacob Javitts Federal Building Plaza, and the Brooklyn Bridge, as well as in numerous city parks and walkways. First quarried in 1858, Stony Creek granite continues to be used throughout the US. Here in the state, you can find its beautiful pink color in the lobby of Naugatuck Valley Community College, in New Haven as the rock on which Yale Peabody Museum's *torosaurus latus* dinosaur sits, in the steps of Woolsey Hall, in the jetties in many of our state's beaches, and, of course, at Stony Creek's Willoughby Wallace Memorial Library (more on that below).

If you'd like to appreciate the granite in its natural state and learn more about the art of cutting it, you can take a hike through the 450-plus-acre **Stony Creek Quarry Preserve** (Quarry Road; scrcog.org), which will take you to a spot high on the yellow trail where you can see the working quarry from afar and will also take you on trails past the abandoned part of the quarry. There are numerous interconnecting trails, and we encourage you to explore them all. Thanks to the efforts of the Branford Land Trust, these lands are preserved and saved for our enjoyment when some of them could have very well become a garbage dump. You can hike **The Branford Trail** and look for the **Selectman's Stones**, explore the more than one hundred acres of the **Van Wie Preserve**, which was made possible through donations from the Van Wie family and is maintained by the Trust, and the smaller **Kelley Preserve**, a ten-acre parcel of land purchased through a gift from Brooks M. Kelley in memory of his son Brooks R. Kelley who loved to spend time on these trails. There are numerous parking options for these trails and detailed directions are given on the website. Properties are open during daylight hours; please be respectful, follow the rules, stay on the trails, and leave no trace.

Another place to see granite in use is the **Willoughby Wallace Memorial Library** (146 Thimble Island Rd.; 203-488-8702; wwml.org), a library that almost wasn't. You see, when Stony Creek resident **Willoughby Adelbert Wallace** died in the autumn of 1946, he left much of his life's treasures to the town of Branford with instructions to build a free public library in Stony Creek. Probably knowing how slow things can sometimes move, he gave the town a deadline of ten years in which to act on his bequest. Should they not take action during that time, then the money would be appropriated to the Congregational Church of Christ to be used as it wished. Old Willoughby knew whereof he spoke, apparently, because it did indeed take the town a decade to make a decision regarding the library, and it was only a few months before the deadline that a town meeting was held in which the issue was heatedly debated. By now, the trust had grown substantially and everyone had ideas of how it should be best spent. Cooler heads prevailed and it was decided to accept Mr. Wallace's money and build the library. Local architect David Orr agreed to design the building for free and the Castellucci Brothers of Rhode Island, owners of the quarry in town at the time, donated all the granite used in the construction. So should you have the opportunity to drop by Willoughby's library, send up a silent thank you to the generous miser who made it possible. Open Mon through Thurs, 10 a.m. to 8 p.m.; Fri and Sat, 10 a.m. to 5 p.m. (until 2 p.m. on Sat during July and Aug); and Sun (Nov through May) 1 to 4 p.m.

A short walk up Thimble Island Road will take you to the Stony Creek Puppet House Theater now known as **The Legacy Theater** (128 Thimble

Island Rd; 203-208-5504; legacytheatrect.org). The Legacy Theater Company purchased the 1903 Stony Creek Theater in 2012 with big plans to restore the building and bring theater back to the area. They certainly had their work cut out for them, however. In the early days, the glamorous theater was home to a silent movie theater, Orson Welles and his Mercury Players, a repertory house, and a summer stock house. It then saw life as a World War II parachute factory, then a puppet house that was home to a world-renowned marionette collection. When the puppet house went out of business, however, the building fell into disrepair and was actually slated for demolition in 2008. It was in sad shape with numerous safety concerns. There didn't seem to be much hope, until Legacy Theater founder Keely Knudsen stepped up, but even then neighbors were skeptical. Knudsen had big hopes for a bright future at a newly refurbished and updated theater, but the reality was there were safety codes to be considered, zoning regulations to be navigated, and modern upgrades to be added. And add up they did, well over the $1 million mark. Legacy is currently in full fundraising mode and Knudsen seems tireless as her team puts on productions across the state even as they continue to raise money for their own theater through private and corporate donations. One can feel her love for this theater and it's difficult to not get caught up in her enthusiasm for her vision to "uplift and inspired the community" with "professional plays, musicals, children's shows, cabarets, and visiting Broadway performances and workshops." Kudos to you, Keely. Be sure to keep your eye on the website for all the latest updates.

stonycreektrivia

People from Stony Creek like to call themselves "Creekers," probably to distinguish themselves from the "Yorkers" who swarm the place in summer. We also have it on good authority that residents of the Indian Neck section of Branford are referred to as "Neckers." We're seeing a trend here.

Continuing on Thimble Island Road for a half mile you'll come to **Stony Creek Museum** (84 Thimble Island Rd.; 203-488-4014; stonycreekmuseum.org). Inside, you'll find exhibits on the marionette collection from the former and aforementioned Stony Creek Puppet House Theater, the town's long history with the quarry and how it shaped its community; an old apothecary store complete with original drugs; and, of course, information on the Stony Creek Fife and Drum Corps, and more. The museum is only open Fri through Sun, 1 to 4 p.m., but you can call ahead and make an appointment to visit at any time.

If it *is* later in the day, why not head to one of the local breweries? **Stony Creek Brewery** (5 Indian Neck Ave., 203-433-4545; stonycreekbeer.com) is located on the water and serves beers that follow their "aggressively laid-back" attitude. They offer a beautiful and spacious indoor/outdoor tap-room with views of their canning and bottling process, there's dock access, and a game pit. What's not to love? Their beers include The Crankies (Cranky, Big Cranky, and Little Cranky IPAs); lagers such as the Black Water Pils and the amber Dock Time; seasonals such as Sun Juice, a Belgian summer ale, Crum, an apple cinnamon oatmeal amber ale, and Snow Hole, a Double red winter seasonal, and more. Their beer names are almost as good as the beers themselves. Open Mon through Thurs, noon to 9 p.m.; Fri and Sat, 11 a.m. to 10 p.m.; Sun, 11 a.m. to 8 p.m.

Thimble Island Brewing Company (16 Business Park Dr; 203-208-2827; thimbleislandbrewery.com) can be a bit tricky to find, but don't give up. Their beers are worth the hunt. Founded in 2010 by two men who had no formal experience in brewing but had a vision, the brewery has now grown into the largest self-distributing micro-brewery in the state. Their first beer launched in the summer of 2012; today they offer a variety, including a Black & Tan seasonal; a Windjammer Wheat seasonal; Ruby, a blonde ale spiked with grapefruit; a citrus and tropical Session Forty Five IPA; a limited edition Ghost Island Double IPA, a nod to the Thimble Islands; and their India Pal and American Ales, both refreshing and delicious. Open Mon through Wed, 3 to 8 p.m.; Thurs, noon to 8 p.m.; Fri, noon to 10 p.m.; Sat, 11 a.m. to 10 p.m.; Sun, noon to 7 p.m. Tours are offered Sat at noon, 2, and 4 p.m., and Sun at 1, 3, and 5 p.m.

The brewery holds different events throughout the year and often has food trucks on the weekends, although they also encourage you to bring your own food and enjoy it with their beverages. Growlers and crowlers are also available with souvenir bottles that you can bring back and have refilled.

DuVig Brewing Company (59 School Ground Rd.; 203-208-2213; duvig. com) opened in Branford in 2014 and was born out of a night when there was nothing else to be done but drink with the neighbors. That's exactly what the Dugas and Vigliotti families did when they were snowbound during the blizzard of 2013. They commiserated over their shared love of homebrewing and realized that their creations were just as good, in fact better, than anything they could find in the craft beer world. From this realization came DuVig Brewing. Today their offerings include such creations as the DuVig Hefeweizen; a Berliner Weisse; a Czech Pilsner; Moxie Ale; Stotch 60, a Scottish Ale; and an American Pale Ale, among others. The Tap Room is open Thurs and Fri, 3 to 8 p.m.; Sat, noon to 8 p.m.; Sun, 1 to 6 p.m.

With all that beer floating around in your system, you might find yourself a bit contemplative. Why are we here? What does it all mean? Who are we, really? There's no better place in the area to contemplate than at the *James Blackstone Memorial Library* (758 Main St.; 203-488-1441) in downtown Branford;

branfordtrivia

The Connecticut Hospice was the first of its kind in the US. Established in 1874 in Branford, the company continues to this day offering palliative care to patients and support for their families.

breathtaking in design and decor, it's been lovingly restored, reflecting the justifiable pride town residents take in this unique building.

The Blackstone Library was built in 1896 at a cost of $300,000. The centerpiece is the octagonal rotunda, paved with a marble and mosaic floor. The fifty-foot dome is decorated with large murals that provide a pictorial history of bookmaking, from *Gathering the Papyrus* to *First Proof of the Gutenberg Bible*. The paintings are illuminated by an ornamental skylight that forms the eye of the dome. Medallion portraits of famous American authors, including Emerson, Hawthorne, Longfellow, Whittier, and Stowe, also adorn the room. The whole building is studded with elegant period detail, including wide marble staircases leading to the second floor and a large, inviting fireplace in the main reading room. Open year-round Mon through Thurs, 9 a.m. to 8 p.m.; Fri and Sat, 9 a.m. to 5 p.m.; Sun (Sept through mid-May), 1 to 4 p.m. Closed Sun May 27 through Sept 2.

North Branford

Northford is a neighborhood located in the town of North Branford. Its center, known as Northford Center, was listed on the Register of Historic Places. Yes, a whole village is on the list. Cool, right? And one of those reasons is the historic buildings that dot the area. The beautiful brownstone ***Northford Congregational Church*** (4 Old Post Rd.; 203-484-0795; northfordcongregational.church) is one of those buildings. Built in 1846, this church was gutted by a Christmas Eve fire in 1906, but was rebuilt and rededicated three years later. You can learn more about this building and others by visiting ***Totoket Historical Society*** (1740 Foxon Rd.; 203-980-9828; totokethistoricalsociety.org), which maintains several properties in the area and works to preserve the town's history. Open Mon through Fri, 9 a.m. to 5 p.m.; Sat by appointment.

Van Wilgen's Garden Center (51 Valley Rd.; 203-488-2110; vanwilgens. com) might seem like a large operation to those who don't know, but it's always been a family-run farm with deep ties to the community. It all started in 1920 when William C. Van Wilgen immigrated to the US from Holland. Settling in the coastal town of Branford, he farmed there for a few years. In 1936, he purchased a larger parcel of land in North Branford. William and his brother, Aart, worked together propagating plants and bushes. The rhododendron called "Wilgen's Ruby," is still available today. In 1960, William's son Cornelius joined the business which had now grown to include landscaping and tree work. Van Wilgen's Garden Center opened in 1977, offering landscaping services and still keeping the retail portion. In 2008, Ryan Van Wilgen, William's great-grandson, joined the business full time and he continues to run things the family way. The business now has two other locations, but hasn't forgotten its roots, always supporting local organizations with donations and sponsorships. Open daily, 9 a.m. to 6 p.m., they offer everything you need for a beautiful garden, including pink granite from Stony Creek Quarry in Branford.

Guilford

Guilford is a shoreline town steeped in history. Purchased from Native Americans in 1639, Guilford is packed with seventeenth-, eighteenth-, and nineteenth-century homes. You'll also find remnants of a strong Native American history reflected in the town's names and stories.

Route 77, otherwise known as Durham Road, travels from Durham all the way down to Guilford, where it turns into Church Street and takes you to the Guilford Green. While mostly residential there are a few restaurants and farm stands scattered along the route as it meanders through farm land and past Quonnipaug Lake (aka Guilford Lake).

A little more than three miles past the lake, you'll find *The Dudley Farm* (2351 Durham Rd.; 203-457-0770; dudleyfarm.com). Built by Erastus Dudley in 1844, the farm's future was uncertain in 1991 with the passing of the farm's last owner, David Dudley. But concerned citizens took action, working together with the North Guilford Congregational Church and the Guilford Probate Court, they helped the North Guilford Volunteer Fire Company obtain ownership of the property. From this collaboration came the **Dudley Foundation**, a not-for-profit organization that now oversees and maintains the *Dudley Farm Museum*. Visitors are able to explore the farm house, barns, and grounds which have been restored to their nineteenth-century charm. Even the resident farm animals are representative of those that would have lived on a farm in that century.

The Dudley Foundation hopes to foster the idea of the nineteenth-century way of life when farmers sold their produce at market and the community came together to catch up with each other and what was going on in the world. In that vein, they offer an almost year-round Farmers Market, giving local artisans and farmers the chance to showcase and sell their products. They want people to return often, to stop and visit with each other, to enjoy the farm and gardens, to slow down and enjoy the life right in front of them. Not much to argue about there. Held on the first Sat of the month, Feb through Apr, 9 a.m. to 12:30 p.m.;

every Sat starting in mid-May (weather permitting) and running through Oct (also 9 a.m. to 12:30 p.m.). You'll find organic baked items, naturally raised meats, honey, jams, jellies, salsa, dried fruits and herbs, and so much more. So stop by and sit a spell. We'll see you there.

There are also multiple opportunities to hike from Route 77, including access to two Guilford Land Trust properties: *Braemore Preserve* (ci.guilford. ct.us), a small part of the Northwoods Trail network managed by the land trust; and *Bluff Head Trails* (guilfordlandtrust.org), a pretty strenuous hike that can be made easier by leaving a car at either end of the trail. Check out their website for details on parking. *Bittner Park* (1390 Durham Rd.; 203-453-8068; guilfordparkrec.com), where there are 136 acres, ball fields, a playground, as well as hiking trails to explore, is also located off Route 77.

For more stops in Guilford, head down Route 77 to the *Guilford Green*, with its eclectic collection of boutiques, eateries, and historic properties. Surrounded by Boston, Park, Broad, and Whitfield Streets, the green is a fun place to spend an afternoon or even a day. You will most likely find street parking along the green, even if you have to park a little bit away from the main collection of stores. The Park Street side of the green is home to a bank, a church, town offices, and the Guilford Free Library, all fine to visit, but not as fun as Whitfield Street, where we suggest you start your trip at the *Marketplace at Guilford Food Center* (77 Whitfield St.; 203-453-4848; themarketplaceatgfc.com). Grab a cup of tea or coffee from Madison's Savvy Tea Gourmet, including Hibiscus Peach, Orange Sunset, Goji Green, Madagascar Black, Lavender Mint and more; many served hot or cold according to your desire. The Marketplace also offers a selection of hot or iced coffee from Branford's Willoughby's Coffee. Choose from mochas, cappuccinos, espressos, and lattes, among others. Many choices coincide with the season, so the menu varies. What the menu always offers, though, are fresh, locally sourced baked goods to go with those drinks. Choose from all-natural breakfast muffins, doughnuts, croissants, breads, scones, and so much more. You can choose to eat in or take your treats with you as you stroll the green. If it's lunch time, there are a variety of fresh-made soups and sandwiches from which to choose. Make it a picnic! Don't forget the smoothies and juices. The possibilities are endless, but there is no wrong choice. Open Mon through Thurs, 7 a.m. to 7 p.m.; Fri and Sat, 7 a.m. to 6 p.m.; Sun, 7 a.m. to 3 p.m.

Then head next door to *The Village Chocolatier* (79 Whitfield St; 203-453-5226; thevillagechocolatier.com) to choose some chocolates to take home with you. You may have to make some difficult choices with this wide array of fudge and specialty chocolates. Did we mention there's ice cream, too? Yup. Open Mon through Sat, 10 a.m. to 6 p.m.; Sun, noon to 5 p.m.

Nothing goes better with rich chocolate than an equally tasty hot beverage. Stop in at ***The Spice & Tea Exchange*** (80 Whitfield St; 203-453-0022; spiceandtea.com), a small shop set up like an eighteenth-century trading post, loaded with spices, herbs, and gourmet teas. Actually a franchise, Spice & Tea Exchanges can be found spread over twenty-six states and the District of Columbia, but that doesn't make them any less special. There is one other Connecticut location in Mystic (6 West Main St.; 860-245-4153).

Booklovers will want to head to ***Breakwater Books*** (81 Whitfield St; 203-453-4141; breakwaterbooks.net). Truly one of the last of a dying breed, this independent bookstore exudes a love of books. There is a lovely collection of local books alongside *NY Times* bestsellers and classics. The children's room is comfortable, welcoming, unrushed, and extensive. They accept online orders as well, so you could have your favorite books waiting for you to pick up and enjoy. Open Mon through Sat, 10 a.m. to 6 p.m.; Sun, 11 a.m. to 5 p.m. Breakwater Books also hosts author signings throughout the year, so be sure to check their website for the latest events scheduled. Don't forget to ask about their Book Lover's card, which will entitle you to $10 off after ten $15 purchases.

With your bags packed with books, head back up Whitfield Street the way you came and stop in at ***Flutterby*** (55 Whitfield St; 203-458-1941; flutterby-ct.com), where you'll find a wonderful assortment of local, handmade, and definitely unique gifts and clothing.

While we haven't named every store on the green, we've given you a pretty good assortment from which to choose. When you're done eating and shopping, save some time to appreciate a little history and burn off some calories with a walk down **Fair Street**, located to the north of the green. Head north up Whitfield and take a left on Broad. Fair is your first right. It's less than a city block long, but in that short distance, you'll see the 1869 ***I.S. Spencer & Sons Foundry*** (18 Fair Street), which has been turned into condominiums but is still a cool building to see; the ***North West Center School*** (85 Fair Street), a former one-room schoolhouse turned residence; and homes representing a variety of architectural styles dating back to the seventeenth century. For detailed information on each of the homes, visit the **Guilford Preservation Alliance** website at guilfordpreservation.org and click on *Guilford: A Walking Guide*.

For more history in the area (it truly abounds here), drive back through the green and farther south on Whitfield Street where you will find the ***Henry Whitfield State Museum*** (248 Old Whitfield St.; 203-453-2457). Built in 1639 as a combination minister's home, stronghold, and meeting hall, the Henry Whitfield House is the oldest house in the state and the oldest stone house in New England. Today, it's a museum where visitors can take self-guided tours through the three floors of seventeenth-, eighteenth-, and nineteenth-century furnishings and artifacts from the town's history. You can also explore the grounds and adjacent educational building where more fun can be had. Parking is free, admission is not. Plan at least an hour to take it all in. There are also interesting events planned here, including a "Halloween Hysterics at Henry's," a Firelight Festival the weekend following Thanksgiving, and a Night Before Christmas story time in December, and others throughout the year. The museum's Facebook page is a great place to check for upcoming happening and available hours. The museum is open May through Oct, Wed through Sun, 10 a.m. to 4:30 p.m.; from Nov through Apr, the Visitor Center is open most weekdays 10 a.m. to 4:30 p.m., with the museum open by appointment during those hours and days. Admission. Blue Star Museum.

For a beautiful water view, follow Whitfield Street south to ***Guilford Harbor*** (Whitfield Street and Old Whitfield Street diverge and then converge again and both head to the harbor, so you can choose your way). There's parking available at the Guilford Point and some large rocks just right for sitting a spell.

If you like old houses or antique furnishings and you haven't overdosed on history yet, there's another little side trip you can take. Head back up Whitfield toward the green. At the intersection before the green, take a right onto Boston Street to the 1690 ***Hyland House Museum*** (84 Boston St.; 203-453-9477; hylandhouse.org), a classic colonial saltbox noted for its unusual woodwork and for no less than three walk-in fireplaces. The house and property has a 500-year history, which is explained in fascinating detail on their website. Today the museum hosts special events throughout the year, including a special tour of the museum's quilts and textiles collection, a class on the basics of hearth cooking, beekeeping demonstrations, and more. The gardens are also a sight to behold, especially the extensive herb garden. The museum also sponsors events throughout the town, so be sure to check in to see what's on tap. Museum hours are June through Sept, Fri and Sat, 11 a.m. to 4 p.m.; Sun, noon to 4 p.m. Admission is free, but donations are accepted. It's always best to check ahead, as the house is sometimes closed for private events.

Also located on Boston Street is the 1774 ***Thomas Griswold House*** (171 Boston St.; 203-453-2263 info; 203-710-5327 tours; guilfordkeepingsociety.com). Maintained by the **Guilford Keeping Society**, this house is another saltbox that has been turned into a museum of local history. In addition to the usual collection of furnishings, this house features period costumes, a barn full of tools, an outhouse, and a restored blacksmith shop. Open by appointment June and Sept, Fri and Sat, 11 a.m. to 4 p.m.; Sun, noon to 4 p.m.; July and Aug,

Wed through Sat, 11 a.m. to 4 p.m.; Sun, noon to 4 p.m. Admission. Blue Star Museum.

If the family is getting antsy from the museum tours, perhaps a trip to the *Guilford Salt Meadows Sanctuary* (Meadowlands Road; 203-264-5098; ct.audubon.org/Guilford-salt-meadows-sanctuary) is in order. Here you will find the one-mile **Anne Conover Nature Education Trail**, which sits amid 235 acres of tidal wetlands and is a family-friendly outing and popular bird-watching location. Many educational displays are located along the trail, and guides are available at the trail kiosk. It's a great place to grab some fresh air and stretch the legs. Keep your eyes peeled for the saltmarsh sparrow. This little bird is increasingly in danger of becoming extinct. These sparrows only nest in certain coastal salt marshes from Maine to North Carolina, and lower Guilford saltmarshes seem to be a favorite stop as, according to the Audubon's website, they "support one of the highest density populations of nesting Saltmarsh Sparrows found anywhere in the world." Pretty cool, huh? To find your way to the sanctuary, follow Meadowlands Road from Clapboard Hill Road in Guilford. In about a quarter of a mile you'll see an open grass field and a parking area on your right. The sanctuary is open daily from sunrise to sunset.

If hiking is what you want to do, you'd do well to explore Guilford's *WestWoods Trail System* (Sam Hill Road; 203-457-9253; guilfordlandtrust. org), located across town from the Salt Meadows Sanctuary and maintained by the **Guilford Land Conservation Trust**. You can get maps from various locations in town, including the aforementioned Breakwater Books, Bishops Orchards, and the town hall. This trail system started with seven miles in 1996; today there are more than twenty miles of mapped trails on 1,200 acres that include cave structures, waterfalls, salt marshes, and an inland tidal lake. Visit their website before you go to map out your route if you so choose.

Sam Who?

Did you notice the name of the road you traveled to reach the WestWoods Trail System (see above). Did it sound familiar to you? While looking for something lost, have you ever heard your parents or grandparents mutter, "Now where in the Sam Hill is it?" And did you ever wonder who *Sam Hill* was and why he'd have a road named after him? Well, he was a real guy who lived in Guilford (1678–1752). Old Sam was the town clerk for thirty-five years, judge of the probate court for twelve years, and deputy to the general court for at least twenty-two sessions. He ran for so many offices that people used to say "running like Sam Hill" when they meant someone was persistent. Poor Sam's name—which had become known throughout the country and sounds so much like the common name for the nether regions—eventually lost that connotation and became a polite euphemism for "hell."

Another town treasure in the area of Westwoods is the **Medad Stone Tavern Museum** (171 Three Mile Course; 203-453-2263 info; 203-710-5327 tours; guilfordkeepingsociety.com), which is not a stone tavern at all but a tavern built by a man named Medad Stone. Located farther away from the green and the town's center of activity, this spot was chosen by Stone in 1803 because he believed the main thoroughfare through town would be routed through here; it wasn't, and Stone never opened his tavern. The land and dwelling were occupied by the Davis family for nearly two centuries, however, as they farmed and maintained the property. Leonard Davis Hubbard lived in the tavern for more than ninety years and even wrote about it in a book titled *Old Tavern Tales*. Upon his death in 2001, Hubbard bequeathed the property to the Guilford Keeping Society, which restored the tavern to much as it was when Stone built it and opened the museum. They like to bill it as "the museum that opened 200 years late." We're sure Medad Stone would be happy to see his dream being appreciated and put to good use.

The Guilford Keeping Society obviously loves and respects history, and they want to teach children to do the same. That's why they host a summer camp at the tavern that invites kids (ages 7 to 12) to come spend the week traveling through history with their American Girl Dolls. They read the historic stories, learn about the times in which the characters lived, and make crafts to celebrate that history. It all culminates with a tea in the tavern's parlor. They also have events, including beer and wine tastings for the adults, throughout the year, so be sure to check out their website for the latest.

Be sure to check out **Armisteadville**, a miniature, handmade village at the tavern museum. Built over the course of thirty-five years, this village features six trade shops, trades that creator Donald Armistead personally learned in order to make his village authentic. And the parts work, too. Armistead donated the village to the Guilford Keeping Society in honor of his wife Dorothy, who was curator at the Whitefield Museum for many years.

The Medad Stone Tavern Museum is open by appointment June through Sept, Sat 11 a.m. to 4 p.m.; Sun, noon to 4 p.m. Admission. Blue Star Museum.

The Keeping Society also supports, in conjunction with **Watershed Partnership**, the **Len Hubbard Community Garden**. Named in honor of the man who left his family's tavern for future generations to enjoy, the community garden's goal is to ensure that future generations can keep and care for themselves and the land they are entrusted with. The Watershed Partnership is a nonprofit group that works throughout Connecticut to promote "safe, healthy, livable communities for present and future generations through education, advocacy, and technical assistance." The Keeping Society allows the community members to have the garden on their property, but there is an extensive list of rules to be followed in order for it to be successful.

If you're of a mind to see more beautiful scenery, follow Sam Hill Road south to Water Street. Head northeast on Water Street and watch for Mulberry Point Road on your right. Follow Mulberry all the way to its end. You can't park at Mulberry Point, but you can see the lighthouse on Faulkner's Island off in the distance.

There is a lighthouse on the island, *Faulkner's Island Lighthouse,* built in 1802. In 1976, the keeper's house was destroyed by fire. The Coast Guard replaced the valuable Fresnel lens in the tower with a modern plastic optic, and the lighthouse became automated. While that move toward modernity may have cost the lighthouse some of its romance, you can still see the old light faithfully announcing its presence from many parts of Guilford and adjoining towns, as well as on vessels navigating Long Island Sound.

If it weren't for the determination of the *Faulkner's Light Brigade* (faulknerslight.org), the Faulkner's Island Lighthouse might have been lost forever. In the early 1990s, this historic lighthouse seemed doomed as a series of storms had worn away the island on which it stood. The structure was on the brink of toppling into the sea until a coalition of local volunteers lobbied their legislators. Eventually, Congress allocated more than $4 million to stabilize the island and save the lighthouse.

The island is part of the *Stewart McKinney National Wildlife Refuge* and is a sanctuary for the rare roseate and common terns that end their long flight from winter homes in South America and the Caribbean to nest and breed there. This means that Faulkner's is off-limits to the public, except for the annual open house in September coordinated by the brigade. Ferry service is offered to the island from the Guilford Town Marina, or visitors can use their own watercraft.

After all this sight-seeing and history appreciation, you may be ready to refuel. If you head back to Route 1 on your way back home, we suggest a stop at *Bishop's Orchards Farm Market & Winery* (1355 Boston Post Rd., Route 1; 203-453-2338; bishopsorchards.com). Started in 1910 as a produce stand, Bishop's has grown to become a sizable cider mill and pick-your-own/cut-your-own farm with sidelines in Vermont cheeses, local honey and eggs, fresh herbs, and, more recently, bulk items such as quinoa, rolled oats, French lentils, and brown Basmati Rice. These are offered in large barrels with scoops to allow you to take as much or as little as you choose. There is also an impressive selection of gluten-free, vegan, and other health-conscious offerings. There's a very old-time farmer's market encased in a more modern supermarket vibe about this place. With fresh baked goods and local produce, you can feed the family from breakfast to dessert here.

Bishop's has also partnered with local Van Wilgen's Garden Center in North Branford to offer seasonal gardening service, making this truly a one-stop shop from Apr through Oct.

The farm market is open year-round, Mon through Sat, 8 a.m. to 7 p.m.; Sun, 9 a.m. to 6 p.m. Closed major holidays. Check the website for the most up-to-date pick-your-own offerings and hours.

While you're at the Farm Market, why not stroll across the parking lot to **Bishop's Orchards Winery** (355 Boston Post Rd., Route 1; 203-453-2338; bishopsorchards.com), which offers daily wine tastings of their own fruit wines and hard ciders. They also supply wines from other farms and wineries across the state. Winemaker Keith Bishop is a fifth-generation Bishop as well as being co-owner and co-CEO—that's more than enough hats for one person to wear. He's good at what he does, though, turning his farm's apples, peaches, pears, strawberries, raspberries, blueberries, and blackberries into unique and delicious wines. The many awards listed on their web page attests to the fact that Bishop knows his trade. The wine bar is open year-round, Mon through Sat, 8 a.m. to 6:30 p.m.; Sun, 10 a.m. to 5:30 p.m. You don't need a reservation for a tasting unless there are more than nine people in your group, in which case they respectfully request you call ahead so they can make arrangements. Tours are offered Sat and Sun at 2 p.m. There is a cost for both tastings and tours; check the web site for the latest information.

Madison

Heading east on Route 1, you'll come to the town of **Madison**, an upscale shoreline community with a great main street and great beaches. But there's history here, too. The 1785 **Allis-Bushnell House** (853 Boston Post Rd.; 203-245-4567; madisoncthistorical.org) in Madison is noted for the unusual corner fireplaces and original paneling that grace its period rooms. The **Madison Historical Society** maintains the house and its collections of toys, dolls, costumes, kitchenware, and china. The museum is organized in such a way to allow visitors to travel through time from the colonial period, through the Revolution, into the Civil War, and then on to the colonial revival era. What a neat idea. The grounds to the museum, including the herb garden in the back, are open to the public year-round sunup to sundown at no cost. The house is open by appointment and for special events and open houses throughout the year. More information is posted on the website.

Another historic home in Madison comes complete with a family ghost. The 1685 **Deacon John Grave House** (581 Boston Post Rd.; 203-245-4798; deaconjohngrave.org), located at Tunxis Farm, was owned and occupied for 300 years by the descendants of Deacon John Grave. Throughout its history, it has served as an inn, a tavern, a military hospital, and even a courthouse, but it is the military hospital where this house's ghost story originates. During that time, Anne Grave lived in the house and helped nurse wounded soldiers back to health. She fell in love with one of these soldiers, and when he was well and had to leave, he promised to return but never did. Every once in a while someone will report seeing the form of a woman walking through the house, items will not be where they were originally placed, a presence will be felt, noises heard. Some speculate that Anne still roams the house waiting for her love to return. Do you believe the ghostly tale? You'll have to visit and see for yourself. Tours are available by appointment.

Hammonasset Beach State Park (1288 Boston Post Rd.; 203-245-2785) is Madison's crown jewel and Connecticut's largest public beach park. With its two miles of beach along Long Island Sound, this beach has been opened to the public since 1920, drawing 75,000 visitors its first year. Today, more than a million beachgoers flock to its sandy beaches and walking trails. There's also a campground that fills up quickly once it opens for the season. Personally, we like the beach at sunset when the crowds are gone and the peace settles in.

hammonasset trivia

According to the DEEP website, "Hammonasset" means, "where we dig holes in the ground."

During World War II, the Hammonasset Beach was closed to the public and loaned to the US government as an army reservation. Meigs Point was used as an aircraft range. Planes flew over Clinton Harbor, fired at the range, and then flew out over Long Island Sound.

Hammonasset Beach State Park is also home to the *Meigs Point Nature Center* (1288 Boston Post Rd.; 203-245-8743; meigspointnaturecenter.org). The center gives visitors an introduction to the sea life found in Long Island Sound, including horseshoe crabs, lobsters, and a variety of fish. It also has some reptiles found in Connecticut, as well as some mounted animals, including a deer and a black bear. The staff is knowledgeable and dedicated; everyone in your party is sure to learn something. A calendar of family and children's activities is offered. Nature walks are almost always on the calendar along with other special activities; be sure to check it out. Open Apr though Oct, Tues to Sun, 10 a.m. to 5 p.m.; Nov through March, Tues to Sun, 10 a.m. to 4 p.m. Hammonasset can get busy during the summer season, so if you can visit in the off-season, we highly recommend it.

Clinton

Relatively new to the scene, *Shanks* (131 Grove St.; 860-669-4224; shanksclinton. com) is a restaurant housed in a 1974 Bruno & Stillman commercial lobster boat. Don't let the outside fool you, this boat—er restaurant—has state-of-the-art equipment and churns out some serious New England fry (yes, you *can* get a burger if you must, we don't know why you would). Not only is the food wonderful, but the views out over the Clinton Harbor from the picnic tables are second to none, especially at sunset. Now you can also enjoy misty mornings on the water, as the restaurant is open for breakfast on the weekends. Open Mon through Thurs, 11 a.m. to 8 p.m.; Fri, 11 a.m. to 9 p.m.; Sat, 8 a.m. to 9 p.m.; Sun, 8 a.m. to 8 p.m.

It's not a boat, but ***Chamard Vineyards*** (115 Cow Hill Rd.; 860-664-0299; chamard.com) is still one of the shoreline's hidden jewels. Owned by famed geneticist **Dr. Jonathan Rothberg**, Chamard produces 6,000 cases of wine a year. The vineyard grounds are beautiful and the lodge rustic and charming. They also have a barn where they host live music and other events, and a bistro where they serve "simple, wholesome, classic food influenced by products readily available from the property and in the region." What a wonderful way to support local businesses. For a fee, you can also create your own wine, from choosing the grapes to fermentation to corking—the process is up to you. The vineyard and wine bar are open Tues through Thurs, 11 a.m. to 5 p.m.; Fri and Sat, 11 a.m. to 9 p.m.; Sun, 11 a.m. to 6 p.m.

The Connecticut River Valley

Old Saybrook

If you're a hardy New Englander, then you know that the best time to visit the beach is in the winter—no crowds, no traffic, no fees. Unfortunately, most of the clam shacks and ice cream stands close in the off-season. That's why it's good to know that ***Johnny Ad's*** (910 Boston Post Rd.; 860-388-4032; johnnyads.com) is open year-round. Johnny Ad's is something of a shoreline landmark. In the summer it's a popular destination for tourists; in the winter the locals have it all to themselves.

oldsaybrook trivia

It is said that General de Lafayette stopped by the James Pharmacy in 1824 to purchase either socks or soap—the facts are uncertain. What is certain is that Katharine Hepburn was a frequent visitor while she lived at Fenwick.

Depending on the season, you can eat inside or take your food outdoors to the picnic tables and fight the seagulls for it. The **lobster roll** is the genuine, butter-drenched shore favorite, and the fried whole-belly clams are crunchy and briny. Open daily at 11 a.m.

If you follow Main Street its southernmost distance, you'll come to ***Saybrook Point,*** where the Connecticut River flows into Long Island Sound. This is ecologically protected National Conservancy topography and the perfect place for lodgings that rank among coastal New England's best—namely, *Saybrook Point Inn, Marina, & Spa* (2 Bridge St.; 860-395-2000; saybrook. com), in business since 1989. The layout includes a dock and marina (large enough for 125 moorings) as well as a spa for fitness workouts, massages, a whole slew of sophisticated beauty treatments, and indoor/outdoor swimming pool plunges. All eighty-two guest rooms are tastefully furnished (Chippendale and Queen Anne styles predominate), with sizable bathrooms, fluffy robes, and ample storage space. If you'd like romantic intimacy, choose one of the two suites nestled in the marina's mini-lighthouse. The inn also has two historic buildings, Three Stories and Tall Tales with more rooms. Details are on the website. *Fresh Salt* is the on-site restaurant here, serving breakfast, lunch, and dinner with a beautiful waterfront view. Brunch, served Sun 10:30 a.m. to 2 p.m., is very popular. They are also only four miles from the Florence Griswold Museum (see write-up later in this chapter).

Essex

With one of the best anchorages on the Connecticut River, *Essex* has always had intimate ties with the river. Essex's Main Street still looks very much like it did in the eighteenth century. Clapboard houses, fan-shaped windows, and fences abound, and in the shops that line the street, purveyors of antiques, clothing, and gifts ply their trade to tourists from around the world.

There used to be two shipyards in the town, and from 1754 there was a West Indies warehouse next to the town dock where goods from Africa and the Indies were unloaded for redistribution across the state. It was next to that warehouse at the Hayden Shipyards that America built its first warship, *Oliver Cromwell*, in 1776.

It is therefore fitting that the *Connecticut River Foundation's Connecticut River Museum* (67 Main St.; 860-767-8269; ctrivermuseum.org) is located at Steamboat Dock. The museum chronicles the history of Connecticut by tracing the evolution of the Connecticut River and of steam power. Among the exhibits is a full-scale working replica of David Bushnell's 1775 *American Turtle*. This is the first submarine ever constructed. The museum also contains nautical paintings, shipbuilding tools, and memorabilia. Special events are held here throughout the year, including an annual holiday model train show, and foliage and other sightseeing cruises. The museum itself is open Columbus Day through Memorial

essextrivia

David Bushnell, designer of the American Turtle, coined the word "submarine" to describe his invention.

Day, Tues to Sun, 10 a.m. to 5 p.m.; Memorial Day through Columbus Day, open daily. Gift shop. Admission. The research archive is open by appointment only.

If you've never visited the 1776 *Griswold Inn* (36 Main St.; 860-767-1776; griswoldinn.com), don't leave Essex without doing so. People who know and love this place often call it the "Gris" (pronounced "grizz"). The inn offers thirty-three guest rooms, a full-service restaurant, and a taproom with full menu and delicious brews.

The Gris is open daily for lunch and dinner, plus a Sunday brunch in the form of the justly famous Hunt Breakfast. This tradition goes back to the War of 1812, when officers of the British army, which was then occupying Essex, forcefully suggested that the establishment start serving a regular Sunday hunt breakfast. Today, the Hunt Breakfast table groans with an array of food that includes fried chicken, lamb kidneys and mushrooms, and creamed ham and eggs over English muffins. It's almost, but not quite, enough to make you forgive the British for burning New London during the same war.

A number of the inn's downstairs rooms have been turned into dining rooms. You can, for example, eat in the book-lined library or in the Steamboat Room, with its lifelike mural of steamboating on the river. No matter where you land, you'll have an interesting experience. The owners even hold art tours and talks about the amazing collection of art that was always at the inn, but never received much attention. Visit the website for available dates; reservations are required. The Gris is open throughout the year except for Christmas Day.

If the river formed Essex's early history, the railroad had much to do with its later development. The *Essex Steam Train and Riverboat* (1 Railroad Ave.; 860-767-0103 or 800-277-3987; essexsteamtrain.com) off Route 154 was chartered in 1868. It still runs a steam train, with an optional riverboat ride, along the Connecticut River. Four or more trains per day make the twelve-mile round trip from Essex to Deep River, and all but the last train connect with the riverboat. Boats make a round trip from Deep River to Gillette Castle and East Haddam. Before or after the excursion, guests can tour a variety of vintage train cars and visit the gift and snack shops (both in old railroad cars). The railroad runs a varying schedule from May through Oct, and from Thanksgiving through Christmas. Tickets can be purchased at the station in Essex. The North Pole Express and Thomas the Tank Engine special events require reservations and sell out fast.

Essex used to be famous for manufacturing piano keys, and nearby *Ivoryton* was the center of the ivory trade that supported that industry. In fact the town's name derives from the fact that it used to import "ivory by the ton." Both the legal ivory trade of olden days and the local piano works have ceased to be. But a salute to music of a different sort can be found at the *Museum of Fife & Drum* (62 N. Main St.; 860-399-6519; companyoffifeanddrum.org), where the Company of Fifers and Drummers is headquartered. Exhibits trace the development of military parades in America from the Revolutionary War to the present day and include many uniforms and musical instruments, including drums dating from 1793. There's a special display of Civil War–era musical instruments. This museum is truly unique. Open by appointment. Admission.

The *Ivoryton Playhouse* (103 Main St.; 860-767-7318; ivorytonplayhouse. org) was the first self-supporting summer theater in the nation. Although cozy and unpretentious, the Ivoryton can boast some of the most famous names in American theater: Marlon Brando, Ginger Rogers, Carl Reiner, Groucho Marx, Helen Hayes, Jerry Orbach, Alan Alda, Mary Astor, and Gene Hackman all graced the playhouse's stage. Katharine Hepburn, who was born in Hartford and lived nearby in the Fenwick section of Old Saybrook, launched her career at the Ivoryton. Today the theater offers a full schedule of great plays— musicals, comedies, and dramas, as well as a wonderful children's summer program of theatrical entertainment.

Deep River

Settled in 1635 as part of Old Saybrook, the sleepy village of *Deep River* is known throughout the state as the site of the *Deep River Ancient Muster*, "the oldest and largest gathering of fife and drum participants and enthusiasts in the world," according to Deep River's website. Held annually the third Saturday of July, this is truly a family-friendly event. The muster is preceded by a parade that starts at 11 a.m. at the corner of Main and Kirtland Streets, proceeds down Main Street, and ends at Devitt's Field, where the muster commences. Roads close at 10:30 a.m., and people arrive early to claim spots along the route. Visit deepriverct.com for more information.

Down the road from Fountain Hill Cemetery, you'll find the 1840 *Stone House* (245 Main St.; 860-526-1449), where the local historical society maintains

Connecticut Freedom Trail

Daniel Fisher was a slave. William Winters was a free man. And somewhere in between the two was a trip from North Carolina to Philadelphia to New York to New Haven and eventually to Deep River. On this journey, Daniel was helped by numerous people, including Deacon George Read of Deep River, along the Underground Railroad. During this journey, Daniel became William. He lived a good life with friends and family in Deep River along Winter Avenue, which was eventually named for him. William Winters died in 1900 at the age of ninety-two. He is buried in Fountain Hill Cemetery on High Street.

a small museum filled with such items as nineteenth-century furnishings, maritime memorabilia, locally made cut glass, and Native American artifacts. Open Tues and Thurs, 10 a.m. to noon. Donations requested.

Killingworth

Hugh Lofting, the man who gave the world the character **Dr. Dolittle**, rests in a little cemetery in rural *Killingworth*, unseen by virtually all who pass by. Lofting was a native of England but moved to tiny Killingworth in 1928 at the height of his popularity as the author of a series of books about a kindly, eccentric veterinarian who could talk to animals. According to a town historian, Lofting wrote some of his books while living here, in a house on River Road. Lofting died in 1947 and was buried in *Evergreen Cemetery*, across the street from his house, now privately owned. The cemetery is on Green Hill Road, and Lofting's tombstone is in the back right-hand corner.

Haddam

Right near the iconic East Haddam Swing Bridge you'll find *Goodspeed's Station Country Store* (22 Bridge Rd.; 860-345-7322; goodspeedsstation.com). Walking through the doors is like walking into another world full of beautiful and unique items to discover—books; gifts; cards; local and international food; old-fashioned candy; farm, shabby chic, and primitive decorations; and so much more! Kris and Ann Marie Pszczolkowski carefully choose their products and do their best to support local artisans, but Kris also imports incredible items from Poland. You'll find tea from **Haddam's Whole Harmony 4 U** alongside authentic Polish pickles and so much more. They are normally open Mon through Sat, 10 a.m. to 6 p.m.; Sun, 11 a.m. to 5 p.m., but check their Facebook page for any changes.

The Blue Oar (16 Snyder Rd.; 860-345-2994; blueoarct.wixsite.com/ctrestaurants) is unique in that when they say BYOB, it means bring your own beer, booze, or boat. Located on the Connecticut River, The Blue Oar has a dock for boaters to use, so that is completely an option. You should also bring your own tablecloths, glassware, and centerpieces if you want to set the atmosphere. You don't have to, though. Once you arrive at The Blue Oar, you can go choose a table, put your stuff down, make your selections from a menu, then go upstairs to order. It's definitely a relaxed vibe around here. And that's all the better to enjoy the scenery, which can be spectacular around sunset or just watching the boats cruise on down the river.

They don't take reservations and they don't take plastic. Cash or check with proper ID only, please. It's also weather dependent, so if you are in doubt, it's always best to call ahead. The Blue Oar opens for the season on Mother's Day weekend and stays open through Labor Day, 11:30 a.m. to 9 p.m. daily. They start to shorten their hours in fall until they eventually close for the season dependent on the weather.

Located about three-tenths from the junction of Routes 81 and 154 on Route 154 north of Higganum Center is a Connecticut institution known as **Higgies** (256 Saybrook Rd.; 860-554-3082; higgiesfoodandicecream.com).

haddamtrivia

Heading south from Middletown toward Haddam, taking Route 9 to Route 154, you'll come upon a large rock set well back from the road. This is **Bible Rock** and its cleft marks the line between Middletown and Haddam. Look carefully because the rock is well back from the road and easy to miss when leaves cover the trees.

This restaurant has been around since 1945 and has a reputation for the "best dogs and shakes" in the area. The owners pride themselves on using only top-quality products. A shake flanked by a couple of chili dogs makes a perfect nostalgic lunch, but the fresh hand-pressed cheeseburgers are also popular. The best way to enjoy a Higgies lunch is outside at a picnic table under the trees. Open early Apr until late Oct, Mon and Wed, 11 a.m. to 7 p.m.; Tues, 11 a.m. to 3 p.m.; Thurs through Sun, 11 a.m. to 8 p.m.

On Route 154 you'll pass some beautiful Victorian, Beaux Arts, and Gothic Revival houses. About two miles out of Higganum Center, there's a former Catholic church, now a private residence, overlooking the Connecticut River, the perfect brooding realization of Gothic architecture.

Sundial Gardens (59 Hidden Lake Rd.; 860-345-4290; sundialgardens. com) is actually a collection of formal gardens, including a seventeenth-century knot garden, an eighteenth-century-style garden, and a topiary garden with a fountain. There's also a tea and gift shop and tearoom on-site, and on Sunday the owners offer "tea talks" that include a tour of the gardens followed by tea and dessert. The tea shop is open in mid-April weekends only, from noon to 5 p.m. The gardens are best visited in June. Their Facebook page is the best source of the latest happenings. Admission.

Durham

Durham is one of those New England treasures tucked almost exactly halfway between New Haven and Hartford, with its main street being Route 17, which then splits into Routes 79 and 77 and points to the shore (Madison and Guilford, respectively). Durham is a small town with a little more than 6,500 residents.

The spirit of this small town and its traditions is epitomized in the **Durham Market** (238 Main St.; 860-788-3335). The market building has been a fixture on Durham's Main Street since 1835 when Leverett W. Leach opened a store here that eventually became known as L. W. Leach & Sons as his sons grew and assisted him in the business. When Leverett died in 1866, his sons continued the business as L. M. & O Leach until selling it to brothers Fred L. and Jesse B. Atwell in 1897. The Atwells expanded the business to include a post office and enjoyed the business until 1934 when John C. Otte and Perley S. Morse purchased the business and ran it as Morse & Otte. The store stayed in the Otte family (John and Perley were brothers-in-law), passed down through the generations, for sixty years until new owners, Chet and Jackie Mounts took over in 1994. The Mounts changed the name to Durham Market and operated it for twenty-three years before selling it to new owners late in 2017.

The new owners came to the purchase with a vision of turning the market into a community meeting center. They have given the store a complete overhaul, adding a smoothie machine and a local merchant corner where local artisans can showcase and sell their wares. Fresh produce is always available along with fresh meat from local farms. There's organic ice cream, fresh-baked bread, and standard groceries as well; they even offer fresh sushi. While the updates are ongoing, there is a true community spirit at the market now as there was in the past. Stop in and see what they have to offer; you won't be disappointed. Open year-round, Mon through Sat, 8 a.m. to 8 p.m.; Sun, 8 a.m. to 6 p.m.

durhamtrivia

When the New York Giants squared off with the New England Patriots in 2012 for Super Bowl XLVI, Durham found itself in the middle of the hubbub. Exactly the middle. The small, central Connecticut town is equidistant from the Giants' MetLife Stadium in East Rutherford, New Jersey, and the Patriots' Gillette Stadium in Foxborough, Massachusetts. Sports channels, newscasters, and sports fans descended on the small town in the wee hours of the morning to celebrate the rivalry. Groups gathered at the high school, faces painted in their team colors and held a pep rally of sorts. No head count was taken, so we're not sure if the majority of residents were happy with the results or not. Either way, a fun time was had by all.

Driving down Durham's Main Street is like driving into the past. The eighteenth- and nineteenth-century homes that line the Historic District have been lovingly restored and maintained. In the short two-mile span, you'll find twenty-five historic buildings, including the 1763 ***Reverend Elizur Goodrich House*** (81 Main St.), home to Rev. Goodrich, a Yale University graduate who mentored students, including Eli Whitney, and worked with the likes of Ezra Stiles, president of Yale (1778 to 1795). The house is privately owned. The 1772 ***Cook-Fowler House*** (119 Main Street), was once home to William

Chauncey Fowler, son-in-law of Noah Webster. It is now privately owned. The 1806 **Lemuel Camp Tavern** (199 Main Street) served as a tavern, a boarding house, a summer residence to Wedworth Wadsworth and his wife, and is now restored as an office building. The 1745 **Elias Austin House** (256 Main St.), also known as the Moses Austin House, is the birthplace of Moses Austin who founded a settlement in Texas. Unfortunately, Moses died before his dream of a state could be realized, but his son Stephen F., stayed on and became known as the "Father of Texas." The house is now privately owned. These are just some of the stories behind the houses. To learn more, visit historicbuildingsct. com/towns/durham.

If you're looking for a gift for a special occasion or just something to satisfy your sweet tooth, stop by **Kim's Cottage Confections** (16 Main St.; 860-349-2256; kimscottageconfections.com). With more than twenty years of experience in the confection industry, owner Kim Terrill is up to just about any challenge you can throw at her. As she says on her website, she does it all—from cookies to tea parties and everything in between. We've seen some pretty amazing cakes come out of her kitchen, and there are fresh-baked cupcakes, cookies, and candies available daily, all made on the premises. You really can't walk by without walking in for something delicious. Open Tues through Fri, 9 a.m. to

The Bridge Below

In 1994, the state enacted plans to repair the 1920s' bridge that carries Route 17 across Allyn Brook in Durham when they uncovered something unexpected at the construction site—a long-forgotten bridge buried beneath the existing structure.

With the help of the Connecticut Historic Preservation Office, as well as, the state archaeologist, local historians discovered that the bridge was most likely the work of East Haddam stonemason Silas Brainerd, who was hired to build the stone arch bridge in 1823. It was made out of brownstone, and since Silas's sons operated the E. & S. Brainerd brownstone quarry in Portland at the time, and it is thought that they may have provided the material for the bridge.

Local officials requested that the state reevaluate their original plans and try to incorporate the historic bridge into the design of the new. Amazingly, the state agreed and delayed construction for a year while they figured out exactly what to do. The historic bridge was carefully excavated and the state simply built the new bridge over the old.

If you want to see the bridge for yourself, park on the side of Old Cemetery Road on the west side of Route 17 on the north side of the bridge. (It's across from the Hill Hollow condominium complex.) Or park at Durham Dari-Serve and walk up Route 17 on the sidewalk, cross at the cross walk and down to see the bridge. There are stairs that lead down to a walkway where you can view the historic bridge that is essentially under the road.

A Sweet Treat on the Way to the Beach

So many travelers use Route 17 to Route 79 to get from points inland to Hammonasset Beach State Park. It's become a tradition to stop on the way back for an ice cream at **Durham Dari Serve** (13 Main St.; 860-349-3367). It can get busy on a summer night, so be prepared to wait a little bit. It's worth every minute, though. There's no indoor seating; it's walk-up window only with a few benches available outside. Most people just hang out on the tailgates of their trucks and enjoy their ice cream. Open mid-May to about mid-Oct daily, noon to 9 p.m. When the "gone fishin'" sign goes in the window they have closed for the season.

---

5 p.m.; Sat, 9 a.m. to 3 p.m.; Sun, 9 a.m. to noon. Her hours can fluctuate with the season, so it's best to check her Facebook page or give her a call before heading out. Kim is flexible and will also meet by appointment.

Another hidden gem in Durham is **Deerfield Farm** (337 Parmelee Hill Rd.; 860-301-7828; deerfieldfarm.org), a small dairy farm that processes its own milk and makes its own cheese and yogurt. There is a small self-service farm store in the barn where you are on the honor system. The farm is also open for tours, but you should call ahead. Open daily 10 a.m. to 6 p.m.

If you're looking for a breakfast sandwich, a fresh salad, a sandwich, wrap, grinder, or delicious Italian pastry, the place to go is **Lino's Market** (472 Main St.; 860-349-1717; linosmarket.com), an Italian specialty market tucked away at the end of Durham's Main Street. You'll find all sorts of fresh bread and other authentic Italian dishes prepared by Lino and his staff. You can even order online and they'll have your order ready for you when you arrive. The parking is tough here, especially around noon and 5 p.m., so be aware. Open Mon through Fri, 7 a.m. to 7 p.m.; Sat, 7 a.m. to 6 p.m. Closed Sun.

Middlefield

Middlefield is home to **Indian Springs Golf Course** (123 Mack Rd., 860-349-8109; indiansprings-golf.com), which offers not only a challenging nine-hole, par thirty-six public golf course, but a family-run, welcoming sort of atmosphere that makes being in a small town so wonderful. They offer a clubhouse, driving range, short-game practice area, and putting green as well as the **Fair Weather Café** with its bar and patio overlooking incredible views. Even if you're not a golfer, it's a great place to stop and get a quick or relaxing lunch and/or dinner. Their menu is fresh and innovative.

While in Middlefield, be sure to check out **New Guida's Restaurant** (484 Meriden Rd., 860-349-9039; newguidasrestaurant.com), home of the famous

10-inch pedigreed hot dog. Guida's has been serving up these delicious dogs since 1946. You can order them plain (but why would you?) or with "everything" (mustard, relish, and onions). Or if you are a true diner aficionado, you can order a chili and cheese dog. Every Mon night, from 4 to 8 p.m., their famous hot dogs are buy-one, get-one free! They also have all the diner staples—wonderful breakfasts that are popular with the locals, ice cream, fried clams, and more. Open Mon through Sat, 7 a.m. to 7 p.m.; Sun, 8 a.m. to 7 p.m. This place can get wicked busy on summer days during lunch, so please plan accordingly.

If you've eaten one too many hot dogs (is that possible?) and need to burn them off, head down the road just over two miles (northeast on Route 66, actually), where you'll find the headquarters of **Connecticut Forest and Park Association** (16 Meriden Rd.; 860-346-TREE; ctwoodlands.org). Commonly known as CFPA, this association of wonderful staff and a huge network of volunteers manages and maintains more than eight hundred miles of hiking trails throughout the state. Yes, these are the folks responsible for all those blue-blazed hiking trails we talk about in this book. The Blue-Blazed Hiking Trail System was created in 1929, a long-term objective to protect land (both public and private) for public enjoyment. Since its first members organized in 1895, CFPA has helped secure more than 100 state parks and forests for the use and enjoyment of outdoor enthusiasts.

One of those uses is right in CFPA's backyard. *Camille's Way* is an easy two-mile loop through 280-acre Highlawn Forest with numerous smaller loops radiating out from it. You can park in the headquarters' spacious parking lot and pick up the trail in the back by the kiosk. The trail is obvious as it follows wide, gravel paths before dipping into the forest. This area is used as a demonstration forest and outdoor classroom, which explains the observation platform with stairs leading down to a vernal pool and the large amphitheater. The trail then winds through the former Christmas tree farm where trees have overtaken what used to be open farm fields. The land is protected by a conservation easement, which CFPA now holds. It is just one example of how the association works to protect and share our land. You will see more evidence of this as you travel throughout the state. You'll likely see CFPA's signposts and parking lots to access points to the blue trails. To see where these are, visit their website for an interactive map, or, better yet, stop into the headquarters and pick up a copy of their *Connecticut Walk Book*. The office is open Mon through Fri, 9 a.m. to 4 p.m.

The organization also hosts a variety of workshops throughout the year. If you'd like to donate to support their ongoing efforts to acquire and save Connecticut's forests and parks for public use, you can do so via their website.

You can also join a volunteer group or purchase some of the nifty swag they offer. That way, when you're on the trails, you'll look like a professional! Sounds like a win-win.

If you're looking for that special gift, be sure to visit **Perrotti's Country Barn** (288 Baileyville Rd.; 860-349-0082), where you'll find a large selection of gifts and collectibles. This family-owned and -operated shop is packed full of the latest trends with such lines as Mantra Bands, Chamilia Beads, Chavez for Charity, Dogeared, Jim Shore, Alex and Ani, Scout Bags, Vera Bradley, Natural Life, and more. They also offer ice cream seasonally at the **Caboose Ice Cream Stand**, which is next door. Open Mon through Fri, 10:30 a.m. to 6 p.m.; Sat, 10 a.m. to 6 p.m.; Sun, noon to 6 p.m.

Middletown

Once a bustling seaport on the Connecticut River, **Middletown** boasts many historic houses and a varied history. The **Middlesex County Historical Society** (151 Main St.; 860-346-0746; middlesexhistory.org) sponsors the **Middletown Heritage Trail**, which features twenty historic sites. Included among these is **Indian Hill Cemetery** (383 Washington St.; 860-346-0452; indian-hill.org), where General Joseph Mansfield is buried. General Mansfield was born in 1803 in New Haven and lived with his family in Middletown. He entered the military academy at the tender age of fourteen and ascended the military ranks until he reached the office of Inspector General in 1853. He had married Louisa M. Mather on September 25, 1838, and they had three children.

In 1862, General Mansfield found himself in the midst of gunfire in Sharpsburg, Maryland, in the Battle of Antietam. He was desperately trying to stop his troops from firing into what he believed was a line of Union soldiers when he was fatally shot. It turns out, however, that his troops were right and had been shooting at members of the Confederacy. Mansfield succumbed to his injuries and his body was transported home to Connecticut and buried in Indian Hill. After his death, Louisa and the children stayed in Middletown. In fact, the family house at 151 Main Street stayed in the family until 1959, at which time it was acquired by the historical society and remains their head-quarters today.

The tour begins at the **Middletown Police Station** (222 Main St.) and can be done at your leisure. Free brochures, which include a map of the trail, are available at the police department, at the society's offices, at **Russell Library** (123 Broad St.), and at the **Middlesex County Chamber of Commerce** (393 Main St.). All but two sites are wheelchair accessible.

Middletown has no shortage of cool little places to eat and shop. Take, for instance, **Perk on Main** (386 Main St., 860-788-2287; perkonmain.com). Owner

Katie Hughes-Nelson has made a commitment not only to the community in which her business belongs, but to the world in which we live. Her mission statement hangs on the wall in the restaurant and proclaims that it is their goal "to help bring forth an environmentally sustainable & socially just human presence on Earth." And she puts her money where her mouth is in buying only fairly traded organic coffee; local products when possible; and using recyclable materials that can be composted, including encouraging customers to bring in their travel mugs for their coffee instead of using paper products that will only end up in a landfill. They even donate the used coffee grounds to local gardens and farms instead of throwing them out.

But recycling isn't even what they do best. Their food is delicious. Choose from berry or veggie smoothies; crepes filled with fresh fruit, or maybe Nutella, if that's your thing; omelets dripping with cheese and meat or vegetables and served with homemade home fries and your choice of many different kinds of bread for toast. For lunch, there are fresh made salads that hit the spot, soups, sandwiches, and more—all made fresh. You can't help but feel as if you're doing a good deed when you purchase a meal from Perk on Main and help Katie help our environment. Also, watch for **Perk on Wheels**, a food truck that is currently parked at the Dairy Serv in Durham, but often makes appearances at many of the area farmer's markets. Check her website for the latest.

If crepes aren't your thing, or if you're looking for something entirely different, how about dining in a restored jail house? At *Bread & Water* (51 Warwick St.; 860-852-5944; breadandwater51.com) you will do just that. Located in a renovated 1850s' jail house, this restaurant serves culinary perfection in an unusual dining destination. You will find things such as grilled Spanish octopus, shaved filet mignon with marinated mushrooms and organic field greens; duck confit with a potato leek emulsion, and beets with goat cheese mousse and pistachio sand. And those are just the appetizers. Chef-owner Carl A. Ciarcia knows his stuff, and he and his staff offer an amazing dining experience from wine to dessert. He changes the menus every few weeks or so, and whatever he chooses to create he gets glowing reviews. The restaurant is open Thurs through Sat, 5 to 10 p.m., or by appointment for private events. Reservations are highly recommended and can be made online.

Another place we highly recommend is *Pocketful of Posies* (386 Main St., 860-343-0123), the creative and eclectic shop in *Main Street Market*. Voted Retail Business of the Year in 2017, this store is the creation of Dottie Smith, formerly of Favorite Things in Durham and Pocketful of Posies in Essex and on Martha's Vineyard. Middletown is her sole focus these days, and what she and her staff create is amazing. From handmade floral wreathes and arrangements to the selection of clothing and home décor; to meaningful jewelry to organic candles, soaps, and creams; to items for your pet or garden, this is the perfect place to find that special gift for someone or maybe even for yourself. Open Tues through Sat, 11 a.m. to 5 p.m.

If you have the littles with you, don't pass up the chance to visit **Kidcity** (119 Washington St.; 860-347-0495; kidcitymuseum.com), where kids (ages 1 to 7) will enter a world just their size. Toddlers can crawl through sea caves (and stay dry) on the lower level; the first floor offers a Space Age Roadtrip, a fishery, a farm, and a Main Street, and more for children a little older to explore. Every room has easily visible entrances and exits so you can relax while you let your children explore; you'll know where they are at all times. This place really is built for them.

There is admission, and we highly recommend if you're going to be traveling the state anyway that you purchase a membership to the museum. This will provide you reduced admission to other kid-friendly museums across Connecticut and also allows you access to members-only hours. It is a great bargain if you think you'll have time to visit them all (or revisit one multiple times). The museum requests that one adult accompany up to four children. Open Sun through Tues, 11 a.m. to 5 p.m.; Wed through Sat, 9 a.m. to 5 p.m. Blue Star Museum.

If you're in the area on a July evening, be sure to stop by the **Wadsworth Mansion** (421 Wadsworth St., 860-347-1064; wadsworthmansion.com) for their Music at the Mansion series. The beautiful back lawn of this historic mansion opens at 5:30 p.m. for a 6:30 p.m. concert every Wednesday evening in July. The concerts are free and open to the public, but donations are accepted and appreciated. Guests are encouraged to picnic, bringing their own food or purchasing from visiting food trucks. They list the schedule on their website along with other events, including tours, teas, outdoor markets, and more. There are also walking trails around the beautiful grounds that are open when an event is not ongoing.

Adventure seekers won't want to pass up a visit to **Empower Leadership Sports & Adventure Center** (2011 S. Main St.; 860-638-4754; leadershipsports. com), a thirty-acre adventure center owned by husband and wife team of Joe and Maureen DeRing and run with the help of manager Dan Jaskot. Individuals and families or groups can zip line through the trees and take part in other team-building and empowering adventures such as a ropes course, rappelling, scavenger hunts, and tree climbing. The idea behind the DeRing's operation is to build confidence with experience, but most of all, it's fun! Reservations are required and can be made online. There are some limitations as to who can participate, and they do close if there's too much wind and/or lightening, so be sure to check their website for information and cancellation policy.

Portland

Brownstone Exploration & Discovery Park (161 Brownstone Ave.; 866-860-0208; brownstonepark.com) is located in a former ***Portland*** brownstone quarry less than thirty minutes from Hartford, New Haven, and Waterbury. Here you'll find challenges for even the most hard-core adventurer in your group. They offer rock climbing up steep walls of brownstone, zip lining, cliff diving, rope swings, scuba diving, wakeboarding, kayaking, a play area for smaller kids to play and swim, and more. Some activities require an additional fee, and some are included with your admission. Visitors are required to wear a life jacket (provided) at all times. You can bring in your own food and beverages, and there is plenty of space to spread out for a picnic. You might even be able to snag one of the floating gazebos (extra charge), which are pretty cool. Open daily mid-May through Oct, 10 a.m. to 7 p.m., weather permitting.

If you'd like a more relaxing time, stop in at the ***Arrigoni Winery*** (1287 Portland Cobalt Rd.; 860-342-1999; arrigoniwinery.com), where you can enjoy live local music on the patio while sipping wine made from the grapes grown on the farm's two hundred acres. Named for the bridge that spans the Connecticut River between Portland and Middletown, this winery was made possible by boxing champion John "Jack LaSalle" Gherlone, who passed his love of winemaking on to his grandson, who is the current owner of the winery. Sadly, Gherlone passed away before the winery opened, but we think he'd be proud to see what his grandson—and now his great-granddaughter—have accomplished. They also host events and a calendar is listed on their website. Just look for the animal statues on the front lawn, head in, and get ready to enjoy a New England evening on the farm. Open Fri, 11:00 a.m. to 9 p.m.; Sat and Sun, 11 a.m. to 6 p.m.

portlandtrivia

Portland supplied so much brownstone for Manhattan town houses that it was called the "city that changed the face of New York City."

East Haddam

East Haddam is the only town in the state to occupy both sides of the Connecticut River, and as you approach the eastern part of the township from across the river, you pass over the longest **swinging bridge** in New England.

This uncommon bridge actually pivots sideways to open a path for passing boats. The first thing you see on the other side is a glorious three-story American Gothic palace that looks like a wedding cake and dominates the East Haddam skyline. This symphony in gingerbread is the ***Goodspeed Opera House*** (6 Main St.; 860-873-8668; goodspeed.org). Founded by William

goodspeedtrivia

Goodspeed more than a century ago, the Goodspeed is widely known as "the birthplace of the American musical," thanks to the number of Broadway hits that received their first tryouts there. The opera house has a fascinating history, including being used as a town garage for years before being saved by a community action group and being restored to its former glory. Goodspeed Musicals' regular season typically begins in early Apr and runs through Nov or Dec depending on extensions and holiday programming. They also offer Festival of New Musicals every Jan and additional programming Feb and Mar, so there's always something going on. Be sure to check the website for latest information.

Right outside the entrance to the Goodspeed, you'll find the **Gelston House** (8 Main St.; 860-873-1411; gelstonhouse.com), a beautiful waterfront restaurant and lodging. The food is wonderful, and the rooms are gorgeous. It's a perfect accompaniment to a show at the Goodspeed, and the two make for a wonderful weekend away. Apparently we aren't the only ones who think so. East Haddam old-timers whisper that the Gelston House, built in 1853, was once a hideout for rumrunners during Prohibition. The restaurant can get busy on show nights. Open Tues through Thurs, and Sun, 11:30 a.m. to 9 p.m.; Fri and Sat, 11:30 a.m. to 11 p.m. Closed Mon.

While you're in East Haddam, stop by the **Nathan Hale Schoolhouse** (29 Main St.; 860-334-2858; connecticutsar.org), a one-room establishment where Hale taught in 1773–1774. Originally called Union School, it was renamed for Hale after he became an acknowledged American hero. Today, the schoolhouse is a museum containing Hale possessions and displays of artifacts relating to local history. Open June through Labor Day, Fri to Sun, noon to 4 p.m.; after Labor Day through Sept, Sat and Sun, noon to 4 p.m. Admission. Blue Star Museum.

Up the road and around the bend a bit is a place unto itself. You can't miss the bright blue and green building with the two large wooden cats at the top. This is **Two Wrasslin' Cats Coffee House** (374 Town St.; 860-891-8446; twowrasslincatscoffee.com), where everyone is welcome and the food is fresh and delicious. You won't find burgers and hot dogs here, but you will find fresh roasted coffee, smoothies, fresh bagels, and a variety of sandwiches and salads. Oh, and there's ice cream, too. The seating is in backrooms of the house with couches or tables, or out on the deck on nice days. Either way, you'll feel comfortable and relaxed and able to do your own thing. Don't be fooled by the size of the building from the outside; there's lots of seating inside, around the corner, and up the ramp. Open Mon through Wed, 7:30 a.m. to 5 p.m.; Thurs and Fri, 7:30 a.m. to 8 p.m.; Sat, 8 a.m. to 8 p.m.; Sun, 9 a.m. to 8 p.m.

Historians don't agree on how the **Devil's Hopyard** (366 Hopyard Rd.; 860-526-2336) in East Haddam got its name, but they do agree that a lot of fascinating legends surround the 860-acre state park outside the town. The most lurid one has Satan himself playing in the house band while the locally renowned Black Witches of Haddam held Sabbat in the area. According to this legend, Mr. Scratch would sit on a rock near the sixty-foot cascade of Chapman Falls in the center of the park and play while his minions cavorted.

Nutmeggers' Yankee forbearers were kind of obsessed with Satan, and the sabbat origin certainly seems reasonable. Sadly, the origin of the park's strange name is probably more commonplace than legend admits. There are those who maintain that a local farmer and noted bootlegger named Dibble once cultivated a hopyard along Eight Mile River and brewed his harvest into a particularly potent moonshine. According to this version, the park's name began as Dibble's Hopyard, which later evolved into Devil's Hopyard.

Whatever the true origin of its name, there is no denying that this isolated, heavily forested, and reputedly haunted park is a truly spooky place at night. During daylight, though, Devil's Hopyard is a great picnic spot, and the big rocks around Chapman Falls are especially nice for spreading a blanket and whiling away a summer's afternoon. There are some picnic shelters scattered around the park, but most people just lay out a spread near the falls. The park is open from 8 a.m. until sunset.

The granite structure that is East Haddam's **Gillette Castle** (67 River Rd.; 860-526-2336) was built over a five-year period from 1914 to 1919 as the retirement home of the famous actor William Gillette, who designed the edifice, including its unique, hand-carved interior furnishings and appointments. Built on 122 acres, the twenty-four room mansion is now a museum, kept almost as it was when Gillette lived there. Among the actor's possessions on display is his collection of more than 100 scrapbooks filled with pictures of cats. Gillette's best-known stage role was as British detective Sherlock Holmes, and Gillette Castle also houses the largest collection of Holmesiana in the world, including a complete re-creation of Holmes's sitting room at 221B Baker Street.

Gillette specified in his will that the property not "fall into the hands of some blithering saphead who has no conception of where he is or with

Do You Hear What I Hear?

The small village of **Moodus** in East Haddam is the site of a curious phenomenon steeped in legend. At more or less regular intervals, loud noises like the voices of the damned can be heard throughout the town. These are the famous "Moodus Noises."

Native Americans said these noises were the voice of an evil spirit who lived on nearby **Mount Tom**. Early colonists believed the noises were the result of an ongoing battle between the Good Witches of East Haddam and the feared Black Witches of Haddam. According to this myth, when the battle between good and evil goes on too long, a benevolent spirit, Old Machemoodus (for whom Moodus is named) awakes and waves his sapphire wand, clearing away the evil witches and ending the battle. The Black Witches of Haddam then gather their powers once again, and the battle is rejoined, causing more Moodus Noises.

According to geologists, the true cause of the noises is the rubbing of tectonic plates against each other along a fault line, a phenomenon known to generate earthquakes. In fact, in 1791, Moodus was shaken by two quakes that were felt as far away as New York and Boston. In March 2011, the area was shaken again by a 1.3-magnitude earthquake. At first residents feared something had exploded, and firefighters and police searched for a cause before they were alerted that there had been a geological disturbance. Another quake is expected sometime during the next few centuries, and there have been predictions that someday Moodus will be swallowed up by the fault and disappear into the earth forever.

what he is surrounded," thus Gillette Castle is now owned by the State of Connecticut. While there is ample parking, the facilities are generally modest, and the rustic beauty of this spot has been well preserved. The view down the Connecticut River from the castle's broad terraces is one of the best in the state. In late winter and early spring, before the facility opens for the season, you can stand on the main terrace in splendid isolation and watch eagles soar above the river.

In addition to his many other passions, Gillette was a train enthusiast. He had two small working trains that used to make loops around the castle grounds, but they long ago fell into disuse. One has since been refurbished and is now on display.

Gillette Castle is open from 10 a.m. to 5 p.m. (last tour leaves at 4:30 p.m.) from the Sat of Memorial Day weekend through Labor Day. There is a modest admission fee for the castle tour, but none to picnic or walk the grounds, which are open year-round from 8 a.m. until sunset. A snack bar and gift shop are also located on the grounds.

Allegra Farm (69 Town Road; 860-537-8861; allegrafarm.com) calls itself a "living history museum." Home to the Horse Drawn Carriage and Sleigh Museum

Chester–Hadlyme Ferry

A cool way to visit Gillette Castle is to take the **Chester–Hadlyme Ferry** (Route 148) from across the Connecticut River in Chester. This is the second-oldest continuously operating ferry in the US (the Glastonbury–Rocky Hill Ferry is the oldest). The views of the castle from the water are great. It runs Mon through Fri, 7 a.m. to 6:45 p.m.; and weekends Apr through Nov, 10:30 a.m. to 5 p.m. The ferry can accommodate up to eight cars at a time. There's a minimal charge for this fun little ride.

of New England, the farm is located on Lake Hayward, where the owners work hard to keep the past alive. Horses and carriages from the farm have been featured in movies such as *Amistad*, *Time Machine*, *Kate and Leopold*, and Cuba Gooding Jr.'s independent film *Something Whispered*, as well as on TV in *Sex and the City*, of all things. The museum, located in a post-and-beam carriage house and livery stables, is chock-full of carriages, sleighs, coaches, and any other horse-drawn vehicle you can imagine. Horse-drawn carriage rides, sleigh rides, or hayrides are available on reservation. All the horse-drawn rides provide refreshments that vary with the seasons, from iced mint tea to hot chocolate served by a campfire. In the spring and summer, carriages from Allegra Farm are a familiar sight carrying wedding parties throughout the Connecticut River Valley. The museum is open by appointment.

Lyme

Sankow's Beaver Brook Farm (139 Beaver Brook Rd.; 860-434-2843; beaverbrookfarm.com) has been in the same family since 1917 and is a wonderful place to visit. The 175-acre property was originally a working dairy farm, but in the early 1980s, owners Stan and Suzanne Sankow tried their hands at sheep farming. Successful at that for nearly twenty years, they then reintroduced cattle. Today the farm is home to more than 600 sheep and a dozen cows. They produce and sell high-quality products such as all-natural woolen scarves, hats, and cute sweaters finished with pewter farm-animal buttons; yarn from their own wool; artisanal cheeses, yogurt, milk, and more— all made from the farm's own herds. If you're interested, they also offer fresh lamb meats and homemade white bean chili and lamb curry stew. If you're partial to making your own, you can take one of the cooking or knitting classes offered.

The farm is open daily from 9 a.m. to 4 p.m. Farm tours are available by reservation. You can also find this farm's products at various farm markets around the area. If you're in the area the weekend after Thanksgiving, check out Farm Day at Beaver Brook Farm for sheepshearing and spinning demonstrations, hayrides, and free samples of the farm's delicious products.

Old Lyme

The *Florence Griswold Museum* (96 Lyme St.; 860-434-5542; flogris.org) is housed in Florence Griswold's ship-captain father's 1841 house, which she turned into a boardinghouse and salon for painters in the nineteenth century. The light is supposed to be particularly good in this part of the state, due to its proximity to large bodies of reflective water; the shore is near, and the Lieutenant River runs behind the house. Anyway, a community of artists ended up boarding at the Griswold home, where they worked, played, and inspired one another to greater efforts.

The doors and woodwork throughout Florence Griswold's home came to be decorated with original paintings by the likes of Willard Metcalf, Henry Ward Ranger, and Childe Hassam. The vast Griswold collection, including the works of local artists, is on public display inside. The museum is open year-round Tues through Sat, 10 a.m. to 5 p.m.; Sun, 1 to 5 p.m. Admission. Blue Star Museum.

Art lovers should also plan a stop at *Studio 80 + Sculpture Grounds* (80 Lyme St.; 860-434-5957; gilbertboro.com). Located next to the **Lyme Academy College of Fine Arts**, Studio 80 is the personal work space of **Gilbert V. Boro**, an international artist, sculptor, architect, and educator who believes art should help people regain the creativity of childhood. He works in a variety of mediums and his pieces are purchased the world over. Studio 80 is open by appointment.

Connecticut Art Trail

The word *impressionism* generally conjures the revolutionary work of French masters Monet, Renoir, and Degas, but Connecticut was where American impressionism began. From 1885 to 1930, American painters were drawn to Connecticut's picturesque landscape. They painted scenes of bucolic beauty and community life in a distinctive style characterized by vivid colors and broken brushstrokes.

Connecticut is home to ten museums, including the Florence Griswold Museum, that display the work of some of the artists who played leading roles in the American Impressionist movement. These museums, along with eleven other museums and historic sites, compose the *Connecticut Art Trail*, a self-guided tour of the diverse art collections within the state. For a complete list of the museums and more information about the trail, visit arttrail.org.

Outside the studio though, are the Sculpture Grounds, set among four and a half acres of land along the Lieutenant River is a collection of abstract sculptural works inspired by nature. Visitors can wander among the statues and appreciate their setting in nature. You are invited to touch and appreciate the structures. Art critic Jason E. Sharma says of the artwork, ". . . the artist includes the viewer in the work. No longer a detached observer, you feel like a child again, wanting to climb and stroke and remain inside the forms. And you are calm. These strong, open, touchable structures are protective but never constricting." It seems Boro accomplished just what he wished. Sculpture Grounds are open daily, 9 a.m. to 5 p.m. Children are welcome and admission is free.

Ferry Landing Park is home to the **Connecticut Department of Energy and Environmental Protection Marine Fisheries Headquarters and Boating Division** (333 Ferry Rd.; 860-434-8638 for boating; 860-434-6043 for fisheries) and offers a way-cool boardwalk with the added allure of that universal kid (and adult) favorite, trains. This is a wonderful, out-of-the-way destination for parents and kids. (Don't be put off by the dead-end sign on Ferry Road. Just go all the way to the end, and turn into DEEP marine headquarters; the parking lot is beyond the main building.)

The boardwalk meanders along the river and ends at a marsh. At the marsh you'll find an elevated platform, ideal for bird-watching or just watching the river flow. Markers along the walk identify the different animals you might see. The fisherfolk who congregate along the river are more than willing to tell tales to anyone who stops to listen of the big one that got away. The boardwalk also rambles under a railway bridge that gives you an unusual view of speeding trains: underneath! The best time of year to visit is spring through fall. Trains cross the bridge mornings (about 9:30 a.m. to 1 p.m.) and afternoons (around 4 to 6:30 p.m.). The site offers free parking, is wheelchair accessible, and has well-maintained picnic tables. The park closes at sunset.

Niantic

You don't have to be a book lover to spend many contented hours at the **Book Barn** (41 W. Main St.; 860-739-5715; bookbarnniantic.com) in the village of **Niantic**. To call this place a used bookstore is like calling the Grand Canyon a neighborhood park. The Book Barn is a compound of six buildings, each overflowing with volumes and, luckily, meticulously arranged by subject—so, for example, one building houses fiction and poetry, while another is devoted to science and history. There is also an area dedicated exclusively to children's books. Best of all, the proprietors want you to stay as long as possible. Chairs, benches, and couches are strategically placed throughout the complex to entice you to linger. There are also picnic tables, beautiful gardens, and a play area, including a playhouse, for children. A dozen cats also live here and truly believe everyone works for them. There is a goat, too, that you can feed.

If all that doesn't convince you to make an afternoon of it, there's also free coffee, doughnuts, biscuits, and juice. Checkers and chessboards are set up for anyone who has the time and urge to play. Paperbacks cost $1, and hardcover novels run about $4 to $5. The Book Barn also purchases books between the hours of 11 a.m. and 6 p.m. Their buying policy is on the website.

The Book Barn's inventory grew so massive that the owners opened three additional locations: the **Book Barn Downtown** (269 Main St.; 860-691-8078), the **Book Barn Midtown** (291 Main St.; 860-691-3371) in downtown Niantic, and **Store Four** (55 West Main St.; 860-739-0277). We wonder where they'll go next! All stores are open daily 9 a.m. to 9 p.m.

A few doors down is the ***Niantic Cinema*** (279 Main St.; 860-739-6920; nianticcinema.com), considered by many to be the best independent movie theater in the area. The five-screen theater shows first-run movies as well as independent films you won't find at your mall multiplex. Ticket prices are reasonable, and the popcorn is actually affordable.

Also nestled in the Niantic is the ***Children's Museum of Southeastern Connecticut*** (409 Main St.; 860-691-1111; childrensmuseumsect.org). Frequently children's museums overflow with activities for kids over five, but fall short for those younger than that, so this interactive educational center is a real discovery. The exhibits and activities are designed to appeal to, but never talk down to, kids and are engaging enough to capture the attention of adults, too. Imagination Station features a lighthouse, fishing boat, and village, encouraging kids to make their own fun. The Discovery Room introduces visitors to the museum's live animals, including a bearded dragon, a tortoise, tree frogs, gecko, and crabs. Did we mention the bee hive you can watch? Need more hands-on activities? Head to Creation Station and build sculptures, learn about magnets, and play a pipe organ!

Throughout the year, the museum hosts a number of special events and classes, including a respected summer camp program that focuses on the environment, science, and the arts. Open Tues through Sat, 9:30 a.m. to 4:30 p.m.; Sun, noon to 4:30 p.m. Open Mon during summer and school holidays. A picnic area is available. Admission; kids under 2 free.

Rocky Neck State Park (exit 72 off I-95 in Niantic) is a great location for outdoor recreation, but one that consistently fills up on hot summer days. Luckily, it can also be enjoyed in the off-season. If you like things historical, be sure to check out the pavilion, constructed as a Works Progress Administration project. For picnics, though, walk out to the end of the rocky point, where you have the waters of Long Island Sound on three sides. This is a beautiful and peaceful place to pitch a blanket and share a meal. Be sure to bring some stale bread or a couple of anchovy pizzas for the gulls; they seem to expect it. The park has a picnic area and a place to cook. Open daily from 8 a.m. to sunset.

Salem

Salem Valley Farms (20 Darling Rd.; 860-859-2980; salemvalleyfarmsicecream. com) near the junction of Routes 11 and 85 in ***Salem*** is another great ice cream stop. "Rich" is one word for Salem Valley Farms' ice cream—rich and, well, eccentric. How else would you describe an establishment that peddles outrageous flavors like ginger and espresso fudge? Actually, the menu features plenty of familiar flavors, as well as an ever-changing menu of innovative items. Everything is made on the premises and they can have close to 80 flavors at any one time in the summer (a little less in the colder months). If you want to know what you'll find, check their Facebook page, as they usually list them there along with any updates on hours. Open Mon through Thurs, noon to 9 p.m.; Fri through Sun, noon to 10 p.m.; shorter hours in cooler months; closed Jan and Feb.

Mohegan Country

Colchester

Located off Route 16, the 1872 ***Comstock Bridge*** (now honorably retired) is one of Connecticut's three remaining covered bridges. It is now used mainly by fishermen and folks just watching the river flow. The wheelchair-accessible area was designed by Peter Reneson, a polio victim who grew up in ***Colchester***.

Lyman Trumbull, a US senator from Illinois, one of the founders of the Republican Party and coauthor of the Thirteenth Amendment, was born and raised in Colchester in the home of his grandfather, historian Benjamin Trumbull, at 80 Broadway St. The house still stands today, but is private and not open to the public.

Lebanon

Jonathan Trumbull was the only colonial governor (1769–1784) to support the American War of Independence. He organized George Washington's supply line almost single-handedly, and it was largely thanks to Trumbull that Connecticut came to be called the "Supply State." Today at least three buildings in Lebanon are associated with the Trumbulls and the governor's historic efforts to support the Revolution. Two are located near each other on W. Town Street (Route 87) on the green.

The *Jonathan Trumbull House* (169 W. Town St.; 860-642-7558; govtrumbullhousedar.org) was once the governor's home. It was built by Governor Trumbull's father between 1735 and 1740. Today it is furnished with period furniture and administered by the Daughters of the American Revolution. Also on this site is *Wadsworth Stable.* Originally located in Hartford, this stable was saved from demolition due largely to the efforts of Katherine Seymour Day, who raised enough funds to have it relocated. In 1954, the Daughters assumed ownership, dismantled the stable, and moved it to Lebanon. Today it serves as a museum and holds numerous antique wagons and farm implements. While we can't say George Washington slept there, we're pretty sure his horse did. Both the museum and stables are open by appointment.

The third Trumbull property, the 1769 *Jonathan Trumbull Jr. House* (780 Trumbull Hwy.; 860-642-6100; lebanontownhall.org/trumbulljuniormuseum. htm), is a center-chimney farmhouse with eight intricately carved corner fireplaces and a gorgeous original cherry staircase with a molded rail. George Washington really did sleep here, on March 4, 1781. Today it is furnished with both reproductions and period antiques. Open mid-May through Columbus Day, Sat and Sun, noon to 4 p.m.

Built in 1727 as the Trumbull Family Store, the *Revolutionary War Office* (149 W. Town St.; 860-873-3399; lebanontownhall.org/war-office.htm) was where the Council of Safety met to plan the logistical effort that kept Washington's army in the field during the Revolutionary War. Today the building is owned by the Sons of the American Revolution and is open Memorial Day through Labor Day, Sat and Sun noon to 4 p.m. Donations accepted.

The home of **Dr. William Beaumont**, the "father of gastric physiology," is also located in Lebanon. The *Beaumont home* (16 W. Town St.; 860-642-6579; james.com/beaumont/dr_birthplace.htm) is maintained by the **Lebanon Historical Society** and houses a display of surgical instruments and a recreated exam room. Open mid-May through Columbus Day, Sat noon to 4 p.m. or by appointment.

Franklin

Tiny Franklin offers the *Blue Slope Country Museum* (138 Blue Hill Rd.; 860-642-6413; blueslope.com), where city slickers can get acquainted with farm implements and tools housed in a Pennsylvania Dutch–style Amish barn on a 380-acre working dairy farm. The museum offers educational programs and demonstrations relative to the importance of farming in this country. Special events in Oct.

Norwich

Located at the confluence of the Yantic and Shetucket Rivers, *Norwich* was founded in the second half of the seventeenth century. By 1776, it was the second-largest city in Connecticut. Because of that, Norwich is an important historical cornucopia that was often overlooked. A group of representatives from organizations across the city decided to change all that and formed **The Norwich Heritage Groups** with the goal of finding the best ways to promote tourism while preserving and protecting the city's resources. In 2015, in collaboration with the **Norwich Historical Society**, the group opened the *Norwich Heritage and Regional Visitors Center* (69 East Town St.; 860-886-1776) as a center of operations.

A large part of Norwich's history comes from the fact that it was a major Patriot stronghold during the Revolutionary War. Among Norwich's sons who fought in that war was **Benedict Arnold**, the infamous American general who tried to turn West Point over to the British and who later burned New London. And although Arnold was a traitor to his country, he is Norwich's traitor and they celebrate this and what it had to teach us. In fact, the center is located in the historic 1787 *Daniel Lathrop School House*, a school made possible and dedicated to Benedict Arnold's mentor Daniel Lathrop. The school house is usually open from the end of Apr to Oct, Wed through Sun, 10 a.m. to 4 p.m. It's always best to check ahead to be sure someone will be there.

Other Arnold sites can be found on the *Benedict Arnold Walking Trail of Colonial Norwichtown* (walknorwich.org/benedict-arnold-trail). This two-mile trail starts at the site of the *Arnold Family Homestead* (corner of Washington St. and Arnold Pl.) and ends at the grave site of Arnold's mother, Hannah Waterman Arnold, who some say died of a broken heart. The website has an amazing narration of the tour, which you can listen to on your phone as you walk the trail. There are twenty-two stops on the trail which takes an estimated forty minutes to complete, depending on how fast you walk.

There are three other walking trails created by Heritage Groups with trail maps and information all contained on their website (walknorwich.org/walk-norwich-trails) and future trails in the works. There's even some cool swag to be had to show your support of this great organization. Free trail brochures are also available at the visitors center, city hall, chamber of commerce, Otis Library, Slater Memorial Museum, and Leffingwell House Museum.

The *Slater Memorial Museum and Converse Art Gallery* (108 Crescent St.; 860-887-2506; slatermuseum.org), on the campus of the Norwich Free Academy, doesn't have the romantic lure of some of Norwich's historical attractions, but it's well worth a visit, especially if you've never been able to get to the Louvre or any of the other great European sculpture galleries.

This imposing three-story Romanesque structure was built in 1888 to house a truly impressive collection of plaster casts of famous Greek, Roman, and Renaissance sculpture. The casts are still the main attraction, but in addition to that collection (one of the three finest in the US), the museum also has displays of antique American and European furniture, Native American artifacts, textiles, and various fine art, including one of the best collections of Hudson River School art in America. Open Tues through Fri, 9 a.m. to 4 p.m.; Sat and Sun, 1 to 4 p.m. Admission, although Sat in July and Aug are free.

New England's old, hallowed cemeteries are among the best places to visit during the fall (or any time of year, really). The headstone inscriptions tell us much about rich and poor families as well as entire social histories. Travelers with proper doses of curiosity can easily get lost in the past. *Old Norwichtown Burial Ground* (Old Cemetery Lane; 860-886-4683) off Town Street reveals a rich colonial history. You'll find the graves of Mrs. Arnold and other Arnold family members, as well as the final resting place of Samuel Hunter, signer of the Declaration of Independence. Open every day until dusk. Brochures are available at the cemetery entrance for self-guided tours.

Early in the seventeenth century, a Pequot subchief named **Uncas** formed a new tribe, the **Mohegans**. During the Pequot Wars of 1638, Uncas and his people sided with the British, beginning a century of intimate involvement in the affairs of European settlers. The Mohegans and Pequots eventually united under Uncas's leadership, and they became a powerful force in southwestern Connecticut. The first major American novelist, **James Fenimore Cooper**, recounted part of their story in his 1826 sensation, *The Last of the Mohicans,* one of his famous Leatherstocking Tales.

Chief Uncas died in 1682. He is buried in the *Indian Burial Grounds* on Sachem Street in Norwich. **President Andrew Jackson** laid the cornerstone of Uncas's monument in 1833.

In the northern section of Norwich you'll find the village of Yantic, perhaps best known for the *Yantic Falls* (210 Yantic St.) on the Yantic River. The area around the falls was once a favored campsite of the Mohegan Indians in the 1640s. The tribe's sachem, **Uncas**, led his people into a battle in the area against their rival the **Narragansetts**. The legend goes that the Mohegan warriors chased the Narragansetts to the edge of the falls, where the Narragansetts chose the deadly leap into Yantic River over surrendering to the Mohegans.

Despite the violent legend, today the falls are beautiful to see. There is a pedestrian bridge that offers photo-worthy views of the falls as they cascade forty feet over rocks to the river below. A train bridge also crosses the river, but does not detract from the view. Exercise caution when exploring the falls, as the volume of water is one of the most powerful in the state.

Montville

In 1931, **John Tantaquidgeon**, a direct descendant of Chief Uncas, founded the *Tantaquidgeon Museum* (1819 Norwich–New London Rd. [Rte. 32]; 860-848-3985; mohegan.nsn.us) in the Uncasville section of *Montville*. Here the culture and history of the Mohegans and other New England Indians are presented in a series of displays featuring artifacts of stone, wood, and bone made by Indian craftsmen throughout the years. Artifacts from other tribes of the Southeast, Southwest, and Plains are housed in their own sections. Open year-round, Tues through Fri, 10 a.m. to 3 p.m. Tours are given by members of the Mohegan Tribe. It's best to call ahead to check their availability.

Just 200 yards from the Tantaquidgeon Museum is the *Mohegan Congregational Church* (27 Church Ln.; 860-848-2029; mohegancongregationalchurch.synthasite.com), a 1831 meetinghouse founded by three members of the Tantaquidgeon family a century before their descendent would create the Tantaquidgeon Museum. The three women, Lucy Occom Tantaquidgeon, her daughter Lucy Tantaquidgeon Teecomwas, and her granddaughter Cynthia Teecomas Hoscoat had the foresight to know that identifying themselves as Christian would help them keep their land. They gave this piece of land on Mohegan Hill to the tribe for the purpose of erecting a church for the community. Their strategy worked, and the church is still in use today. Services are every Sun at 9:30 and all are welcome to participate.

West of Mohegan Hill, off Raymond Hill Road, is the ninety-two-acre *Cochegan Rock Forest*, now owned by the Mohegan Tribe and closed to the public. The tribe was able to reacquire this land, which is sacred to them, from The Boy Scouts of America in 2007. The tribe purchased the tract of land with revenue from their casinos, as they have done for other sacred sites in the state. One of the reasons this land is so important to the tribe is that it is the site of **Cochegan Rock**, the secret meeting place of Uncas and his counselors. This rock is huge, although reported measurements vary, and is believed to be the largest freestanding rock in New England. The tribe allows the Scouts to continue to use the land, but it is closed to the general public because of past vandalism and illegal activities.

Farther north, near the village of Mohegan and across the street from *Mohegan Sun Casino* is *Shantok, Village of Uncas* (Fort Shantok Rd.), formerly known as Fort Shantok State Park. The land on which this park sits was an early settlement of the Mohegan tribe under their Sachem Uncas. They lived on this land from mid- to late seventeenth century. During that time, Uncas allied with the English, which didn't make him popular with the other tribes. In 1645, the Sachem used the fort here as a stronghold against members of the warring Narragansett Tribe. Uncas may just have succumbed to the Narragansetts if Thomas Leffingwell had not come to his aid. Today, there is a memorial to Lieutenant Leffingwell acknowledging his help. The history of the land is murky, with the general truth being that the state of Connecticut seized the land through eminent domain in the early twentieth century. In 1994, the Mohegan Tribe was allowed to regain their land from the state through the 1983 Land Claims Settlement act, at the cost of $3 million. In 1998, the tribe began to restore the land resulting in the beautiful setting that exists today, which includes a playground, walking trails, ball fields, barbecue pits and grills, and an outdoor amphitheater. The area, however, is still sacred ground, containing more than 100 graves and a Mohegan tribal cemetery. So while they urge people to enjoy the area, they also ask that sacred areas be respected.

A small stand of pines known as **Freedom Forest** can also be found in the Shantok village. This tiny forest is dedicated to those who fought in **Operation Desert Storm**. It seems this land gives us more than one reason to reflect. Open daily, dawn to dusk.

Montville also offers an attraction of a different sort from an earlier time in our history. **The Dinosaur Place at Nature's Art Village** (1650 Hartford–New London Tpke.; 860-443-4367; naturesartvillage.com) features a forty-foot tall brachiosaurus and more than forty of his friends who roamed the earth millions of years ago. There are one and a half miles of trails through the woods where visitors encounter life-size prehistoric surprises. There is also a splash pad, children's playground, a replica silver mine, mini-golf, outdoor picnic area, and ice cream shop. Open daily Apr through Labor Day, 10 a.m. to 6 p.m.; reduced hours before and after the peak season. Last ticket to the park is sold 1 hour before closing. Admission.

The Eastern Shore

Ledyard

In **Ledyard,** on Route 214, you'll find the eleven-acre property on which sits the **Ledyard Powered-Up–Powered-Down Sawmill** (Iron Street; 860-464-2575; ledyardsawmill.org), an unusual restored 1860 water-powered vertical sawmill. The park also has a working blacksmith shop, a two-acre mill pond, an 1878 "Lane" shingle mill, ice-harvesting equipment, and a picnic area. The park is staffed by volunteers and the saw operates when the water level is sufficient, usually Apr, May, and mid-Oct to Nov; open to the public Sat 1 to 4 p.m. during those times.

Spooky Seaside Sanatorium

The now-defunct *Seaside Sanatorium* (36 Shore Road) occupies thirty-six amazing acres on Magonk Point on Long Island Sound in Waterford. But as beautiful as it appears, it's past is dark and it's future unsure.

The building was designed by noted architect **Cass Gilbert** (of NY Woolworth Building fame) and opened in 1934 as a hospital to treat children with tuberculosis. They thought that sun and fresh salt air would be good for patients. Following the widespread success of the TB vaccine in the 1950s, the hospital was no longer treating patients, and in 1958, the facility was converted into senior housing. In the early 1960s the facility found a new purpose as a home for the mentally disabled and it continued to serve as a sanatorium until allegations of abuse and a few too many suspicious deaths forced its closure in 1996.

The property passed from developer to developer without receiving much, if any, love. Eventually the state gained ownership and in 2014 the property was declared a state park, the first one on Long Island since Bluff Point State Park was established in 1963. The buildings have all been recognized by the **National Register of Historic Places**, and in 2018, Connecticut DEEP put out a request for proposals for a "partner to help restore and reuse" the buildings on the property. We'll have to wait and see what happens, but in the meantime, visitors are welcome to visit and walk the grounds, which are open from dawn to dusk.

Entering the buildings is strictly prohibited, and despite the obvious safety reasons, there might be another good reason to keep your distance. Considering the Seaside Sanatorium and its various buildings have remained vacant for at least two decades, it's not surprising that stories of strange happenings and possible hauntings have circulated. All the usual characters of paranormal investigators have visited the site with various experiences. In 2007, the New England Paranormal Video Research Group claimed to have captured some EVPs (electronic voice phenomenon), and a few spirit orbs appeared in their photos. Maybe the former patients roam the halls and grounds, still hoping the fresh air and salt water will heal them. Maybe it's one of the abused patients who met an untimely death and wants someone to hear his story. Whatever the case, it's up to you if you want to visit these hauntingly beautiful grounds and see for yourself.

New London

Between 1784 and 1907, New London was home port to 196 whaling vessels, over twice as many as ventured from all other Connecticut ports combined. The industry peaked in 1846 and died off rapidly thereafter.

This history is reflected in the city's ***Whale Oil Row*** (105-119 Huntington St.), a series of four Greek Revival houses built by **Charles Henry Boebe** between 1835 and 1845. Originally built for Ezra Chappel, the homes were the private residences of leading businessmen of the time until they were turned into commercial office space in the mid-twentieth century. The four buildings were listed on the National Register of Historic Places in 1970. They are still beautiful to behold, a piece of history that carries some of the aura of those days when Connecticut whale oil helped light the lamps of America.

New London's twenty-six block ***Historic Waterfront District*** (City Pier behind Union Train Station) has so many great things to see and do. To follow in the footsteps of such figures as Nathan Hale, Benedict Arnold, and Eugene O'Neill is an experience in itself, but there's also shopping and dining galore.

If you're more of water fan than a land lubber, visit the granite-walled 1833 ***Custom House Maritime Museum*** (150 Bank St.; 860-447-2501; nlmaritimesociety.org), the oldest operating custom house in America, where you can book a variety of cruises and peruse centuries of maritime history. There may be a wait for some of these cruises after you purchase your tickets. It can be hot during the summer and your spot in line isn't in the shade. Just be prepared.

Be sure to check out the museum's front doors, which were assembled from planks taken from the frigate USS *Constitution* (Old Ironsides). Open Jan through Mar, Thurs to Sun, 1 to 5 p.m.; Apr through Dec, Wed to Sun, 1 to 5 p.m. Admission.

As a way to highlight the history that is New London, the Copp family and the staff at the ***Avery-Copp House*** in Groton (see write-up below) put the wheels in motion to create the ***Thames River Heritage Park*** (1 Waterfront Park; thamesriverheritagepark.org). Billed as "a new kind of state park" the Thames River Heritage Park pulls together a way for people to visit eighteen national and historic sites along both shores of the Thames River. It includes sites in both New London and Groton and includes four centuries of our nation's history.

Opened in 2016, the Thames River Heritage Park is the only heritage park in the state. Perhaps the coolest part of the park is that it's all tied together by water taxi. Boarding and disembarking is available at three of the sites: Fort Trumbull State Park in New London (on the hour), City Pier in New London (twenty minutes after the hour), and Thames River Landing in Groton (forty minutes after the hour). Parking is available at these locations as well.

This is a relaxing way to explore these sites. Visitors travel at their leisure between stops, spending as much time as they'd like at each. The taxi runs in a continuous loop, and people hop on and hop off on their way to and from the sites. Each ride takes about fifteen minutes.

A complete list of the sites and their history is on the park's website. You can choose to visit them all, or just a few. There is so much history in this one area, it will be a tough decision to make! You can purchase round-trip tickets online or on the boat. The taxies are not handicapped accessible at this time and there are no restrooms aboard. Bikes are allowed if there is room. Dogs are welcome, but must carried or able to navigate the ramp onto and off the boat.

The taxi runs Fri, noon to 10 p.m.; Sat, 10 a.m. to 10 p.m.; Sun, 10 a.m. to 9 p.m. Holidays follow a Sun schedule. After a last stop at Fort Trumbull at 7 p.m., the taxi runs between City Pier, New London, and Thames River Landing, Groton, every twenty minutes beginning at 7:20 at City Pier. Operation is contingent on the weather, so be sure to check the website before heading out.

Some of the New London sites you can reach by water taxi include:

- *Nathan Hale Schoolhouse* (19 Atlantic Street; 860-334-2858; connecticutsar.org/sites/nl-schoolhouse.htm) where Nathan Hale taught from 1774 to 1775.

- *The Shaw Mansion* (11 Blinman St.; 860-443-1209; nlhistory.org), home of the **New London Historical Society**, as it has been since 1907. No, that's not a typo. Founded in 1870, this society is the oldest historical organization in eastern Connecticut. Considered the cradle of the American navy, the Shaw Mansion was built in 1756 by Captain Nathaniel Shaw and served as Connecticut's naval office during the Revolutionary War (we're not sure if George Washington slept here, but he definitely visited). This is one of the few structures to survive Benedict Arnold's burning of the city. Five generations of Captain Shaw's family lived here until it was turned over to the historical society. Today the mansion is home to an impressive collection of items.

- The 1678 *Joshua Hempsted House* (11 Hempsted St.; 860-443-7949) also survived Arnold's burning 1781. This home of the famous Connecticut diarist, Joshua Hempsted, is now the oldest surviving house in New London. One of the interesting features of this home is that it is insulated with seaweed. Owned by Connecticut Landmarks, it houses a collection of abolitionist papers. Hempsted's diary can be seen at the museum at the Shaw Mansion.

- *Fort Trumbull* (90 Walbach St.; 860-444-7591) was originally built to protect the harbor from the British, but the structure that stands today was constructed sometime between 1839 and 1852. The views from the fort over the harbor are second to none. You can walk the grounds and the interior of the fort. There are multimedia exhibits showing the movement of Benedict Arnold's troops in 1781. The fort also has a great fishing for striped bass, bluefish, weakfish, and tautog.

- *Monte Cristo Cottage* (325 Pequot Ave.; 860-443-5378; theoneill.org/mcc) is the boyhood home of **Eugene O'Neill**, arguably America's greatest playwright. Named for O'Neill's actor-father's best-known stage role, Monte Cristo Cottage is a pretty gingerbread structure that looks like it should be filled with light and laughter. Alas, the years O'Neill and his brother Jamie spent there were more like one of the Grimms' darker fairy tales. Both father James and brother Jamie were heavy drinkers. O'Neill's mother, Ella, addicted to morphine from O'Neill's birth, battled her own demons throughout his childhood. She is said to haunt the tiny cottage.

- *Lyman Allyn Art Museum* (625 Williams St.; 860-443-2545; lymanallyn.org) was established in 1926 at the bequest of Harriet Upson Allyn, the youngest of whaling captain Lyman Allyn's six children. The museum opened six years later with a small collection Today the museum contains multiple galleries of more than 15,000 works, a research library, offices, and more. Also located on the museum grounds is the historic Deshon-Allyn House, a nineteenth-century mansion that was home Lyman Allyn.

- The sea has always been at the heart of New London, so it's no surprise that it is home to the *US Coast Guard Academy* (31 Mohegan Ave.; 860-444-8400; uscga.edu). Visitors are welcomed year-round to tour the academy, but they need to make arrangements ahead of time through a link on the website. The public is also invited to attend public events, but are subject to security measures (be sure to check the website so you'll have all the necessary paperwork). Also of note, any time you pass a marching formation on campus, they have the right of way. Do not pass them, just stop and stay out of their way.

- *Ledge Lighthouse* (ledgelighthouse.org) rises out of Long Island Sound at the beginning of the Thames River. Sometimes shrouded in early-morning fog, the lighthouse can have an eerie countenance, which fits right in with the rumor that the light is haunted by a ghost named Ernie. Some believe Ernie was a light keeper who, depressed by marital problems, cut his own throat and jumped off the structure. Some reports say the ghost is a tall, bearded man dressed in a slicker and rain hat. The ghost has been known to untie boats, hide coffee cups and radios, and slam doors. The lighthouse is atop a sixty-five-foot, three-story square building in the water at the meeting of the Thames River, Fisher's Island Sound, and Long Island Sound in New London Harbor. It was abandoned in 1987, and the structure took a beating from the elements. Once again, Nutmeggers jumped into action and the New London Ledge Lighthouse Foundation was formed to save the iconic landmark. Today, fully renovated, the lighthouse once again stands in glory, complete with an interpretive museum and small theater. The foundation offers tours from July through Sept, details on their website. The New London Maritime Society and Cross Sound Ferry offer a variety of lighthouse tours that include Ledge Lighthouse. They can be pricey, but check them out.

Groton

The Thames River Heritage Park tour continues into neighboring Groton. There's so much history in this area, we think you'll need more than one day pass to the taxi! Thank goodness, season passes are available.

Some of the Groton sites you can reach by water taxi include:

- *Fort Griswold Battlefield State Park* (Park Avenue; 860-445-1729) is the site of a 1781 massacre of American troops at the hands of a force of 800 British soldiers under the command of traitor Benedict Arnold. At that time, Yankee privateers based in New London were a thorn in the side of the British in New York, and Arnold came to burn the town, which he did, destroying 150 buildings. The part of his force that advanced up the east bank of the Thames suffered heavy casualties assaulting Fort Griswold, which was held by a force of 150 militia under the command of Colonel William Ledyard. When Ledyard finally surrendered, he was murdered with his own sword, and eighty of his men were slaughtered. Many of Fort Griswold's old emplacements remain, and there are some interesting historical displays. The 134-foot monument tower provides a nice view of the coast.

- *The Avery-Copp House Museum* (154 Thames St.; 860-445-1637; averycopphouse.org) is the little museum that started it all. They are the force behind the Thames River Heritage Park. The historic house in which they are located was built in the early nineteenth century by Rufus Avery. Remarkably, the house remained occupied by the Avery family for generations, with the last family member living there until his death in 1991 at the age of 101. Many of the original furnishings remain, providing a unique window into their lives.

- *Submarine Force Museum* (1 Crystal Lake Rd.; 860-694-3174; ussnautilus.org) houses the world's first atomic submarine, the *USS Nautilus*. The museum includes extensive exhibits tracing the history of America's submarine fleet and offers a pair of top-notch multimedia shows in two different theaters: one tracing the history of the submarine force from the days of David Bushnell's **Turtle** to the machines of today, and one dealing specifically with *Nautilus*.

If you're out with the kids (furred or otherwise) and don't have time for the water taxi tour but need to burn off some energy, Groton has some great state parks. **Haley Farm State Park** (Haley Farm Lane; 860-444-7591) is a great place to explore. It has two hundred acres filled with trails near Palmer Cove. There is a bike trail (also wheelchair accessible) that winds its way along beautiful former farmland. The stone walls you see scattered across the property were a hobby of former owner Caleb Haley, who farmed the land in the late nineteenth century into the twentieth.

From Halley Farm you can reach **Bluff Point State Park** (Depot Road; 860-444-7591) on a bridge over railroad tracks. Bluff Point is an eight hundred-acre coastal reserve that offers a boat launch, shell (permit required) and salt-water fishing, and hiking. This place is also pet-friendly, and a wonderful way to spend a day.

It's the strange place with a strange name. **Gungywamp** in northern Groton is shrouded in mystery. Theories as to who created the strange rock formations on this land range from usual Yankee ingenuity to aliens. The fact that the land has not been readily accessible to the public added to the mystique. Archaeologists as well as ghost hunters have had their say. Strange phenomenon has been reported at the site, including sunlight strategically pouring through certain places of the stone chambers at certain times of the day, suggesting the chambers and stone rings were ceremonial. There's a large cliff called the **Cliff of Tears** that seems to elicit strong feelings of sadness or apprehension in some. Whatever the case, the stones have been dated and are considered to be centuries old; nearby pottery shards and arrow heads have been dated to the Paleo and Woodland time periods.

As of July 2018, the property has officially been turned over to the state and—barring any legal issues—it will become a state park. Connecticut DEEP officials, Denison Pequotsepos Nature Center, the State Historic Preservation Office, and the Office of the State Archaeology are putting their collective heads together to decide the best course of action to take for the land. They want the archaeological resources to be preserved while still allowing the public to see, enjoy, and learn from them. There's also the issue of entrance to the site, which is pretty much surrounded by private property, so easements will have to be secured.

In the meantime, you can take a virtual tour on the nature center's website (dpnc.org/gungywamp) to see what people are fighting to save and learn about the history of the land.

Mystic

Mystic Whaler Cruises (mysticwhalercruises.com) also conducts cruises out of New London from June through Oct. Choose from lobster dinner cruises, Sunday brunch cruises, sunset cruises, or even sailing vacations. Sail for a few hours or a few days.

The forty-five acre *Coogan Farm* (162 Greenmanville Ave.) is the last parcel of undeveloped land in the village of *Mystic*. Obtained by **Denison Pequotsepos Nature Center** (109 Pequotsepos Rd.; 860-536-1216; dpnc.org), this land and its history are being preserved. The farm began with **Captain John Gallup** receiving five hundred acres from John Winthrop, Jr. for his work in the Pequot War. Parts and parcels of the land exchanged hands throughout the years, but today the farm can be enjoyed by everyone, with walking and biking trails throughout the property. The trails are free for the public to use year-round from dawn to dusk.

The nature center operates two nature stores, one at the DPNC headquarters on Pequotsepos Road and the other at the Coogan Farm. All profits from the stores support their environmental education programs. You'll find a range of products, including bird feeders, nest boxes, books, items from local artisans, and more. The nature center is open year-round, Mon through Sat, 9 a.m. to 5 p.m.; Sun, 10 a.m. to 4 p.m. The store at the farm is open Sat and Sun, 10 a.m. to 4 p.m. Admission. Blue Star Museum.

mystictrivia

Mystic derives its name from the Pequot Native American word *mistuket.*

Mystic Drawbridge Ice Cream (2 Main St.; 860-572-7978; mysticdrawbridgeicecream.com) is a cute ice cream parlor that locals claim has the best ice cream around. The Mystic Mud, Mystic Turtle, and Seaport Sally Swirl are Drawbridge originals. Summer hours: daily, 11 a.m. to 11 p.m. Fall and Spring hours: Sun through Thurs, noon to 10 p.m.; Fri and Sat, 11:30 a.m. to 11 p.m. Winter hours: Sun through Thurs, noon to 6 p.m.; Fri and Sat, noon to 9 p.m. By the way, that cute drawbridge is called a *bascule* (French for "seesaw"). You'll have plenty of time to contemplate its rare beauty because car traffic along Main Street goes into gridlock when it's raised to allow boats to pass.

The *Hoxie Scenic Overlook*, between exits 89 and 90 on the northbound side of I-95, offers a postcard view of Mystic Seaport. To the east you can see the seaport, home port to the *Charles W. Morgan* whaling ship, the *L. A. Dunton*, and the square-rigged *Joseph Conrad*, among others. The bluff on the right is where the Pequot Indian War was fought.

Stonington

Stonington is perched on a mile-long peninsula so narrow that you can stand on some cross streets and see the ocean on either side. Were it not for the town's protected harbor, it is unlikely that anyone would ever have chosen to build in such a confined space. That harbor, however, made Stonington a center of New England's whaling and sealing industries in the first half of the nineteenth century. It also helped make Stonington an important railroad terminus. In the early days of railroading, before rail bridges crossed the state's major rivers, Stonington was on the most direct route between Boston and New York, and seventeen separate tracks once converged on the town. In those times, passengers arriving by rail from Boston had to board steamboats in Stonington Harbor for the trip to New York.

At the height of Stonington's fortunes, the town's two main streets were packed cheek by jowl with commercial buildings and the fancy homes of wealthy merchants. When whaling and sealing fell off, the railroad moved on, and Stonington, which lacked the real estate to expand into a bedroom community, was left frozen in the mid-nineteenth century. Most of the beautiful federal and Greek revival homes are still there, only now they're B&Bs, restaurants, antiques stores, and crafts shops.

In 1820, Captain Nathaniel Palmer left from Stonington harbor and embarked on a sailing trip that resulted in the discovery of Antarctica. You can visit the 1853 *Captain Nathaniel B. Palmer House* (40 Palmer St.; 860-535-8445), which Captain Nat, as he was known, built with his brother, Alexander. Built in the late federal style, the home has fourteen rooms and a cupola that looks out over the shipyard and lighthouse. The worn floorboards of the lookout tower are a testament to how often worried family members paced the floors watching for sea captains returning from their trips. A restored outbuilding with an icehouse and workshop is located on the grounds, along with a genealogy library and a collection of oil portraits. This National Historic Landmark also has a permanent exhibit that traces the Palmer family's role in the state's maritime history. Changing exhibitions relate to Palmer, Stonington, and maritime history. The home is bordered by water on three sides, and the property has been naturalistically landscaped. Visitors are encouraged to stroll the grounds and bring a picnic lunch. The Palmer house is open May to Oct, Fri through Mon 1 to 5 p.m. Admission.

Cannon Square, toward the south end of Market Street, marks the site where the Stonington militia successfully fought off the British in August 1814. It and the surrounding streets are the center of Stonington's historic district.

Stroll up Main Street from the square (away from the point) and admire the architecture of the 1827 **Old Customs House** and the elegant 1780 **Captain**

Amos Palmer House, both worth more than a passing glance, although privately owned. In fact, **James MacNeill Whistler**, who painted *Whistler's Mother,* spent part of his boyhood in this house.

Down at the end of Water Street is an especially popular local landmark, the **Old Lighthouse Museum** (7 Water St.; 860-535-1440; stoningtonhistory. org/visit/the-old-lighthouse-museum). It was constructed in 1823 but was moved to its present location in 1840 to protect it from erosion. It is now a museum housing six rooms of exhibits, whaling and nautical displays, a collection of pre-1835 pottery made locally, an ice-harvesting exhibit, and the popular lighthouse display, featuring a fourth-order Fresnel lens and photography of the lighthouses of Long Island Sound. There is also a children's room with an antique dollhouse. If you care to climb the stone steps to the top of the lighthouse, you'll be rewarded with a stunning view of Long Island Sound, including Fisher's Island. If you're at the museum around day's end, linger awhile to see a spectacular sunset over Stonington Point. Open May to Oct, Thurs through Tues, 10 a.m. to 5 p.m. Admission includes a tour of the Captain Nathaniel B. Palmer House.

The **Mashantucket Pequot Museum and Research Center** (110 Pequot Trail; 860-396-6800; pequotmuseum.org) on the Mashantucket Pequot Reservation in Mashantucket is without a doubt one of the most beautiful, stunning, and moving museums in all of Connecticut.

Mashantucket Pequots invested $135 million of the monies earned from the nearby Foxwoods Casino into building this state-of-the-art museum and research center. The museum brings to life the story and history of the Mashantucket Pequot people, a history spanning 20,000 years, from the last ice age to today, and that of other Native American tribal nations.

The life of woodland Native Americans is portrayed in stunning detail with dazzling multisensory dioramas and exhibits. Based on years of scholarly research and the works of Native American artisans, re-creations of life in a sixteenth-century Pequot village, a seventeenth-century Pequot fort, and an eighteenth-century farmstead were created. You can hunt caribou along simulated glacial crevasses—complete with howling winds and the sounds of creaking ice. When you visit the village, you'll hear the sounds of children playing and women working and smell the smoke of many campfires. The detail of each diorama is magnificent, especially the life-size, hand-painted Indian figures, cast from living Native Americans. In a specially designed theater, you can watch a thirty minute film called *The Witness*, which recounts the 1637 massacre of six hundred Pequots at the Mystic fort.

Don't miss the 185-foot stone-and-glass observation tower, which gives you a sweeping view of the area. In fall, this is one of the best places in the

ANNUAL EVENTS IN COAST & COUNTRY

FEBRUARY–MARCH

Eagle Watch Cruises
Essex
(860) 662-0577
ctriverquest.com/portfolio/wintereagle

JUNE

Antique & Classic Boat Rendezvous
Mystic Seaport Museum
75 Greemanville Ave., Mystic
(860) 572-0711
mysticseaport.org

JULY

Guilford Art Center Craft Expo
411 Church St., Guilford
(203) 453-5947
guilfordartcenter.org/expo

North Stonington Agricultural Fair
21 Wyassup Rd., Stonington
northstoningtonfair.com
(860) 535-3956

Sailfest
New London City Pier
(860) 444-1879
sailfest.org

AUGUST

Potato and Corn Festival
Augur Field
290 Forest Rd., North Branford
nbpotatofest.com

Lebanon Country Fair
122 Mack Rd., Lebanon
lebanoncountryfair.org
(860) 642-6012

CT Renaissance Festival
Lebanon County Fairgrounds
122 Mack Rd., Lebanon
(860) 478 5954
ctfaire.com

Ledyard Fair
740 Colonel Ledyard Hwy., Ledyard
ledyardfair.org
(860) 464-9122

Pumpkins n' Pooches Autumn Fair and Dog Festival
Colchester Town Green
(860) 334-6511

Schemitzun
Mashantucket Reservation
(800) 369-9663
schemitzun.mptn-nsn.gov/gcphome.aspx

CT Maritime Heritage Festival
239 Bank St., New London
(860) 447-2519
ctmaritimefest.com

Lebanon County Fair
Lebanon County Fairgrounds
122 Mack Rd., Lebanon
(860) 642-6012
lebanoncountryfair.org

Hamburg Fair
Sterling City Rd., Lyme
Hamburgfair.org

SEPTEMBER

Durham Fair
24 Town House Rd., Durham
(860) 349-9495
durhamfair.com

Guilford Fair
Guilford Fairgrounds
Stone House Ln. and Lovers Ln.,
Guilford
(203) 453-3543
guilfordfair.org

Preston Scarecrow Festival
Preston City Congregational Church
321 Rte. 164
(860) 887-4647

Cruise, Blues, and Brews Festival
Chester Fairgrounds
11 Kirtland Terr., Chester
cruisebluesandbrews.com

Chester Fair
Chester Fairgrounds
11 Kirtland Terr., Chester
(860) 582-5947
chesterfair.org

Haddam Neck Fair
26 Quarry Hill Rd., Haddam Neck
(860) 267-5922
haddamneckfair.com

OCTOBER

Chowder Days
Mystic Seaport
75 Greemanville Ave., Mystic
(860) 572-0711
mysticseaport.org

Portland Fair
Exchange Club Fairgrounds
1348 Main St., Portland
(860) 342-0188
portlandfair.com

DECEMBER

Holiday Magic
Mystic Seaport
75 Greemanville Ave., Mystic
(860) 572-0711
mysticseaport.org

state to take in the brilliant reds and golds of a New England autumn. It's best to visit the tower before going through the museum. Somehow seeing the sweep of the Pequot homeland makes the exhibits and dioramas all the more meaningful.

The museum is open Apr to Oct, Wed through Sat, 9 a.m. to 5 p.m. (last admission at 4 p.m.); Nov, Tues through Sat, 9 a.m. to 5 p.m. (last admission at 4 p.m.). Closed major holidays. Admission.

North Stonington

On Route 2 in **North Stonington** is the **John Randall House** (41 Norwich–Westerly Rd.). This is a house with a history. The Randall family's original clapboard building dates to 1685, with additions made in 1720 and 1790. The house is a landmark on the National Register of Historic Places as well as a stop on the Connecticut Freedom Trail. In the past, it has been a home, a restaurant, and an inn.

For years, the house sat empty and abandoned until Jovial Foods, Inc. purchased the property and began breathing new life into it. According to the Facebook page for Randall's Ordinary, restoration work will soon begin and the field behind the house has already been prepped for organic farming.

And it seems those living in North Stonington aren't the only one excited about the home's restoration, according to a recent post on the Randall's Ordinary page: I heard a story from our warehouse the other day. One of our employees saw a man pass by the window, but when he went to check outside, no one was there. He returned to packing e-commerce orders, and the very next order was being to shipped to a customer named John Randall. Coincidence? We've had a few other friendly signs that John Randall is with us."

So be sure to watch to see what happens next.

Griswold

What do you do with an acre of sunflowers? They're pretty, sure, but they don't have much use except for feeding the cows. The owners at **Buttonwood Farm** (473 Shetucket Tpke.; 860-376-4081; buttonwoodfarmicecream.com) had another idea. They started the Sunflowers for Wishes fundraiser to benefit the Connecticut chapter of the Make a Wish Foundation. The following year, they planted ten acres that produced approximately 300,000 blooms. They sold those for $5 a bundle, and 100 percent of the $500,000 they raised went to the foundation. Now they are up to fourteen acres. The event usually runs the third week of July, 10 a.m. to dusk. All bouquets are on a first-come-first-serve basis. When they're gone, they're gone.

The farm also offers homemade ice cream and other products and sponsors events Mar through Oct. Summer hours: Mon through Fri, noon to 9 p.m.; Sat and Sun, 11:30 a.m. to 9 p.m. Hours vary depending on the time of year, so check their website before heading out. Be prepared to wait in line for the ice cream; it's often out to the parking lot. But the setting is so pleasant you really don't mind.

Places to Stay in Coast & Country

IVORYTON

Copper Beech Inn
46 Main St.
(860) 767-0330
Expensive
copperbeechinn.com
1890-vintage main building
with four guest rooms
with antique and country
furnishings and a carriage
house with nine rooms
with a mix of more modern
amenities. Full American
breakfast comes with all
rooms

MADISON

Madison Beach Hotel
94 W. Wharf Rd.
(203) 245-1404
curiocollection3.hilton.com
Expensive
Beautiful beach resort/hotel
right on the water

Tidewater Inn
949 Boston Post Rd.
(203) 245-8457
thetidewater.com
Moderate to expensive
A former stagecoach stop
offering eight guest rooms
Off-season rates are more
reasonable

MYSTIC

Hilton Mystic
20 Coogan Blvd.
(860) 572-0731
www3.hilton.com
Moderate to expensive
Good bet for lodging
with children; close to
local attractions. Open
year-round

House of 1833 B&B
72 N. Stonington Rd.
(860) 536-6325 or (800)
FOR-1833
houseof1833.com
Moderate to expensive
An elegant and romantic
Greek revival mansion

OLD LYME

Old Lyme Inn
85 Lyme St.
(203) 434-2600
oldlymeinn.com
Expensive
Six rooms, all with private
baths. Jazz club on
premises

OLD SAYBROOK

The Deacon
325 Main St.
(860) 395-1229
thedeconbnb.com
Expensive
Five guest rooms, each
with bathroom and
fireplace

**James Pharmacy Bed &
Breakfast**
2 Pennywise Ln.
(860) 395-1229
jamespharmacybnb.com
Expensive
1790 general store turned
inn turned B&B, three
guestrooms

PRESTON

**Roseledge Country Inn
and Farm Shop, LLC**
418 Rte. 164
(860) 892-4739
roseledge.com
Moderate
Guests receive organic
farm-to-table dining

Places to Eat in Coast & Country

BRANFORD

Stony Creek Market
178 Thimble Island Rd.
(203) 488-0145
Inexpensive to moderate
This local hangout is
a great place to have
breakfast on the deck or
pick up sandwiches and
salads for an impromptu
picnic

COLCHESTER

NuNu's Bistro
45 Hayward Ave.
(860) 537-6299
nunusbistro.com
Moderate to expensive
Charming bistro located in
a cute Victorian carriage
house offering traditional
Sicilian and American
cuisine. BYOB

EAST LYME

Flanders Fish Market and Restaurant
22 Chesterfield Rd.
(860) 739-8866
flandersfish.com
Moderate to expensive
Unpretentious place with good seafood, friendly service; other items on menu as well

GROTON

Paul's Pasta Shop
223 Thames St.
(860) 445-5276
paulspastashop.com
Inexpensive
You can take home prepared food or buy your own pasta and sauce

MIDDLETOWN

It's Only Natural
606 Main St.
(860) 346-9210
Inexpensive
Award-winning natural food

Udupi Bhavan
749 Saybrook Rd.
(860) 346-3355
Inexpensive
Authentic Indian cuisine that is purely vegetarian

MYSTIC

Captain Daniel Packer Inne Restaurant & Pub
32 Water St.
(860) 536-3555
danielpacker.com
Moderate to expensive
Located in a 250-year-old inn; several menus to choose from; children's menu available

OLD LYME

A.C. Petersen
113 Shore Rd.
(860) 598-9680
Inexpensive to moderate
Great place to stop for ice cream. Window service, outdoor seating

OLD SAYBROOK

Al Forno
1654 Boston Post Rd.
(860) 399-4166
alforno.net
Moderate to expensive
Fine Italian cuisine and pizzas

Pizzaworks
455 Boston Post Rd.
(860) 388-2218
pizzaworksoldsaybrook.com
Moderate
Located in Old Saybrook Railroad Station, literally next to the train tracks so you can watch the trains come and go

WESTBROOK

Cafe Routier
1353 Boston Post Rd.
(860) 399-8700
caferoutier.com
Expensive
One of the best French bistros in the state

Lenny and Joe's Fish Tale Restaurant
86 Boston Post Rd.
(860) 669-0767
ljfishtale.com
Moderate to expensive
Best fried clams around, huge servings

Haywire Burger Bar
730 Boston Post Rd.
(860) 391-8479
haywireburgerbar.com
Moderate
Family-owned and -operated restaurant, hand-formed 100 percent Black Angus beef burgers, meat ground in-house daily Almost 30 local craft beers on a rotating basis to complement those burgers

The Quiet Corner

East of Hartford is an area the state's tourism promoters have nicknamed "the Quiet Corner." Bounded on the north by Massachusetts and on the east by Rhode Island, the Quiet Corner encompasses the lightly populated, slightly bucolic uplands of Tolland and Windham Counties. It is an area of peace and tranquility that has escaped both the bulldozers of the state's developers and the attention of the chic set. In truth, the Quiet Corner has such an air of serenity that in many places you can easily imagine that this is the way all of Connecticut looked 350 years ago. Fertile farmland abounds, and herb and flower gardens are among the region's most popular attractions. There are country inns that wouldn't be out of place in France. With some exceptions, the antiques here are neither quite as antique nor nearly as pricey as those sold in the trendier stores across the state in Litchfield County. And if other regions have more to offer the casual traveler, for the patient, the Quiet Corner has its own rewards.

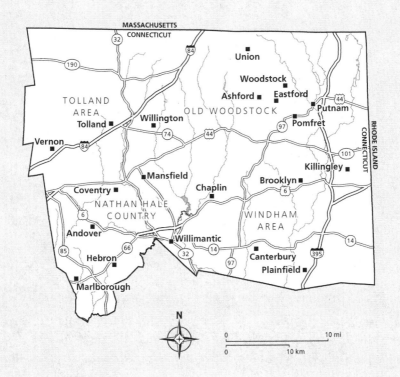

Nathan Hale Country

Marlborough

Seeing a small cluster of picturesque shops around a pond in **Marlborough** means you've reached the **Shops at Marlborough Barn** (45 N. Main St.; 860-295-1114; shopsatmarlboroughbarn.com) Actually, it's several barns and outbuildings that contain nearly twenty-five merchants. This is the place to shop for country furniture, crystal, antiques, knits, quilts, ironware, stoneware, collectibles, and more; many works are by local artisans. There's always something to pique your interest in the beautifully decorated room settings. Open Sun, 10 a.m. to 4 p.m.; Tues through Fri, 11 a.m. to 5 p.m., Sat, 10 a.m. to 5 p.m.

Hebron

Hebron is a small town along Route 66 that is home to another example of Connecticut's roadside rock art, **Eagle Rock**, on the border with Marlborough. This rock had previous lives as a frog, a box turtle, and others, but it became an eagle in 1989 thanks to the talents of graduating RHAM High School student, Jason Sawyer. Others now maintain the majestic bird, adding their initials and dates to its side.

Andover

Once in Andover, you will come across the **Hurst Farm** (746 East St.; 860-646-6536). If your kids have never seen livestock up close and personal, then we suggest a visit. The farm boasts gardens, hayrides, and a country store. You'll also find lots of standard farm critters, such as cows, goats, and lambs, as well as some of those exotic chickens with the punk-rocker hairdos. Adults will probably find more than enough to interest them at the food shop with James Hurst's own salsas, jams, and dried-herb blends, and lots of "only in Connecticut" food products. In fall, there are pick-your-own pumpkin and dig-your-own chrysanthemum patches. Open Mon, Tues, Thurs, and Fri, 9 a.m. to 5:30 p.m.; Sat and Sun, 9 a.m. to 4 p.m.

AUTHOR'S FAVORITES

Woodstock Fair, Woodstock

Memory Lane Countryside Antique Center, Coventry

Willington Pizza House, Willington

UConn Dairy Bar, Storrs

Diana's Pool, Chaplin

Coventry

At the junction of US 44 and Route 31 North is ***Memory Lane Countryside Antique Center*** (2224 Boston Tpke.; 860-742-0346; memorylanesantiques. com). This multidealer shop consists of a house and two barns full of antiques. Fifty dealers have items on display here, so a wide variety of styles and tastes are represented. The large, airy barn is mostly furniture, organized into separate displays. The house also contains furniture as well as smaller items: jewelry, glassware, tools, and the like. Even if you don't purchase anything, the stroll down the aisles is like a walk through history. Seeing familiar items from your childhood is always a bonus. The owners are knowledgeable, too, so don't be afraid to ask questions. Open Wed through Sun, 10 a.m. to 5 p.m.

Next to this store, ***Memories Too*** (2208 Boston Tpke.; 860-742-2865) and ***Aunt Ree's Country Store*** share space in a 2,200-square-foot building. The antique side carries antique and vintage items from a variety of dealers. The inventory changes constantly, so if you see something you like, don't delay! The country store side carries things you'd expect to find in a country store, old-fashioned soda and candy, handmade soaps, local honey, locally made products, and home decor items. Open Tues through Sun, 10 a.m. to 5 p.m.

Nathan Hale is Connecticut's official state hero, and there are Nutmeggers who feel about him kind of the way Tennesseans feel about Elvis. Hale (Yale class of 1773) was a fervent patriot who left his position as a local school-master to join the rebellion against the British as soon as word arrived of the doings up at Lexington and Concord. He fought with the Continental army through most of 1776. In September of that year, he slipped into New York to gather information on British strength and deployments. After being caught (possibly as a result of being betrayed by a cousin), Hale was hanged by the British for spying. He was just twenty-one. Our history books always reported his last words as "I only regret that I have but one life to lose for my country." However, the diaries of British captain Frederick MacKenzie, who witnessed Hale's execution, report young Nathan's final remarks as, "It is the duty of every good officer to obey any orders given him by his commander in chief."

The ***Nathan Hale Homestead*** (2299 South St.; 860-742-6917) was once Hale's home, which is sufficient to make it some sort of landmark. Today, Hale might not recognize the house in which he grew up: It was rebuilt the year he died in the then-fashionable Georgian style. He'd probably recognize the surroundings, though. The house sits in the middle of the 1,219-acre ***Nathan Hale State Forest***, a wooded setting not too dissimilar from the surroundings of Hale's boyhood three hundred-acre farm. The farmhouse holds a collection of colonial antiques, including many of the personal possessions used by two generations of Hales. The homestead is the site of a haunted corn maze the last Fri and Sat of Sept and first Fri and Sat of Oct, and *The Coventry Farmers' Market* June through Oct on Sun 11 a.m. to 2 p.m. The homestead is open in May, Sat and Sun, noon to 4 p.m.; June to Sept, Thurs through Sat, noon to 4 p.m.; and Sun, 11 a.m. to 4 p.m.; Oct, Sat and Sun, noon to 4 p.m. Admission. Blue Star Museum.

While the nearby *Nathan Hale Cemetery* (Lake Street) in Coventry is a nice enough old graveyard—there's even an impressive marker for the man—Halee isn't buried there. After they hanged him, the British dumped his remains in an unmarked grave that now lies somewhere under 66th Street and 3rd Avenue in Manhattan.

Mansfield

Ballard Institute and Museum of Puppetry (1 Royal Circle, Ste 101B; 860-486-8580; bimp.uconn.edu), located on the University of Connecticut's Storrs campus, boasts a collection of more than 2,500 puppets and one of the country's largest collections of videotapes, films, and media about the art of puppetry. The institute is named for Frank W. Ballard who was hired as a set designer and technical director of the Jorgenson Theater when it was new in 1956. In 1962, Ballard added puppetry to the Drama, Art, and Music curriculum, which resulted in more than 400 student productions. He was responsible for the creation of the National Institute and Museum of Puppetry, which has morphed into the institute as it is today. More than half of the puppets in the institute's collection were created by Frank Ballard. Puppets and puppet lore dominate here. Some of the puppets are beautiful and charming; others are dark and disturbing; all are exquisite. Professor Ballard passed away in 2010, and the institute carries on in his memory. They offer workshops, tours, lectures, and performances year-round. Open Tues through Sun, 11 a.m. to 7 p.m. Admission by donation.

With all the attention showered on UConn's famed basketball program, it's easy to forget that the school is also widely known for its excellent agriculture department. An offshoot of that department's activity is the *UConn Dairy Bar* (3636 Horsebarn Hill Rd. Extension; 860-486-2643; dining.uconn.edu/uconn-dairy-bar), which has been around since the 1930s and has been scooping up fountain treats at the current location since the early 1950s. Every day, about twenty-five flavors of frozen treats are on the menu, with old favorites such as chocolate, vanilla, strawberry, and coffee. Specialty flavors like Jonathan Supreme (named for the school's mascot) and peanut butter–swirled vanilla with chocolate-covered peanuts show up from time to time. According to more than one pistachio ice cream fanatic, the Dairy Bar is one of the few places in Connecticut that still churns up his favorite flavor with real pistachios, instead of green-dyed almonds. Servings are colossal. Open June 22 to Labor Day, Mon

Groovy Like a Drive-in Movie

Like other states, Connecticut has a proud history as the one-time home of many drive-in movie theaters. There were at least forty of them during the peak years of the 1950s. But, as has happened in the rest of the country, the drive-ins have gone dark town by town, leaving just three survivors. They're worth the trip.

The Pleasant Valley Drive-in (47 River Rd.; 860-379-6102; pleasantvalleydriveinmovies.com) in Barkhamstead is a vintage site that feels almost like the year it was built: 1947. You will be treated to bonus cartoons and get a chance to feast on hot dogs, fries, and pizza at the concession stand. The movies start at dusk, Apr through Oct (Thurs to Sun during spring and fall).

Mansfield Drive-in (228 Stafford Rd.; 860-423-4441; mansfielddrivein.com) in Mansfield Center has been operating since 1954. It has three screens, all with double features. Open Apr through Sept, Fri, Sat, and Sun; early June, Fri, Sat, Sun, and Wed; mid-June through Aug, daily; Sept through mid-Oct, Fri and Sat only. Gates open fifteen minutes before show time. The theater also hosts an indoor/outdoor flea market mid-March through Thanksgiving every Sun from 8 a.m. to 2 p.m.

Southington Drive-in Theater (935 Meriden-Waterbury Tpke; 860-276-6219; southingtondrive-in.org) opened in 1955. It has a single screen and operates May through Sept. If their parking lot fills up, they welcome you to park your car in a recreation area down the road and bring chairs and/or blankets in to their pavilion area to watch the movie. There's a per-person charge, with a family maximum equal to the price of a car load. It should also be noted that the Southington Drive-in as a business ceased to operate in 2002. Today the theater is owned by the town and is completely run by volunteers. All the profits go to various civic groups in the area. While they may not show current blockbuster movies, their line-up usually includes past favorites.

Regardless of which drive-in you choose, plan on arriving early, the parking lots can fill up fast.

through Sun, 11 a.m. to 10 p.m.; Labor Day to Oct 28, Sun through Thurs, 11 a.m. to 8 p.m.; Fri and Sat, 11 a.m. to 10 p.m.; Oct 29 to April 1, Mon through Sun, 11 a.m. to 7 p.m.; April 2 to May 23, Mon through Sun, 11 a.m. to 8 p.m.; May 24 to June 21; Sun through Thurs, 11 a.m. to 8 p.m.; Fri through Sat, 11 a.m. to 10 p.m.

Chaplin

A short distance from the busy UConn campus at Storrs, the Natchaug River rumbles through a shallow gorge and pours over a small waterfall into a clear pool at the center of a secluded, sun-dappled clearing. Winding over, under, and around the tumbled boulders on either shore are a handful of gentle walking trails. This is *Diana's Pool*, and it is a secret picnic ground used mainly by local fisherfolk and UConn students.

Diana's Pool isn't easy to find, but it's worth the effort. Take US 6 and look for signs directing you to South Chaplin or Sherman Corners. Turn right onto Diana's Pool Road. This is a dead end, but about one hundred feet up the road there's an unmarked parking area on the left (look for a no swimming sign). From there walk about one hundred feet down the trail; it branches a couple times, and if you're not sure which branch to follow, walk toward the sound of the water. At the end of the trail you'll find yourself in a sylvan glade so perfect, you'll expect to see dryads and fauns frolicking. If you want to picnic, you'll have to do without picnic tables, but the sun-warmed rocks above the pool are a great place to spread a blanket and watch the play of sunlight and shadow on the water. Diana's Pool is relaxing at almost any time of the year. Cool autumn temperatures kill off the mosquito population and the fall foliage is in full color. Be sure to wear proper footwear for walking and rock climbing.

Tolland Area

Willington

Don't miss a meal at **Willington Pizza House** (25 River Rd.; 860-429-7433; willingtonpizza.com); it's a little slice of heaven with its small-town setting and decor running to carousel horses. Don't be fooled, though—the pizza selection is definitely big-city sophisticated. There's a broad selection of pies and toppings, including some low-fat pies for people watching their cholesterol. But the reason most people make the pilgrimage to Willington is the delicious Red Potato Pizza. This was the pie that gained nationwide attention. Although pizza pros in New Haven would disown it, the crunchy crust, garlicky roasted potatoes, and sour cream topping make for a rich and different pie that needs to be judged (repeatedly) on its own merits. You're always liable to come across picky pizza-pie mavens who claim that the only way to eat a Red Potato Pizza is with a side dish of iced caviar for topping each yummy slice. If nothing else, the folks at Willington Pizza give you choices. You'll find both the Heart Wise Pizza (tomatoes, onions, peppers, mushrooms, garlic, and broccoli on a red pizza; *no* cheese) and the Widowmaker Pizza (pepperoni, sausage, hamburger, bacon, Canadian bacon, cheddar and mozzarella cheese, all topped with Caribbean jerk spice). The choice is yours. Open daily at 11 a.m. There's now a second location, **Willington Pizza Too** (11 Phelps Way; 860-429-9030), because it's just that good.

Tolland

The lights are on, but nobody's home at **Tolland's Daniel Benton Homestead** (160 Metcalf Rd.; 860-974-1875; tollandhistorical.org/daniel-benton-homestead).

A ghostly figure in a military uniform seems to appear at the front door. Footsteps echo through the east wing and then gradually trail off into silence. Occasionally the whole house shakes without making a sound.

A spokesman for the Tolland Historical Society, which acquired the Benton Homestead in the late 1960s, enigmatically notes that an old house plagued by a flying squirrel "can produce a lot of noise" but refrains from speculating on the subject of the supernatural. The society prefers to concentrate on the house's unusual architectural details, original paneling, and period furnishings, and the fact that it was the ancestral home of former US senator William Benton and used to house Hessian prisoners during the Revolution.

Area ghost watchers, on the other hand, have an abiding interest in the place and eagerly place the blame for certain strange goings-on at the homestead squarely on the shoulders of one Elisha Benton. In 1777, patriot Benton contracted smallpox while being held in a British prisoner-of-war camp. Sent home to Tolland to die, he was nursed by his seventeen-year-old sweetheart, Jemina Barrows. A little more than a month after Benton died in this house, Jemina succumbed to the same disease. Their graves lie forty-eight feet apart on the west lawn of the homestead.

During the years since this incident, the Benton Homestead is said to have played host to various ghostly activities. A member of the household staff claimed to have seen a weeping apparition in a white dress; a guest once reported having heard inconsolable sobbing at midnight; a common story has a uniformed figure wandering the house with arms outstretched as if pleading. The Benton Homestead is open mid-July through Oct, Sun 1 to 4 p.m. Closed Labor Day weekend. Donations appreciated.

Two other historic buildings in Tolland have a less lurid past. In colonial times, the ***Hicks-Stearns Museum*** (42 Tolland Green; 860-875-7552) was first a tavern, then a private home. It was later made over in the Victorian style, a form it retains today. The building now houses a collection of Victoriana, including faux bamboo furniture and a collection of children's toys. The museum sponsors various events throughout the year, including a summer concert series. Open by appointment.

The 1856 ***Old Tolland Jail Museum*** (860-872-7718) on the green at the junction of Routes 74 and 195 housed prisoners until 1968. Today, the intimidating iron-and-stone structure houses the Tolland Historical Society's collection of antique manufactured goods, farm implements, furniture, and Native artifacts. The museum is open June through Sept, Sun 1 to 4 p.m., or by appointment. Admission. Blue Star Museum.

The Tolland Military Museum (749 Tolland Stage Rd.; 860-803-0034) opened in 2018 and includes the collection of Ashford resident Richard

J. Provencher, including items relating to World War I, World War II, the Korean War, the Vietnam War, and Operation Desert Storm. Provencher is a retired Connecticut National Guard member. The museum is located in the building behind the Old Tolland County Jail and Museum and is open May through Sept, Sun noon to 3 p.m. Donations appreciated.

Vernon

As a rule, Nutmeggers understand deli about as well as New Yorkers understand chowder. Which is to say that neither understands the other very much at all. The pleasant exception is ***Rein's Deli-Restaurant*** (435 Hartford Tpke.; 860-875-1344; reinsdeli.com) on Route 30 in ***Vernon***. This is a large, noisy place, with brisk service and small tables that would be right at home in Gotham. The only reminders that you're still in Connecticut are the signs making witty references to New Yorkish things and places (with the restrooms naturally located in Flushing).

But never mind the decor. What counts is the authentic deli food you wouldn't be surprised to find at Manhattan's famed Carnegie. The half-sour pickles are crisp and briny. The firm, fat chips arrive smoking hot. The turkey, pastrami, and corned beef are eminently respectable; same for the combo sandwiches. And the Reubens rival the ones you get at the Manhattan deli from which that sandwich gets its name. If your taste doesn't run to deli meats and sandwiches, don't worry. The menu here is huge, and everything on it seems to be available all day. No matter when you stop by, you can get anything from blintzes to bagels, to lox and eggs, to a full dinner, to a diet plate. And all of it has that special deli touch. If you've ever wondered why New Yorkers rave about deli, here's your chance to find out without traveling to New York. Open Sun through Thurs, 7 a.m. to 10 p.m.; Fri and Sat, 7 a.m. to midnight.

Union

North of Stafford, near the Massachusetts line, is Connecticut's smallest town, the diminutive settlement of ***Union*** (population 620). Most travelers pass it by, but for bibliophiles, it's a standard stop en route to Massachusetts. For here resides one of the state's unique eateries, the ***Traveler Restaurant*** (1257 Buckley Hwy.; 860-684-4920). First and foremost a place for good, home-style cooking at decent prices, The Traveler has one special little twist.

Not only can you order a decent meal here, but customers are invited to pick out three books from the shelves lining the walls, read while eating, and then take them home. That's right: Buy a meal, get a book. Children are well treated, and the supply of kids' books is great. The owners estimate they give away thousands of books a week. The Traveler does breakfast, lunch, and dinner. Open Sun through Thurs, 7 a.m. to 8 p.m.; Fri and Sat, 7 a.m. to 9 p.m.

Eastford

Buell's Orchard (108 Crystal Pond Rd.; 860-974-1150; buellsorchard.com) in nearby *Eastford* is a century-old farm stand par excellence. Starting in June with strawberries, the stand sells fresh produce throughout the growing season. August brings fresh peaches. Apples appear during the fall and can last well into the winter, depending on the size of the apple crop. The stand also sells cider, Vermont cheese, and pumpkins. The caramel apples are made with a special caramel sauce into which are dipped "firm late apples." We guarantee that they are among the best you've ever tasted. The season for caramel apples starts about Labor Day and ends around Halloween. On Columbus Day weekend, the Buells celebrate the harvest with an open house that includes

Gentlemen (and Women), Start Your Engines

If the death of car-racing legend Dale Earnhardt in 2001 taught us anything, it's that you don't have to live in the Heartland or south of the Mason-Dixon Line to care a lot about NASCAR racing; it's a hugely popular spectator sport nationwide. Here in Connecticut, it also offers a welcome alternative to all the scenic vistas, quaint shops, historic homes, and nautical lore. In addition to Lime Rock, the racetrack that attracts the biggest names both on the track and in the stands, three other cozy, family-friendly NASCAR tracks in Connecticut offer weekly schedules of qualifying rounds, featured races, and special events:

Stafford Motor Speedway
55 West St.
Stafford Springs
(860) 684-2783
staffordmotorspeedway.com

Thompson International Speedway
203 E. Thompson Rd.
Thompson
(860) 923-2280
thompsonspeedway.com

New London–Waterford Speedbowl
1080 Hartford Tpke
Waterford
(860) 442-RACE
speedbowlct.com

hayrides and free cider and doughnuts. Summer hours through Labor Day are Mon through Fri, 8 a.m. to 5 p.m.; Sat, 8 a.m. to 3 p.m.; Labor Day through Halloween, Mon through Sat, 8 a.m. to 5 p.m.; Sun, 1 to 5 p.m.; Nov through Christmas, Mon through Fri, 8 a.m. to 4 p.m.; Sat, 8 a.m. to 3 p.m. Winter hours are Mon through Fri, 8 a.m. to 4 p.m. As always, opening can be contingent on the weather, so be sure to check ahead.

Now that you've stocked up on yummy apples, cheese, and other goodies, you need a good place to have a picnic. Why not follow in the footsteps of tons of people and eat with the Frog. Yep, we're talking about another one of those great roadside pieces of rock art, only this one is probably the oldest in Connecticut and isn't exactly on the road anymore. The brainchild of **Thomas Thurber**, a legislator in the 1880s who used to pass this rock every day, **Frog Rock** was on the side of the original Route 44. The story is that Thurber used to see it and envision a frog, so one day he stopped and painted it the way he saw it. It's been a frog ever since. Because it was along a heavily traveled road, it became a popular place for travelers to stop and picnic. When the new Route 44 was built, it no longer followed the same path and Frog Rock faded into the background. In 1997, a group of Thurber's descendants gave Frog Rock a fresh coat of paint and included a memorial to their ancestor. Today, the Frog has company; in fact, he's pretty much presiding over a party these days.

The **Frog Rock Rest Stop** (212 Pomfret Rd. [Rte. 44]; 860-942-0131) now includes a children's playground with climbing equipment, a restaurant with standard roadside foods (burgers, fries, fried seafood, ice cream, etc.), and a gift shop with all the touristy items you'd expect. There's even live music sometimes. The picnic tables are still there as well. While the Frog is always open, the rest stop is open Thurs through Sun, 11 a.m. to 8 p.m.

Old Woodstock

Pomfret

Christ Church (527 Pomfret St.; 860-315-7780; christchurchpomfret.org) on Route 169 in ***Pomfret*** is definitely not the traditional white New England church with pointed steeple. Instead, this is a stone-and-brick building with a certain Byzantine influence. The interior, decorated in what one might call "High Victorian camp," makes an ideal backdrop for 6 extraordinary stained-glass windows, designed by famed Arts and Crafts designer **Louis Comfort Tiffany** early in his career and installed in the church in 1882.

Tiffany, a native of nearby Killingly, created the windows before moving to New York City, and all but one is an original Tiffany design. It is believed that Tiffany copied the Saint George window from an original Venetian design.

Interestingly, the dedications and inscriptions in all six windows are rendered in lead, not in the more common paint, and the glass used is chunkier and more faceted than later Tiffany efforts. The themes here aren't typical to Tiffany, either. Instead of the common Tiffany floral and pastoral compositions, these items feature religious subjects. Besides Saint George, there are two crosses, one with a stylized peacock, of all things. There's also a window depicting the Parable of the Wise and Foolish Virgins and one depicting the Parable of the Talents, with the inscription, "Well done, my good and faithful servant." Finally, there is a rose window depicting Ezekiel and the wheel. Visit about an hour before sunset to get the full effect through the rose window. Call ahead or e-mail (christchurchpomfret@gmail.com) the church office for a tour between 3 and 6:30 p.m. Mon, Weds, Thurs. Make sure you take a good look at the church's interior. It's a haven for gorgeous Arts and Crafts wood carving and tile work. Well done, indeed.

Route 169 weaves south from Woodstock through Pomfret, Brooklyn, and Canterbury and has been officially dubbed one of the ten most outstanding **scenic byways** in the US. This section of the book wouldn't be complete without making adequate reference to Pomfret's favorite hangout, the ***Vanilla Bean Cafe*** (450 Deerfield Rd.; 860-928-1562; thevanillabeancafe.com). Housed in a renovated nineteenth-century barn, this is one irresistible place for lunch, dinner, or a midafternoon cup of cocoa. The soups here are fabulous—nothing fancy, just delicious freshly prepared simple blends. The tomato Florentine paired with a salad is ideal for summertime weather. When winter comes, go for a warmer-upper, such as cheese-topped chili with beef or a vegetarian alternative. The black bean or herbed chevre burgers will fit the bill. The turkey sandwiches taste like the best of part of Thanksgiving dinner: day-after leftovers. They also offer a host of gluten-free options. The Vanilla Bean is run by Barry and Brian Jessurun, and chances are you'll run into them when you visit. Unless you wind up being too full for dessert, the homemade ice cream really hits the spot after a chili lunch. In the evenings, patrons are often treated to entertaining poetry readings, folk concerts, and poetry slams. (The UConn campus at Storrs is close by, so creative talents abound.) Open Mon and Tues, 7 a.m. to 3 p.m.; Wed and Thurs, until 8 p.m.; Fri, until 9 p.m.; Sat, 8 a.m. to 9 p.m.; Sun, 8 a.m. to 8 p.m.

Martha's Herbary (589 Pomfret St.; 860-928-0009) on Route 169 at the junction of US 44 and Route 97 is a sweet-smelling treasure snuggled in the carriage house and servants' quarters of an eighteenth-century house. The gift shop is packed to the rafters with potpourri, soaps, essential oils, cooking herbs, and lotions. Cooking demonstrations and classes take place in the kitchen in the back. Outside, the gardens overflow with perennials, heirloom vegetables (vegetables grown from old strains of the plant, many dating back to colonial times), edible flowers, fish ponds, a sunken garden, and row upon row of herbs. Classes are offered throughout the year on a variety of topics, but reservations are required. The shop is open Tues through Sat, 10 a.m. to 5 p.m.; Sun, noon to 5 p.m.

The *Brayton Grist Mill & Marcy Blacksmith Shop Museum* (147 Wolf Den Dr.) off US 44, at the entrance to Mashamoquet Brook State Park, showcases two establishments that in 1857 made an agreement to jointly support a dam and flume on Mashamoquet Brook.

The four-story Brayton Grist Mill is a reminder of long-ago days when every town on a river or creek had a water-powered mill to shell corn and grind grain. The gristmill on Mashamoquet Brook was operated by William Brayton from 1890 until his death in 1928. The equipment on display includes the turbine, the millstone, and a corn sheller patented in 1888.

The Marcy Blacksmiths also plied their trade in a shop along Mashamoquet Brook; in fact, the area became known as Marcy Hollow. In 1830, Orin Marcy of Pomfret opened the shop, which used a water-powered bellows and trip-hammer. The next two generations of Marcys prospered, perfecting their craft. Darius, Orin's son, won first prize for his horseshoes at the Chicago World's Fair in 1893. A number of antique tools are displayed at the blacksmith shop; some are farrier's tools, and others are wheelwright's tools. Several tools are specially made and stamped "O. Marcy." The museum doesn't have a telephone, but it is open May through Sept, weekends 2 to 5 p.m. Admission is free.

woodstock& pomfrettrivia

During the mid- to late nineteenth century, Woodstock and Pomfret were dubbed "inland Newports" due to their popularity with the rich and ostentatious, who trained up from New York or down from Boston to build lavish summer "cottages" in the Quiet Corner.

Ashford

Continuing west along US 44, you'll wind up in the quaint community of *Ashford*, home to a wonderfully thrifty, only-in-New England version of recycling: a library in the old town dump! It's a metaphor for the regional motto, "Use it up. Wear it out. Make it do or do without." Which makes this "library" at the *Ashford Transfer Station* such a practical idea. It happened this way: A few years back, folks began remarking that a lot of perfectly good books were being sent to the dump, so the people down at the town's *Babcock Public Library* put their heads together to come up with a way to get some more mileage from these castoffs. What they came up with was an "annex" of the library at a central location—the, er, dump—where people could drop off or pick up used books free of charge.

So the Ashford Transfer Station, where residents take their recyclables and trash, gained a plywood shed with simple plank shelving. Now, when residents drop off their recyclables, more often than not they stop by the "annex" to browse the shelves and pick up a couple novels. The arrangements are simple. Books are divided into broad categories such as "mysteries," "westerns," or "romance," with titles running the gamut from those of Stephen King and Tom Clancy to books of philosophy and children's books; drop off what you've read and take as many other books as you want. People from outside of Ashford—such as you—are welcome to use the library, but trash services are for Ashford residents only. The transfer station "library" (232 Upton Rd.; 860-429-3409) is open Wed, 2 to 8 p.m.; Sat, 8 a.m. to 4 p.m.; Sun, 10 a.m. to 4 p.m.

Woodstock

Merchant and publisher **Henry Chandler Bowen** had two great obsessions: roses and the Fourth of July. He indulged both at his summer residence in the center of **Woodstock**, in the northeastern corner of Connecticut. There, in 1846, he built himself a board-and-batten-sided, gingerbread-encrusted Gothic Revival palace. Outside he planted a rose garden, and inside he upholstered much of the furniture in pink. The house itself he painted a fashionably subdued light lavender, but it was later repainted pink with green shutters and dark green and red trim, reminiscent of the flowers that Bowen loved. He named this classic Victorian "painted lady" ***Roseland Cottage*** (556 Rte. 169; 860-928-4074; historicnewengland.org/property/roseland-cottage), but today, most folks in Woodstock just call it "the pink house."

It was at Roseland, during the latter half of the nineteenth century, that Bowen held the most extravagant series of Fourth of July celebrations that America had ever seen. On the day before each celebration, prominent guests from all over the country would arrive by train in neighboring Putnam, whence they would be transported by carriage to Woodstock for an evening reception that featured (what else?) pink lemonade. The next day, a huge American flag would be displayed on one side of the house. The guests would then parade down Route 169 to Roseland Park, where they would amuse the public and each other with exchanges of high-flying rhetoric until it was time to return to Roseland for further diversions

gloriousfalldrive

In the Quiet Corner, there's no prettier fall drive than Route 169 North. Start at the intersection of Rocky Holly Road in Lisbon and head off to Woodstock and points north.

of a nonalcoholic nature. (Bowen was a temperance man.) What makes all of this so remarkable is that no fewer than four US presidents—Benjamin Harrison, Ulysses S. Grant, Rutherford B. Hayes, and William McKinley—participated in these shenanigans; two of them—Harrison and Grant—while in office, the others while they were congressmen.

Today, Roseland Cottage and its grounds and outbuildings are maintained by Historic New England and are open to the public. Everything is much as it was in the glory days. The rose garden is still there, along with an 1850s maze of boxwood hedges, and so is most of the original Gothic Revival furniture. The famous flag is displayed in its traditional location each Fourth of July. Even the bowling alley out in the barn, thought to be the oldest such facility in a private residence in America, is still as it was. One can almost imagine Ulysses Grant—who seems to have coped well at Roseland despite the fact that he was most definitely not a temperance man—bowling his famous strike there during his July 4 visit.

Roseland Cottage is open Memorial Day through Aug, Wed through Sun, 11 a.m. to 4 p.m. (last tour at 4 p.m.). Admission.

The Christmas Barn (835 Rte. 169; 860-928-7652) is more than just a red barn full of Christmas paraphernalia. The year-round display of Christmas decorations upstairs is balanced by displays of country furniture, crafts, lace curtains, curios, collectibles, quilts, craft supplies, and Victoriana suitable for all seasons. Besides, owners Joe and Kris Reynolds are that rare breed of people who seem able to keep the Christmas spirit alive all year. Open June through Dec, Thurs, Fri, and Sat, 10 a.m. to 5 p.m.

No Clothes, No Kidding

Solair Recreation League (65 Ide Perrin Rd., Woodstock; 860-928-9174; solairrl. com) is what our mothers in their most shocked voices used to call a "nudist camp."

It's been around since the 1930s and offers 360 acres of wooded solitude. Amenities include a lake, rental cabins, pool, tennis and volleyball courts, and a social hall.

Visitors are welcome provided you make reservations in advance. If you're interested in learning more, the office welcomes visitors daily but suggests you come in on a weekend between 10 a.m. and 2 p.m. to meet with a staff member who can show you around.

You'll find the Solair Recreation League off English Neighborhood Road in Woodstock. Before dropping in, call for directions, hours, more information, and reservations. Open June to Labor Day, Mon through Thurs, and Sat, 9 a.m. to 4 p.m.; Fri, 9 a.m. to 6 p.m.; Sun, 9 a.m. to 3 p.m.

Stone Walls

When you venture off the beaten path in Connecticut, one of the first things you'll notice is the labyrinth of stone walls that snake across the landscape. Some were built with the precision of Egyptian pyramids; others look like daycare projects. Whatever the level of construction skill, the origin of these natural building blocks is yet another reminder of the limitless power of Mother Nature.

Glaciers that inched their way across the region close to 20,000 years ago scraped the earth as they went, carrying tons of rocks and boulders with them. Farmers had to remove this debris so they could till the soil and plant their crops. The mortarless stone walls you see throughout the area were originally built to make use of the rocks that had been liberally deposited everywhere and to mark field boundaries. Today they serve as elegant property accents, adorning many of the state's most opulent homesteads. These days, craftsmen who have mastered the ancient art of stonewall construction are well compensated.

Putnam

Woodbury may boast Connecticut's "Antique Avenue," but in **Putnam** you've got a whole Windham County town full of antiques shops. Okay, some carry merchandise that's somewhere just above "tag-sale stuff" on the antiques food chain, but most are chockablock with high-quality, well-maintained furnishings, collectibles, and jewelry.

When its main industries quite literally went south, the community and its citizens could have held a pity party and thrown in the towel. Instead, they transformed Putnam into one of the hottest antiques shopping districts in New England. Now more than 400 dealers do business here; most are scattered throughout the Main Street area in a former mill, the old courthouse, and an 1880s Victorian department store.

The anchor attraction is the four-story **Antiques Marketplace** (109 Main St.; 860-928-0442; antiquesmarketplace.tumblr.com) in what used to be the C. D. Bugbee Department Store. Jerry Cohen, a transplanted Californian, accomplished the changeover. There are 350 dealer spaces in the 22,000-square-foot building and the vendors are as varied as the goods they carry. Their profiles are on the marketplace's website and if you read them, you'll see the wealth of knowledge and passion they bring to the items they collect. A trip here is as much about learning as it is about shopping. The entire antiques district is open Wed through Mon from 10 a.m. to 5 p.m.

Arts and Framing (112 Main St.; 860-963-0105) is the place to visit for antique mirrors and frames, custom hand-gilding, and glass as well as some antique furniture and accessories. Open Tues through Sat, 10 a.m. to 5 p.m.

Jeremiah's (26 Front St.; 860-928-0666) is a large, multidealer shop, with an ever-changing display of estate jewelry, china, and glass, in addition to Victorian and country-primitive furniture. Open Wed through Mon, 10 a.m. to 5 p.m.

If all that walking has left you a tad peckish, central Putnam offers a modest selection of handy eateries for lunch and light noshing. A recommendable luncheon choice, with homemade soups and a selection of artful sandwiches, is the *Courthouse Bar & Grille* (121 Main St.; 860-963-0074; courthousebarandgrille.com). Open daily 11:30 a.m. to midnight.

If you tend more toward a snack, try **Mrs. Bridges Pantry** (292 Rte. 169; 860-963-7040; mrsbridgespantry.today), featuring food, teas, and British gifts. You'll also find such "Brit stuff" as tea cozies, lemon curd, and imported cards. You can order a Farmhouse Tea, which includes an individual pot of tea, your choice of tea sandwich, and a scone, or a Fireside Tea, which comes with your pot of tea, baked beans or spaghetti on toast, and a scone. Tough choices but no wrong choices. Their orange or lemon squash cordials make for a refreshing pick-me-up after a long afternoon of serious antiquing. The tearoom is open daily (except Tues) 10 a.m. to 6 p.m.

Windham Area

Killingly

You know you've found *Zip's Dining Car* (Route 101; 860-774-6335; zipsdiner. com) when you see the neon sign that towers over the building advertising with commendable brevity: eat. Located at the junction of Routes 101 and 12 (exit 93 off I-395) in the Dayville section of *Killingly*, Zip's is an original O'Mahoney diner, built in 1954.

The diner is actually a New England invention. Its progenitor, the lunch wagon, was invented by Walter Scott in 1872 in Providence, Rhode Island. More improvements followed, and in 1906 the Worcester Lunch Car Company was born. It soon was the primary popularizer of the Art Deco, neon-crowned, nickel-alloy (later stainless-steel) structure that we now associate with the American diner.

Zip's is one of the last of the original stainless-steel diners still in operation and is especially notable for its pristine condition. The quilted and beveled stainless steel and the blue-accented chrome just gleam. This is a family-run restaurant that has been in the same family for three generations.

Zip's menu is diner classic, featuring freshly prepared food, most of it made from scratch. The roast turkey with all the trimmings and the Yankee pot roast are both big dinner favorites. For lunch hoist a huge Zip's Burger (an especially good cheeseburger on a bulky roll) or a turkey club (made with freshly roasted turkey); these examples of the sandwich-making art are as well executed as you will find anywhere. Open daily 6 a.m. to 9 p.m.

Head south from Zip's on Route 12 and you'll hit *Logee's Greenhouse* (141 North St.; 888-330-8038; logees.com), has been a family operation since 1893, so when it comes to plants, they speak gospel truth. The six greenhouses feature a range of plants, including herbs, house plants, passion flowers, bonsais, and more. Logee's publishes a mail-order catalog that's available at a small charge. Logee's is open daily 10 a.m. to 5 p.m., with longer hours (to 6 p.m.) Apr through Memorial Day and shorter hours (to 4:30 p.m.) Nov through Feb.

Plainfield

If you're into fishing, consider putting *Plainfield* on your itinerary. The modern *Quinebaug Valley Trout Hatchery* (141 Trout Hatchery Road; 860-564-7542) in the township's Central Village is one of the largest hatcheries in the east. The operation is open to the public year-round, 8 a.m. to 3 p.m., and visitors can view the hatchery through a big glass wall. The state allows restricted fishing in the nearby waters weekends from Mar through Memorial Day. And there's a fishing pond at the hatchery that is often stocked.

Keep driving west from the Plainfield area on Route 14A until you're almost in Rhode Island. There, in the hamlet of *Oneco* (where Route 14A is known as Pond Road), you'll find something called *River Bend Campground* (41 Pond St.; 860-564-3440; riverbendcamp.com), which offers the Lucky Strike Mine and Gemstone Panning Sluice. While you won't exactly find the treasure of the Sierra Madres here, children can don miners' hats and delve into an aboveground man-made mine in search of gemstones, fossils, or shells, or try their luck panning the sluice. Open early Apr through mid-Oct, 9 a.m. to 5 p.m. Admission.

Moosup (pronounced MOOSE-up) may be Connecticut's most patriotic village. On the Sunday closest to August 14 (V-J Day, the day Japan surrendered), the entire town turns out for its *"Victory over Japan" Parade.* Sadly, this is the last of its kind in the country. You'll see flags, brightly costumed marching bands, and baton twirlers, but the day really is for the vets. You'll probably have to brush away a tear or two as you watch these brave men, some wearing chestfuls of beribboned medals, walking in the parade or lining the sidewalks. The marchers parade from N. Main Street to Prospect Street. The parade starts at 1:01 p.m. (the time Japan surrendered) and lasts until around 3:30 p.m. The parade is free; come early and bring your own lawn chairs. Call (860) 564-8005 for more information.

Canterbury

In 1832, at the request of the community, **Prudence Crandall** opened an academy on the *Canterbury* Green to educate the daughters of local wealthy families. The school flourished until the following fall, when Crandall admitted Sarah Harris, a twenty-year-old African-American woman. Outraged parents withdrew their daughters, forcing the school to close. But Crandall reopened it as a school for the education of "young ladies and little misses of color." The state responded by passing the "Black Law," which made it illegal for Crandall to run her school. Crandall was arrested and spent one night in jail. She was taken to court, but the case was dismissed for lack of evidence. Despite her legal victory, she ultimately closed the school after it was attacked by a mob.

ANNUAL EVENTS IN THE QUIET CORNER

FEBRUARY

Essex Ed Parade
Main St., Essex
essexct.org

MARCH

Hebron Maple Festival
22 Main St., Hebron
(860) 423-6389
hebronmaplefest.com

JULY

Willimantic Boombox Parade
Main Street, Willimantic
(860) 465-3046.

AUGUST

Brooklyn Fair
15 Fairgrounds Rd., Brooklyn
(860) 779-0012
brooklynfair.org

Annual Podunk Bluegrass Music Festival
Hebron Lions Fairgrounds
347 Gilead St., Hebron
(860) 913-1354
podunkbluegrass.net

SEPTEMBER

Hebron Harvest Fair
Hebron Lion's Fairgrounds
347 Gilead St. (Route 85)
(860) 228-0892
hebronharvestfair.org

Woodstock Fair
Routes 169 and 171
(860) 928-3246
woodstockfair.com

Four Town Fair
56 Egypt Rd., Somers
(860) 749-6527
fourtownfair.com

NOVEMBER

Northeast Connecticut Region Ember Art Festival
nectrct.org

Although Crandall's school was open for less than two years, it stands as a powerful symbol in the fight for racial equality and civil justice.

The 1805 building in Canterbury where Miss Crandall's academy was housed is preserved as the **Prudence Crandall House Museum** (1 S. Canterbury Rd.; 860-546-7800), a site for both permanent and changing exhibits on the history of black Americans in pre–Civil War Connecticut. There are also exhibits dealing with the life of Prudence Crandall and the development of Canterbury. The museum has a gift shop and a research library. Open May through Oct, Wed through Sun, 10 a.m. to 4 p.m.; Nov to April, Mon through Fri by appointment only. Admission. Blue Star Museum.

Brooklyn

Creamery Brook Road in bucolic **Brooklyn** is bordered by the usual Quiet Corner collection of quaint stone walls and verdant pastures. That's as expected. What's completely unexpected is the herd of shaggy bison. After all, Connecticut isn't exactly known for being where the buffalo roam—except that they do now. Austin and Deborah Tanner started out buying one bison for their dairy farm and ended up with a small, shaggy herd of American bison on their **Creamery Brook Bison Farm** (19 Purvis Rd.; 860-779-0837; creamerybrookbison.info).

The Tanners offer prearranged tours of their working farm, you just need to call and schedule. They also sell healthful, lean, red bison meat, and you can purchase various cuts of bison meat at the farm or you can order online and have it shipped. The Tanners suggest bison burgers are a good way to start. Fresh eggs and souvenirs are also sold at the farm store. The Tanners participate in local fairs and hold events throughout the year. A complete calendar can be found on their website.

The **Brooklyn Town Hall** (4 Wolf Den Rd.; 860-779-3411) was built in 1820 as the Windham County Courthouse. It was here in 1833 that Prudence Crandall was tried for violating the "Black Law" by running a school for African-American students in nearby Canterbury. Taking a stand against discrimination, Crandall pleaded not guilty and refused to post bail. She defiantly spent a night in a cell in the basement of the courthouse, but she wasn't alone. Mary Benson, daughter of prominent abolitionist George Benson, volunteered to stay with her. The next day, George Benson and Rev. Samuel May paid the bond for her release. Benson and May were staunch supporters of Crandall. In fact, when Crandall first envisioned opening the school, Reverend May spoke for her at a Canterbury town meeting since at that time it was not considered appropriate for women to do so. Benson allowed her to remain at his house during her two-day trial.

You can still see the **Benson family home** (60 Pomfret Rd.), where Reverend May officiated the 1834 wedding between George Benson's daughter

Helen and William Lloyd Garrison, the publisher of *The Liberator* of Boston. You can also see the **Unitarian Meeting House** (7 Hartford Rd.), the first church of its denomination in the state, where May served as the first pastor starting in 1822. **May's home** (73 Pomfret Rd.) still stands as well. All these places are on the Freedom Trail. While you can visit the town hall and meetinghouse, please respect the privacy of the owners of the Pomfret Road homes, which are not open to the public.

Windham & Willimantic

Willimantic ("Willi" to locals), a village in Windham, is home to the largest thread mill in America and is sometimes called the "Thread City." So where else would you locate a museum dedicated to the history of the textile industry? The **Windham Textile and History Museum** (411 Main St.; 860-456-2178; millmuseum.org) occupies two 1877 buildings inside the mill complex of the old Willimantic Linen Company on Main Street. Dugan Mill is a two-story brick building housing a factory setting re-creating conditions of a century ago. There's a fully equipped shop floor with a spinning frame, carding machine, loom, and 1880s cast-iron proof printer. Overlooking the shop is an 1890-vintage overseer's office.

The museum's three-story main building houses a re-creation of the company store that once occupied the site; it's now set up as a gift shop. The museum also offers re-creations of a nineteenth-century mill owner's mansion and a mill worker's home. The Dunham Hall Library, on the third floor, contains a one-of-a-kind collection of books, photographs, and manuscripts, including a collection of old textile industry pattern books. Open Fri, Sat, and Sun, 10 a.m. to 4 p.m. Guided tours offered second Sun of the month at 2 p.m.; self-guided at other times. Admission. The museum sponsors special events throughout the year.

The sleepy village of **Windham** isn't well known these days. Two centuries back, however, the **Windham Frog Pond** was famous throughout England and her colonies. During the long hot summer of 1754, war and drought endangered Windham. As that summer drew to a close, ponds and streams across Connecticut were almost dry, a catastrophe for an agricultural community. That year, though, Windhamites had other worries. With the French and Indian War in full swing, they could expect especially ferocious Indian raids at the end of summer. One hot night, worried residents heard an uproar coming from a marshy pond outside the village. It sounded, they thought, like the chanting of hundreds of Indians working themselves up to an attack. Some even thought they heard someone utter the words "Colonel Dyer and Elderkin, too." Dyer and Elderkin were the community's leaders.

All night long the sound continued as the town marshaled its defenses. In the last hour before dawn, the noise rose to a crescendo before dying out at first light. Their nerves drawn taut as bowstrings, the desperate colonists prepared to fend off the expected attack. But it never came. After a while, a scouting party crept through a swamp to the pond from whence the startling noises had come. There, they found not the expected French and Indians, but thousands of dying bullfrogs choking in the shallow waters of the pond. No one could explain what had happened, but it was a wonder and no mistake. Some speculated that the nightlong noises were the sounds of the frogs fighting for territory in the restricted waters, but it was only speculation.

The Frog War story eventually became well known in Europe, so much so that it was made into a popular operetta that brought notoriety, if not fame, to the small town of Windham. In honor of the frogs, the town renamed the site Frog Pond. Windham Frog Pond can be seen today about a mile east of Windham Center on the Scotland Road (Route 14); the pond is on your left as you cross Indian Hollow Brook.

A few years ago, Windham announced that it was adopting a new town seal. The winning entry featured—you guessed it—a frog.

To that end, the town has another frog attraction: ***Frog Bridge*** just outside of downtown Willimantic. Completed in 2000, this bridge cost the city $13 million. On this bridge are four eleven-foot frogs atop spools of thread. The bridge crosses the Willimantic River and connects Routes 66 and 32.

Places to Stay in the Quiet Corner

COVENTRY

Daniel Rust House B&B
2011 Main St.
(860) 742-0032
thedanielrusthouse.com
Moderate to expensive
Located in a lovingly
restored pre-Revolutionary
homestead on two acres

WOODSTOCK

Inn at Woodstock Hill
94 Plaine Hill Rd.
(860) 928-0528
woodstockhill.com
Moderate to expensive
Twenty-one guest rooms,
eight with working gas
fireplaces

Places to Eat in the Quiet Corner

PUTNAM

85 Main
85 Main St.
(860) 928-1660
85main.com
Moderate to expensive
New American fusion
cuisine, including a full
sushi menu

The Stomping Ground
132 Main St.
(860) 928-7900
the-stomping-ground.com
Moderate
Pub grub and live music;
craft beer

MANSFIELD

Fenton River Grille
135A Storrs Rd.
(860) 786-7870
Fentonrivergrill.com
Moderate to expensive
Twenty draft lines plus local
craft brews, flatbreads,
salads, seafood, burgers

WILLIMANTIC

Willimantic Brew Pub
967 Main St.
(860) 423-6777
willibrew.com
Moderate
Located in a former 1909
post office, seven-barrel
brewery

Index

About the Author

Cindi D. Pietrzyk is a freelance writer and editor based in Connecticut, where she has lived since she was four years old. She is the author of several books, including Globe Pequot's *Short Nature Walks in Connecticut* and *Boston's Freedom Trail*. She and her family enjoy exploring history on back roads and in small towns as well as in cities with all the culture they offer. Follow her on Facebook and be sure to let her know about your adventures in our state.